the last
footman

Gilles Macbain

9-10- 2019

Gilles Macbain

in memory of
miss synnott's domestic employment agency – middle abbey street

the last
footman

Gillies Macbain

THE LILLIPUT PRESS DUBLIN

First published 2019 by
THE LILLIPUT PRESS
62–63 Arbour Hill
Dublin 7, Ireland
www.lilliputpress.ie

A CIP record for this publication is available from
The British Library.

10 9 8 7 6 5 4 3 2 1

ISBN 978 1 84351 765 8

The Lilliput Press gratefully acknowledges the financial support
of the Arts Council / An Chomhairle Ealaíon.

Set in 12pt on 15.5pt Monotype Bembo Pro by Niall McCormack
Printed in Poland by Drukarnia Skleniarz

CONTENTS

dublin

the bus that brought me from the mailboat pier in dun laoghaire into dublin was dark green, a double decker with an open platform at the back. i sat in the rearmost, sideways facing seats. the bus conductor rode standing, on the platform. at every stop he greeted each female passenger as they got on, with a kiss – nothing disrespectful, just a light kiss on the cheek. i was mesmerized. english bus conductors did not treat their passengers so. was he drunk? no. the women seemed to expect and cautiously accept it. we travelled a long meandering route through south dublin suburbs still sleeping in the watery winter sunshine. were we lost? no. did we hurry? not at all. at baker's corner a dog lay asleep in the middle of the road.

this really happened to me on my first day in dublin. what would be the point of making it up? it happened, but what did it mean? i do not know. perhaps that is why i remember, when so much else is forgotten. it is a loose end in a tale of loose ends – in fact a loose end in a life of loose ends.

my first sight of ireland, that morning, had been of the tall painted houses of dun laoghaire, through a slight sea mist. i had come to dublin with no money, or to be more precise, with thirty shillings, most of which had gone on the single fare for the boat. before i could afford to travel on any further, or even eat, i had to make my way to the city centre. there in grafton street, on the corner of anne street, i found my way to the premises of louis wine, the jeweller. there on the glass counter above the antique rings and watches i laid my only valuables, a pair of gold cufflinks bearing my father's initials. louis wine himself looked closely at this offering with an expression of sorrowful disdain, which at the time i found wholly convincing. he announced that he would give me four pounds.

i was twenty years old, but a very immature twenty. too inexperienced to haggle, i was quickly shown out of the door and on to the pavement again, with four pounds in my pocket.

dublin these days has become a sophisticated city, cosmopolitan and full of strangers. then it was an easy-going, rather run-down place with horses in the streets and the sounds of the gulls from the rooftops. they did things differently then. there were irish country barmen in the pubs, and irish country girls waitressing in the cafés. for me the past is not the foreign country – it is the present which is the alien place. the past is where i am from, the place whose ways and language i understand. the homeland i would long to return to.

i walked on down grafton street, hoping to find a bus to bray, to take me out of dublin and put me on to the road south.

nineteen sixty-three was one of the most severe winters of the twentieth century. two days earlier, in england, hitch-hiking in the dark over a pass in the pennine hills, i had travelled between banks of deep snow piled up higher than the cars. here, in ireland, as i hitch-hiked slowly southwards along the foot of the wicklow mountains, there was still snow, but the main roads were clear, and there were soon only thin drifts here and there in the shadow of the hedgerows.

as the day wore on, i made my way to wexford town, and then to waterford, obliged to go by whatever routes the drivers would offer me. finally, nearing dusk, i got down from my last lift, a gravel lorry, beside a pub familiarly called 'the cats' on the southern slopes of the knockmealdown mountains. my objective was the monastery of mount melleray.

i had read in a pre-war travel guide, *in search of ireland,* that the cistercian monks of mount melleray offered hospitality in the mediaeval tradition to anyone who knocked on their door. from 'the cats' bar i took the road up the hill in the gathering darkness, not knowing whether this tradition would still hold good thirty years after the book had been published.

at a cottage beside the road i saw a woman with a spade going in from her vegetable garden, and called out to ask her if i was going the right way.

'the gate is up the road on the left,' she said, 'but hurry, the monks will be gone to bed.'

i hurried. i was sweating now, carrying a large suitcase, and clueless as to what i would do if refused admittance. i came to a wide stone gateway, went up a long avenue, and sensed rather than saw ranges of buildings in the wintery darkness. at a small gothic doorway was a single light, and a bell. now there was silence except for my own breathing. after a while, and from somewhere within, came the sound of shuffling feet. an old man in a brown habit opened the door and i began to explain that i needed somewhere to stay the night.

'would that be one night?' he asked, cutting short my story.

'maybe more,' i said.

he turned and gestured me to follow him down the stone passage. no other words passed between us. he put on a light in what seemed to be a sitting room or small waiting room, and asked me had i eaten. learning that i had not, he left me there to sit beside the dying embers of a small turf fire. i was twenty, tallish and lean, and suddenly, after two days and two nights of constant travelling, i was aware of deep silence. only now did it come home to me that i was going to leave england, for good. i was alone in the world.

after what seemed like ten or fifteen minutes the old monk returned. he put down at the table a tray, with poached eggs on toast, home-made brown bread, home-churned butter, home-made strawberry jam, and a steaming pot of tea. he closed the door silently behind him. i sat down in front of this feast, put my head in my hands, and wept.

mount melleray, county waterford

i awoke in the morning in a small bare room, not unlike the study at the boarding school that i had left three years before, except that this room was centrally heated. i had no idea of the time but felt that i had been allowed to sleep on. the gothic window opened out on to an enormous walled vegetable garden, and in the garden below me a man – a labourer, not a monk – was ploughing with two horses: a brown and a grey. beyond the garden wall were tall pines, and beyond that again to the south were low hills in a slight morning mist where i sensed lay the sea.

a soft knock came on the door and a voice summoned me to breakfast, informing me that if i wanted any i would have to come now. this was my introduction to brother declan. meeting him was a mild form of culture shock. a monk does not 'meet you halfway.' he remains embedded in an order and a routine that has been several hundred years in the making. he stays put. as a guest you enter his world, and if you are dressed as i was, your sports jacket and loud yellow tie suddenly feel ridiculous and out of place.

the cistercians were a silent order, but there were rules that allowed essential conversation to each monk, particularly in whatever was his particular place of work – the kitchen, the garden, the workshop, the farm or the bakery. of all the things that impressed me in those first few days, two things stood out – firstly that brother declan, though a vegetarian himself, could nevertheless cook meat and fish for the visitors to perfection.

the second thing was that no one asked me why i was there, or how long i intended to stay. not being at that time a catholic, i had somehow expected to be subjected to a little subtle or not so subtle catholic propaganda – but not a word. the cistercian hospitality appeared to be unconditional. this drew me in to the community's way of life far more effectively than any attempt at persuasion could ever have done.

4

by lunchtime i had decided that the way to acknowledge this kindness was not to behave as a bed and breakfast tourist, but to partake fully in the routine of the monks.

to the visitors, work in the garden or attendance at the services in the abbey church was optional, and by the time the visitors' breakfast was served, the monks would have several hours of prayer and plainsong already behind them. my fellow guests were few in number, but included a couple of recovering alcoholics and a yugoslavian priest on retreat. the presence of this priest quickly taught me the differences between a priest and a monk, as this priest was a nervous, driven, and egotistical man, totally lacking the serenity of those who leave the world completely behind them.

so i began to follow the routine of the monastery, attending the services that punctuated the day just as they had done since the middle ages, and borrowing a brown habit to cover my own clothes while working in the garden. (the brothers wore brown habits, whereas the ordained priests, addressed as 'father', wore black and white.) father luke, the guestmaster, met me thus attired at the door to the garden and said teasingly –

'they'd be starting to get worried at home, if they could see you now!'

if my first impression of the monastery had been of the deep silence, it was nothing as compared to the depth of silence of the abbey church in the small hours of a february morning. the monks filled the lighted stalls in the nave, while the balcony allocated to the guests – in which i stood alone – was in darkness except for the reflection of the soft light from below. after a period of prayer and plainsong there followed a period of meditation. there are few places as completely quiet as the knockmealdown mountains two hours before dawn in late winter.

i was fasting – not fasting from food, as i began to eat like a horse – but fasting from noise, from stress, from tension, frustration and confusion.

on the third or fourth day, i was taken for a walk around the flower garden by father luke, who engaged me in gentle conversation. not being a catholic and thus not availing of confession, i was tactfully being offered the chance to ask for counselling, or simply to ask for advice, or to get things off my chest. for this i thanked him, but i had not at that time acquired the habit of openly expressing my feelings. however, the chance to step out of my accustomed world had already served to give me a new perspective on my life. from this place and at this distance it was easy to see that my existence in england was shallow, self-centered, and congested. i was also feeling oppressed there by the constant burden of other people having ambitions for me that i would never be able to fulfill.

by the tenth day i had arranged for a little money to be sent to me by post, and received an envelope containing ten pounds. i was already resolved to go back to england, pack up my furniture and few possessions, and to return to ireland for good.

dublin, summer, 1964

i went back to england until the summer of the following year. i settled down to sitting all over again the examinations that i had failed when at school. to support myself while doing this i taught latin in a prep school as an (unqualified) assistant teacher. i also applied for a course in trinity college in dublin and was accepted, subject to achieving certain grades in my results.

as soon as the exams were over, i once again took the boat to dun laoghaire, being determined that by the time the results came out i would already be committed to life on the other side of the irish sea. this was a wise precaution, as it turned out.

this time i travelled with a bicycle that had my suitcase strapped on the back, as well as a small borrowed tent. on the morning of arrival i made my way inland through south county dublin to clonskeagh, which my map showed as open countryside. the map was one of those cloth-backed ones and must have been some years out of date, as clonskeagh turned out not to be the little village i expected, but a built-up continuation of the dublin suburbs. nevertheless, i found a place to pitch my tent on a grassy bank on waste ground behind a pub. in the morning i would ride into town and enquire about a job for the summer …

miss synnott

on the marble mantlepiece of miss synnott's employment agency, a single room up three flights of stairs in middle abbey street, stood a faded, printed notice –

butlers £1
footmen 15/-
pantryboys, chambermaids, parlourmaids 10/-

these were the fees – or one-time fees – charged by miss synnott's agency to the new employer when staff were found a position. miss synnott seemed to approve of me immediately. perhaps she simply saw me as young, fresh, and easy to place.

it was only much later that i learned how miss synnott was a power behind the scenes in the fading world of the big houses of anglo-ireland. to those whom she considered good employers (and her memory was known to be a long one), she sent proven domestic servants. these she met rarely, matching loyal and long-serving cooks with kind and considerate employers. the difficult and temperamental cooks she sent to the difficult and temperamental employers – those who were always quarrelling with their domestics and firing them. it was these latter, of course, who paid her fees most often and kept her in business.

miss synnott was a woman not to be trifled with. from the lips of disappointed and recently-dismissed servants she would know the below stairs politics of certain big houses better than did the owners themselves. she knew of the current goings-on in distant counties in which she had never even set foot. she was a power in the land.

thus it was that miss synnott, after drawing a blank with a club in saint stephen's green that might need a waiter, telephoned sir dermot, in county wicklow, and got me accepted for a position as pantryboy, sight unseen. there was no need for an interview. in fact, later that same afternoon, when i pedalled my bicycle up sir dermot's tree-lined avenue, he was not even at home.

it was late july. i had travelled nine miles on the bicycle. at the front of the house i came into gravel so deep that i had to dismount and push my bike from there to the stable yard. i was entering the world of those who wake on summer mornings to the sound of the gravel being raked beneath their bedroom windows.

sir dermot's house was grand, but not exceptionally large. in its heyday, in edwardian times, it had had its own opera house, and even its own railway station. now the city's housing estates had come out to meet it, but a golf course on one side, and the sea on another, and its own fields on a third, saved it from being swallowed up by the suburbs. it was at its core a georgian house but much altered and improved. it was the sort of house that estate agents, rather than architectural historians or romantic novelists, are inclined to admire.

in the absence of sir dermot i was let in by the kitchen door by seamus the houseman and maura the upstairs maid, a 'girl' of about forty or forty-five. 'oh look what they've sent, would you!' said seamus, clapping his plump little hands.

maura brought me down to the staff dining room in the basement. the comings and goings of temporary staff were nothing new to them.

on the staffroom table were the remains of teatime, several bowls of sherry trifle, all half-eaten, and a box of jacobs' best assorted biscuits. seamus offered, and poured out, a teacup of fairly flat champagne. he talked all the while. there were several more bottles of champagne on a tray, all opened. they had very smart white and gold labels.

'that stuff'd sicken you,' said maura.

she and seamus each poured themselves a cup of tea. this was my introduction to woodstream house. i was immediately happy there.

after an uncomfortable night in the borrowed tent, i was glad to settle for a bed, clean sheets, and three meals a day – with four pounds ten shillings wages, and half a day off, each week.

i slept that night in a store room. in the morning sir dermot had still not returned. seamus took me up the back stairs and into a long linen room high in the attics. there he rummaged about in long shelved cupboards full of sheets and table cloths and linen napkins, emerging eventually with a bundle of dark blue velvet.

'you'll have to see if these fit you,' he said.

'these' turned out to be a pair of velvet knee britches that, as it turned out, i could only just manage to squeeze my bottom into. how on earth would i be able to breathe, let alone work, in these? it was not until seamus opened the door again, and maura poked her head around, and the two of them nearly burst themselves with squeaks and cackles of laughter – that i realized they were only having me on – footmen had not appeared in the dining room in full velvet livery for years and years. i had been hired, in fact, to be the pantryboy, but my promotion from pantryboy to first (and only) footman took place that very morning.

someone was reclining out on the lawn in the sunshine – fergus, the temporary footman. he was from county offaly. taking advantage of sir dermot's absence, he was drinking his employer's orange squash and stuffing himself with custard-filled biscuits. he too had no taste for champagne. as well as that, he was homesick. he had only been prevailed upon to stay on until my own arrival by the entreaties of lynch the butler, who had not wanted to be left to do a big dinner all on his own.

in smaller houses most butlers worked single-handed, and might even double as chauffeurs or (god forbid) gardeners, but the ground floor of a big house was traditionally run by several men. footmen appeared with the butler in the dining room, while the pantryboy polished glasses and silver and other such jobs behind the scenes, without emerging from the pantry. on the ground floor the housework too was done by men, upstairs the female staff were in charge, while the

9

big kitchen in the basement was under the sole control of the cook. a cook might be a tyrant but only down within her own department, and a cook appearing upstairs was a sign of a dire emergency, like the oily-handed engineer of a ship suddenly appearing on the bridge.

sir dermot was a kindly man who took an interest in his staff. as soon as he arrived home, he sent for me, asked me questions about myself, and promised me a better bedroom in the basement of the main house.

'i think there's a room down here,' he suggested, opening a door in the basement passage. i was flattered by his attention and very impressed by the idea that someone might not know all of the rooms in their own house. he liked things done properly. under his watchful eye i soon learned the ways of the dining room and the little servery beside it. the servery was entered by a narrow door which closed flush with the wall in the dining room. that wall was painted with italian scenes, so that when the door was shut it was hard even to see that it was there.

lynch the butler was temporary, as were almost all of the woodstream staff. like some of the house's fine but threadbare linen tablecloths, lynch had been hauled out of retirement, to do just one more summer season. when the family upstairs sat down to lunch all together they were six, including the old french governess. downstairs we were thirteen – butler, footman, houseman, cook, chauffeur/gardener, and various maids. the servants' hall always ate *before* the family upstairs. this put an automatic time limit on our lunch break, and avoided tensions if lunch or dinner upstairs went on longer than expected.

sir dermot was a diplomat, and spent only the long days of summer at woodstream. they had houses in other countries and he returned to ireland for only a few weeks each year. this was his old family home. his wife chose the menus, but on those occasions when he was at woodstream alone he had us serve the treacle puddings, rice puddings, and other nursery food of his childhood days. this was his self-indulgence. even when the food being served was simple, all plates had to be properly warmed and placed on the table from the left, with the pattern the right way up. tables were completely cleared and polished between every meal and the next, until they shone like glass. all cutlery and glasses were laid out in precise position and order. if for any reason i forgot to warm plates, lynch would send me to put twenty or thirty in scalding hot water in the servery, and immediately dry them again. occasionally, if no one had remembered to uncork wine in time to warm up naturally in the dining room, bottles of claret got the same treatment.

the knives at woodstream were plain steel knives. we are now so used to stainless steel knives that it is almost forgotten that knives were once, before these, of plain steel. such knives had to be scrubbed regularly with an abrasive powder to make them shine. i soon realised that these knives were a kind of statement. the reason for stainless steel knives is that they are labour saving. old knives make the opposite statement – that a family has been around for a while, and has enough servants that there is plenty of time to sacrifice in the afternoons to such routine tasks. unfortunately it was my task, and so it was my afternoons which were sacrificed.

there were perhaps fifty years in age between lynch the butler and myself. real life butlers, unlike their counterparts in fiction or in plays and films, are often nervous men, more intimidated than intimidating. they do not make judgments on their employers' guests, indeed they are seldom even told who their employers' guests are, so they assess them solely by the quality of the wine that is ordered up from the cellar to put before them. 'twenty-four for dinner,' lynch would say, 'nine o'clock. the wine is sent up.' the wine would be sitting waiting in the little wooden lift that conveyed the food and wine up from the kitchen and the cellar. that was all you needed to know. the longer the passages in a house, the more important it was to keep everything from going cold.

all butlers hate two things – one is surprise parties, which dismay the staff just as much as they delight the guests. the other is childrens' high tea, which can leave a dining room table all crumbs and honey and jam an hour and a half before dinner. there is another thing that staff dislike, and it is the parties that are so successful that the talk in the dining room goes on and on, and the washing up can't be started.

all irish butlers have one anecdote. it is this: it is about footmen in a particular irish peer's house who used to retire to the staff hall to play cards when dinner was over but the dining room still occupied, leaving the butler to keep watch upstairs. as soon as the gentlemen finally got up from the dining table the butler would shout down the lift shaft –

'the buggers are out.'

one night when the talk upstairs was prolonged, and a footman off sick, the butler was persuaded to join the card players downstairs to make up a fourth, and failed to hear the dining room above being vacated. the butler was busy relieving the footmen of a portion of their wages when the voice of their employer came clear as a bell down the lift shaft –

'the buggers are out.'

i have also heard this story told *up*stairs.

it was mid-summer, and the two boys of the family were home from eton. their long-haired languid friends came and went, and when parties were held, pretty girls seemed to appear from nowhere, an endless supply of them.

at the dinner table sir dermot gave out advice to his sons, liberally – on their manners, on their friends, on sexual and financial matters, and on people and their peculiarities. he was open and frank, but if the conversation strayed into particularly sensitive territory, he would lapse into french in the belief that his irish servants would not understand what he was about to impart. servants anyway quickly lose interest in their employers' conversation, even though it continues all around them as they wait at table. (the hot gossip often arrives at the servants' hall first, in any case, carried there by visiting chauffeurs and others.)

sir dermot's french was not fluent, but was exactly the same brand of english 'public school' french that i had acquired myself. so whenever i heard the phrase *'pas devant la domesticité'* – ('not in front of the servants') – i stopped thinking my own thoughts and took notice. it meant he was about to come out with something really interesting.

sir dermot lived a life of disciplined pleasure. even after parties that went on late into the night he rose at eight o'clock in the morning. he took a full hour to get up, but this included a swim in the pool in the conservatory.

one morning i brought him his coffee in the library. he was opening his post, which was often large. he wore a dressing gown, but stylishly, as though it were a full dress uniform.

'what are you going to do, gillies?' he asked.

i had recently received the letter which informed me that my two examination results, although they were both passes, were not of sufficient grades to admit me to trinity college.

'i think i will stay as i am sir, and be a butler.'

his paper knife paused in mid slice, but only fractionally. his own eldest son also had his name down and was destined to go to trinity.

'you are either mad,' he said, 'or very wise. personally, i would love to be a butler.'

later in the summer i met him in the small drawing room on my way to close the shutters in the ballroom, tend to the fire, and replenish the ice bucket.

'where are you going?'

'fire and ice, sir.'

'sounds very biblical.' and then out of the blue, he said –

'how would you like to work as a footman at buckingham palace?'

never expecting this question, but flattered, i said

'yes, sir.'

(if i had stopped to think about the implications of this – going back to england, and worse, living in london – i would have said, 'no, sir.')

'lord plunkett is a friend of ours in london, i will have a word with him.'

before the summer was over, lynch the butler gave in his notice, and as there were only a few weeks left, sir dermot suggested that i would be able to carry on alone, with a little help behind the scenes from seamus. i was willing, and suggested that i could press my own dinner jacket into service, but he would not hear of this and took me into the town of bray to have me measured for a suit. in fact one suit a year was part of the footman's customary conditions of employment, along with the four pounds ten shillings and the half day off on tuesdays.

seamus himself never let sir dermot buy him a suit. he knew that without one, he could never be lured 'temporarily' back into serving in the dining room, which he disliked.

seamus was a backstairs person, and he had been at woodstream long enough to be known by most of sir dermot's regular guests. one of these even had seamus trained to bring him grapes, on a silver tray, in his bath in the mornings. everything went everywhere on a salver, grapes as much as letters. you carried the salver with your hand flat beneath it. you never showed your thumbs. the baths at woodstream were those edwardian ones, with hoods, which are able to squirt hot or cold water at you from all directions. a jacuzzi effect. they had a mahogany rail around them.

in august came the dublin horse show. sir dermot was in the habit of block booking tickets in advance, and then giving away those of them that he wasn't going to use as a bonus to the staff. we all got stand seats. i had heard of the horse show's reputation for parties and hunt balls. i had decided to go one better than the other staff, and had bought myself a ticket to a ball in the shelbourne hotel that was to be held later on the same evening.

i enjoyed the first part of the day out, the afternoon at the horse show, but before i even went up the steps of the hotel that evening, i realized that it was a mistake to be heading for the ball. i would know no one, and the few people of my own age that i did recognize would almost certainly be friends or acquaintances of my employer sir dermot's sons. but, to my surprise, the first face that i met in the hotel lobby was familiar, an english journalist with whom i had occasionally had a drink in my teaching days.

'what are you doing here?' he asked, astonished.

'i am a domestic servant. i am going to be a footman in buckingham palace,' – i said, triumphantly – 'what are you doing?'

he trumped my ace – 'i am william hickey.' he replied.

'william hickey' was not his own name, but the name of the gossip column in the *daily express* that he was that day representing. he had been sent over from england specially to cover the ball. like me, he knew of the dublin horse show's reputation, but he had never been to ireland.

we sat on two high stools beside the door of the horseshoe bar, and settled down to watch the most beautiful girls in the country, whom we did not know (nor had much hope of knowing), come and go. we had a drink or two.

bit by bit, in the manner of his kind, he extracted my recent life story from me. he listened attentively, and at one point he said –
'i think i could use that.'

we removed ourselves to the balcony of the ballroom where there were tables set for the dinner which was included in the ticket. while being careful not to disclose any personal information (except what was already public knowledge) i began to point out on the dance floor below some of the people that i had recently handed around the pudding to at woodstream, and in particular lady arabella coblington, who was staying for the whole week of the show. she was a beauty, a favourite of sir dermot and his sons and deservingly admired by all. the drink was taking its effect, and i was beginning to show off.

we did find partners to dance with in the end, but the third 'dance' (a tune which william hickey failed to recognize) was in fact the national anthem. the night was already over and my three guineas were spent and gone.

i sobered up on the nine-mile ride back to woodstream on my bicycle.

breakfast went on later than usual during the horse show week. breakfast was not served at table, it was just laid out in advance on a sideboard from which they all helped themselves as they came down, one by one.

two mornings after the ball, i was clearing away cereal bowls when i heard my name spoken – not someone asking for more milk, or fruit, or kedgeree – but my own name in conversation. somebody coughed, deliberately, and lady arabella stifled a giggle.

the morning paper was lying open on the breakfast table, and as soon as they had left the room, i took a look –

oh dear. i had always suspected that the gossip column in the *daily express* was made up on a bar counter – now i knew for certain. over a large photograph was the headline – 'lady arabella dances the night away' – and under the photograph, further down but in two long columns, was a garbled version of my own life story – embroidered, misunderstood and misquoted, and with a fair helping of ordinary everyday misprints thrown in.

the younger members of the house party had gone off to the horse show, again, sailing down the avenue in a cream and open-topped vintage mercedes. they went to the show for a while every day that it was on, and were invited out to both lunch and dinner on most days. my own half day was already spent, and for me it was back to work for the rest of the week, and the weekend too. the house was quiet. lynch had gone. seamus was away on the bus to county laois, visiting his old mother. i would have the day to myself.

that same evening i was filling up the ice bucket in the small drawing room. sir dermot was to have a cold supper, alone. the *daily express* was still there, open beside the drinks tray. some instinct told me that buckingham palace was off the menu for the foreseeable future. sir dermot saw me take away the newspaper. he said in his diplomat's voice:

'very amusing ...'

(which actually meant – *not amusing at all*.) i suspected what was coming –

'... but i don't think they would take people who talked to the newspapers ...'

that was all he said, but i knew what he meant, and nothing more was said on the subject of buckingham palace.

i told my story to seamus and maura down below over the usual tea and leftover flat champagne. seamus was scornful as usual.

'they're only mad because they weren't in the feckin' papers themselves, and them at the ball.'

maura said,

'you'll get a position someplace, don't mind them.'

and seamus added encouragingly –

'you have th'appearance.'

so here i was, the course of my life no longer dependent upon trying to pass exams. i would have to learn to live on my wits. i was destined to be a domestic servant – a clean and presentable appearance my only recommendation.

the yacht *clonsilla*

as the time for sir dermot to leave ireland for the winter drew near, his wife and her personal palestinian maid having gone on ahead, the house was winding down. ever since the retreat of the ancient lynch, i had been acting butler, but the duties were not difficult. the day came when the silver, which had been counted and checked out of the strongroom for the summer, was all to be counted back in.

sir dermot had found me a position in one of the few big houses in dublin that he himself did not know well — the household of lady honor, a daughter of the late earl of iveagh, and a director of the guinness family brewery. she was the owner of a small georgian house, phibblestown, on a stud farm, and a large motor yacht, and currently in need of a single-handed houseman. recently promoted to butler, i might have been reluctant to allow myself to be downgraded to 'single-handed houseman' had it not been for the outside chance of being asked to work on a yacht in the mediterranean.

i was engaged by lady honor's secretary, on exactly the same terms as before — four pounds ten shillings per week, half a day off on a tuesday, a fortnight's holiday and one new suit, each year. as a single-handed houseman, i still acted as butler, but in a much smaller household which had no other indoor staff. peggy the all-purpose house maid was a daily and came over on a bicycle. lady honor's mother-in-law, who was elderly and spoke little english, lived with me in the basement and acted as cook. this was an awkward arrangement, as it breached the traditional upstairs/downstairs dividing line.

lady honor was a great traveller, but where she went i did not know. much of my role was to mind the house while she and her eastern european second husband were away. i sat out the autumn and winter, and waited in hope of an offer of employment at sea. lady honor was a reader of books, and on the quieter days when i had finished *the irish times* i worked my way steadily through her library.

the life of a formal house, even a small one, is like a theatrical play at which the stagehands get to know the scenery and cues and occasional lines. working backstage, you know many intimate details of the performance, but are often in the dark as to the characters and the plot. why lady honor lived near dublin, i do not know. she did not seem to go there very much. she owned horses, here beside the house in the stable yard, but i never saw her out among them. she had one son by her previous marriage, but he came seldom, and though very polite, did not engage us much in conversation. he was in the british cabinet or something. why she was married to an eastern european refugee airman, why she kept her mother-in-law in the basement, why she wore a black velvet mask over her eyes at night, why she smoked when it made her cough in the mornings – all of these things were a complete mystery to me. perhaps life can become quite strange when you can afford to do anything that you want. by that i mean, do the things that you really prefer to do, not just those outward things which are done to impress other people or indicate to them your privileged status.

my only real friend in the household apart from the dogs was peggy, the maid. peggy lived out and came in at eight o'clock in the morning, and worked until ten o'clock at night, but went home in the middle of the day. she was married but had no children of her own. her twin sister had seven children, one of whom peggy had on a kind of permanent loan, which suited all parties. peggy's 'only child' was well behaved, while her sister's remaining six were more or less untamed. to quote peggy herself – they were always 'flying wild on bicycles and into every kind of divilment.'

one late afternoon peggy was plucking a goose in the basement kitchen. i was idling away the time by threading goose feathers into her tightly rolled hair from behind her chair. every so often she pulled them out and said, 'would you ever go on out of that.' eventually i managed to thread in several so smoothly that she did not feel me doing it. but then, while i was momentarily out of the room, the bell rang from upstairs …

peggy appeared above in the drawing room where afternoon tea was in progress, to say 'yes, milady?' – with a halo of large goose feathers sticking out of the back of her head in all directions.

servants laugh about these things. their employers probably laugh about these things too – but not in front of the servants.

no comment was made. how to explain that? perhaps, even if you fear that your staff are going mad, you do not readily upset the ones you are used to, in case they have to be let go – and you are left having to train in new and unfamiliar ones, who then may turn out to be dishonest, or indiscreet – and indiscreet is considered a lot worse than just being mad.

in the spring the longed-for invitation came. would i like to learn to be the assistant steward on the yacht, now lying in tunis harbour? yes i would. so that was that. wages would be the same – fly out on friday. deal done.

lady honor went off to london, and her secretary was left to get me a seat on a flight to tunis. at this late hour, as it turned out, all flights were booked. the only available way to get to tunis that friday was from amsterdam, first class. i was downcast, sure that this would be the end of the adventure, but mrs beatty the secretary knew her employers better than that. the following morning without even asking them she put me on the aer lingus flight to amsterdam, to make the connection.

my weeks in the mediterranean were not happy ones. we sailed where the other yachts did not go. no sitting in the marina at monte carlo for us. we sailed southwards, down the featureless coast of tunisia. we sailed in the early hours of the morning, while the owners and their current guests were still asleep in their cabins, and we sailed every day.

the guests were english, irish, and american. the crew were maltese and greeks, and myself. the captain was a red-faced lancashire man, an alcoholic of the strictly controlled type. in the evenings he stayed up late to drink with the owners, and in the early morning, which he did not enjoy, it was my job to wake him. the owners got the benefit of his obsequious late-night charm, and i bore the brunt of his early morning foul temper.

the yacht was a modern steel one, and equipped with an electronic automatic pilot. if we travelled at night, the captain set the automatic pilot and went off to his bunk. the youngest maltese deckhand was left on watch, only to wake the captain if a cruise ship or oil tanker appeared to be on a convergent course. woe betide the watch if he made the wrong call and woke the captain unnecessarily!

we were an ill-assorted crew and ill at ease. the three greek deckhands did not speak english, but that did not mean that they could not have a blazing row with the maltese. they also had a comprehensive range of manual gestures which most mediterranean deckhands would understand. the greeks indicated by signs that they considered that the two maltese were thieves and homosexuals. i considered that they were probably right on both counts. the maltese steward and cook ignored them but pointedly dined on their own, in the galley. the owners and their guests ate in the saloon. the crew, including myself, dined below, and the captain dined alone on the bridge. four separate dinners on one one-hundred-and-fifty-foot yacht. it was not a happy ship.

'this man very fucking captain' was the opinion of the little greek engineer, who did have some basic english.

i learned never to empty wastepaper baskets off the upper deck, and i learned how to carry two bowls of soup at a time down a heaving ladder. (you come down frontways, sliding your elbows down the highly polished sides.) going up a ladder at sea, you can't carry full bowls of soup, unless you have worked in the circus.

we wore white gear with short trousers, rather like naval officers do in the tropics. polishing the silver and polishing wine glasses went on much as back at home. in the calm waters of an anchorage the table was laid as formally as it would be on land. at sea, most breakable things lived in tight cupboards with rails to hold them in if we hit unexpected bad weather.

the north african heat, in a confined metal ship, is almost unbearable. i was immediately homesick for ireland, for cool damp fields to walk in in the afternoons. here the imprisonment was total. the yacht carried three smaller boats on the upper deck – a motor boat, a lifeboat also with its own motor, and a dinghy. the dinghy was for use as a platform for cleaning or painting the hull of the yacht by floating around the outside. in the more isolated places the yacht often dropped anchor a couple of hundred yards off a beach, and the owners went ashore for the day in the motor boat. i felt that i should still be entitled to my weekly half day off when at sea, but for me that couple of hundred yards might as well have been a couple of hundred miles, and i did not get it.

it was only later, when tied up at quaysides for water and diesel, that i had any chance of going ashore. once in sfax in tunisia we tied up behind a cargo ship registered in cardiff, and i went over for a bit of chat with the welsh deckhands, but they turned out to be all west indians and black. (these were still the days when manchester united and arsenal fielded teams of eleven local white men.)

lady honor, almost alone among her distinguished family, was a catholic – a convert. one of her more frequent guests in ireland and on the yacht was father philip caraman, a novelist and a jesuit priest. she had him flown out at her expense, and he shared in the pleasures of the voyage, but often sat and read on the shaded side of the upper deck in the afternoons, while other guests went in search of more worldly amusement ashore.

one day that we spent anchored off the palm-fringed island of djerba, far to the south of tunis, was a sunday. most of the crew, though of different nationalities, were catholics, or if not, they were greek orthodox. the steward was ordered to cover the saloon dining table with a cloth, to make an altar from which father caraman could say mass. it was blazing hot. for once the volatile and quarrelling greek deckhands were silent. sailors are often religious, not to mention highly superstitious. the participation of all present was genuine and fervent.

i think that i may have been suffering from mild sunstroke at the time. the mass in the saloon seemed strangely unreal – the white glare of the sky, the white glare of the sea, the motionless yacht with the ensign of an earl hanging limp at the stern, the crew bunched kneeling on the saloon carpet with heads bowed, the uneasy guests, and the thin, clever priest. how was he paid or persuaded to go along with this bizarre arrangement? on what terms did the church and his order release him to go cruising? and what did he make of the two elegant english guests who were clearly not married – at least, not to each other – and equally clearly sharing a tiny sweaty cabin?

over several weeks we sailed from tunisia to malta, and from malta to greece, and through the greek aegean islands to turkey. the places that we went to were invariably off the beaten track, and even where there was a quay the owners might decide, for quietness sake and to be away from harbour smells, to anchor a little out in the bay.

no one told us, the crew, where we were going, until the night before. we sailed each morning well before breakfast time (motored would be a better word), and did fifty nautical miles or so, and each afternoon we sweltered at anchor, rocking in the slight mediterranean swell. a free daily issue of 'foster's hop leaf ale', an australian lager, went unopened. all the crew craved was ice-cold tea, made with water from a tap beneath a tank built in to the bottom of the enormous fridge. at a small aegean port in western turkey the owners and their guests were invited by the mayor of the town to go on a wild boar shoot. as usual we knew nothing of this until late in the evening, when a large boar was delivered to the quayside and we had to string it up by the legs, between lifeboat davits at the stern, until it could be butchered. in the mediterranean heat this butchering had to be done fairly promptly.

the following evening in the saloon the silver was polished, the table laid, and a quantity of pink champagne brought up as usual from the refrigerated storeroom below. the mayor, who was invited, was suitably impressed, and dinner was a great success. wild boar meat is darkish, somewhat more like venison than like pork.

in the days that followed, we the crew had to finish up what was left. the maltese steward, who was on a contract, wasted nothing. we had roast wild boar, wild boar stew, wild boar sandwich, and wild boar soup. wild boar quickly became as unpopular as the tins of sticky australian lager.

in due course we came to istanbul, by way of the sea of marmora, and moored in the bosphorus. so i have seen the great city of istanbul, but i have never set foot in it. we moored at a buoy just fifty yards offshore, near enough to hear the steward haggling on the owners' behalf with the turkish taxi drivers. fifty yards of a bosphorus full of jellyfish and oil slicks – a great highway for an endless procession of russian tankers. it was fifty yards too far.

lady honor, unlike sir dermot, had no interest in her staff. even now, when she is long dead, i feel a slight disloyalty in saying so – but my loyalty was something that she had no particular need or wish to earn. had i accidentally fallen in among the jellyfish and oil slicks, she would have expressed regret, but then sent to mrs beatty in ireland for a replacement to be hired and flown out on the next available flight.

the maltese steward was employed on a contract. the system was that he had an allowance of so much money per month to feed the crew, thus anything he could manage to save could be kept for himself. this was the one-time system of the royal navy, which he had joined straight from reform school at the outbreak of the second world war. some way into our voyage i realized that he was seriously fiddling the rations and cheating the crew. when we docked in valetta, his home port on malta, he went ashore many times with mysterious boxes and packages. i foolishly voiced my suspicions to his cabin mate the maltese cook. would we report the steward to the owners?

the cook informed me that the steward had been reported to the owners many times already, and they did not want to know. it seemed that although they knew that he systematically cheated them, he was also a useful match for the roadside stall holders and taxi drivers and could haggle in either maltese, greek, arabic, or turkish on his employers' behalf. when they had seen some desirable item in a bazaar, they could retire back aboard the yacht for drinks, leaving the steward behind for as long as it took to wear down the sellers on shore. this man could fill his bag from a food stall under the eyes of a delighted vendor, only to stack it all back again when he heard the price demanded. where there was no vocabulary in common, he had an expression of utter sneering disdain that could intimidate any haggler across any language barrier.

the steward came to dislike me. had the cook spilled the beans? the maltese people live on a mediterranean island crossroads, and can combine the best of the italians, the arabs, and the british armed services – or sometimes, as in his case, the worst. the captain disliked me too, particularly since the morning i had opened his cabin wardrobe by mistake and a clatter of empty gin bottles fell out. i wore my hair longish, like the students in dublin. in harbour on the island of rhodes he sent me to have it cut, knowing well that his greek barber would cut it almost to the bone and that i would have no way of communicating counter instructions. no doubt the captain and the steward had themselves suffered abuses in their time, and this was the only way they knew of relating to subordinates.

eventually came the day of my release. the voyage ended in piraeus, the port of athens, in greece. there in the sun-battered harbour i helped the steward serve lunch, and just had time to wash up in the galley before we, the owners, and the luggage were put into a couple of taxis for athens airport. we flew from athens to london, and made the connection with an aer lingus flight for dublin, where two more taxis were waiting for us. as soon as we were back home at phibblestown, i had to go upstairs, lay the table for two, uncork the wine, and then announce and serve dinner as though nothing in particular had happened that day.

i never saw lady honor even mildly disturbed, even when the stabilizers on the yacht failed in a choppy sea and all the loose items started crashing around the saloon, and her husband and the captain were shouting at each other like lunatics. the rich are different, not only from the rest of us, but from each other.

sir dermot to the rescue

the one thing that the mediterranean voyage had taught me was that when i had grown homesick, it was a homesickness for ireland, not for anywhere else. if i could, i wanted to avoid ever leaving ireland again. as soon as my employers next went abroad, i got out my bicycle, rode down to the post office, and rang seamus at woodstream. seamus told me that sir dermot and the family were back in ireland, but the staff were already hired for the summer and there was little chance of them taking on any more, but he thought that sir dermot might 'know someone.'

half an hour later i was alone back at the house when the telephone rang. it was sir dermot himself.

'i might be able to help,' he said, briefly and smoothly. 'walk down as far as the gates of luttrellstown castle, and i will meet you there in twenty minutes.'

surprised, but encouraged by this personal attention, after months of lady honor's neglect, i walked quickly and was at the gates just as he arrived. he turned his ancient station wagon, i got in, and we drove back in the direction of the phoenix park. he had the kind of car that you would never need to lock up. the anglo-irish tended to have a deep contempt for showy motor cars, and his, though chauffeur-maintained, was probably worth less than he would spend on some occasions in a single evening to give a good party.

when we came to the park, sir dermot pulled the car over on to the grass, and plied me with questions. indebted to him for driving over, i was in no position to refuse to answer, and i found myself, against my better judgment, divulging the workings of my employers' household, to all of which he listened with intense interest.

he then told me that he had arranged for me to go for an interview with his old friend miss rose talbot, in malahide castle.

i said that i would go. he seemed pleased. he put his hand on my knee and said –

'it seems that you were less than happy on the yacht?'

i could make no reply. i had suddenly, as if waking up from a dream, realized where we were: we were under the trees on a back avenue of the phoenix park – a well-known rendezvous where all the lovers go … i sat, frozen with embarrassment, and without sufficient savoir faire to bring the moment to an end. 'better get you back before anyone misses you,' he said, totally unruffled.

– and that was that.

malahide castle

'the honourable' miss rose talbot was so styled apparently by special permission from the queen of england. as the sister of a baron, but the niece (not the daughter) of his predecessor, she would not normally be entitled to that distinction, but no one deserved the honorary appellation 'honourable' more than she did.

servants live in intimate proximity to the virtues and vices of their employers, and cannot help but have strong feelings about them. if a man or woman can be a hero to their valet, they are a hero indeed.

miss talbot became my heroine.

in a servery, when dinner is over but the dining room is not yet vacated, or down in the servants' hall where visiting chauffeurs and bodyguards toy with a cup of tea or a bottle of stout, servants talk to servants.

nothing is sacred in the staff hall back-chat, in the course of which those below stairs demolish the pretensions of those above – but it was here that i became miss talbot's champion.

most of the time the rich, the clever, the ambitious, and the powerful, maintain facades which they present to the outside world as they calculate their advantage and watch for their next move. miss talbot, on the other hand, was miss talbot, through and through. i wanted to work for her from first meeting her. in fact on the day sir dermot took me over for interview (getting an invitation to lunch for himself, into the bargain) i did not leave with him when he went home. i began that same day, as footman, under nugent the butler.

nugent had been there so long that he had worked for the last lord talbot before the war. times had been hard then at malahide, as indeed they had been in many places, but formalities were observed nevertheless. nugent said that 'the old lord' used to change for dinner and have it announced to him in the drawing room, even if it was scrambled eggs on toast and he was eating alone.

malahide castle now belongs to dublin county council, so i had better explain what it was like when i saw it first. the talbots had lived at malahide for almost eight hundred years. lord talbot was a reserved man, but kind, a bachelor in his fifties, and a man who loved the garden, which extended over six or seven acres. he was 'lord talbot de malahide, admiral of malahide and the seas adjoining.' this latter part was a mediaeval title, still extant even though by now meaningless – but then that could also be said presumably of all titles.

in tasmania, australia, some earlier younger son of the talbot family had built up an extensive estate and also called it 'malahide'. in time this man had died and willed the new estates back to his family of origin, so there was a malahide in each hemisphere of the world, and plants were exchanged between the gardens of the two. lord talbot, who was referred to by the six gardeners in the garden as simply 'the lord', had one of the best collections of southern hemisphere plants to be found in the northern hemisphere of the world.

inside the mid-eighteenth-century house with its encrustation of victorian additions, lay a core of the older castle, with unexplained thick walls deep in the kitchen passages and basement. the talbots of malahide had lasted about as long as the roman empire, and about twice as long as the british empire. they were now perhaps in decline, but while they had lived there, secure in malahide, nations had risen and flourished, and empires fallen, and gone. i was immediately curious as to whether lord talbot, the owner of a house rich in books and pictures, but above all rich in history and tradition, did not harbour any ambition to leave it all to an heir? one day after lunch, in the servery, i cautiously raised the subject with nugent.

'i suppose,' said nugent drily, 'if he could grow one in the garden, we would have one.'

so, sadly, the talbots of malahide were now doomed to disappear, after lasting so long. on the walls of the dining room, which was a mediaeval hall in origin, hung the portraits of talbot ancestors. some were disquietingly similar to the living talbots, while others were remarkably different. property went as straight as it could down a senior male line, but dominant genes are in no way so restricted. looking down upon the dining room, in total, there were the painted faces of sixty-three people, and three dogs. most of these were oil paintings from the seventeenth and eighteenth centuries. when you went in to draw the curtains, light the candles, or turn on the hotplate on the carved mahogany side table, over one hundred painted eyes followed you around the room.

years later, at the auction in 1976, odd objects or pictures that i knew so well (because i dusted them every morning) went for enormous prices. pop stars, millionaires, and museums nearly cut each other's throats to bid for the battered tables at which i had ladled soup, kept scrambled eggs warm, or half-filled a hundred polished glasses with medium sweet sherry.

as with everywhere else that i worked, we were never told who was coming to dinner. why would we possibly want to know? sometimes a chauffeur or bodyguard declined to come into the staff hall, and sat instead in a car or lurked in the shrubbery outside the front door, and we guessed that it was the british ambassador or some such. but mostly we were just told the menu, to have the right plates and silver, and the wine. lord talbot had three kinds of wine in quantity – the best red, the second-best red, and the rosé. he did not distinguish chateau from chateau for his guests. in the servery i fell into the habit of classifying the rich people of the english-speaking world into three great classes: best red, second red, and rosé.

nugent would come into the servery at morning coffee break. 'twelve for lunch. second red.' occasionally he would come out of the dining room with his own assessment of the company. he might say laconically 'ambassadors', or 'sir dermot and them', or occasionally, when miss talbot was entertaining languid and interesting young men 'beatles'. he did not approve of the current new fashion for long hair. anyone under thirty with hair that came over the tops of their ears was a 'beatle'.

but i have got this far without mentioning miss funshion, the cook. she was mad. some of the best cooks are mad. in fact if a cook of long-standing, many employments, and years of service in big houses, is still sane – it usually goes along with being not a very good cook.

on the very first day that i went to malahide miss funshion took me aside and confided in me –

'there's going to be a war!'

this was alarming news, i waited for her to tell me why she thought so. she explained that colonel watson (her one-time employer) had disappeared again, just as he had done before the second world war and before the first world war. he was apparently the man charged with training the hawks that intercepted the enemy carrier pigeons. thus in any war he was always the man to be called up first. so everybody knew that when he was sent for, that was the sign. there was going to be a war.

miss funshion glared at me, triumphantly.

the cook's kitchen helper was anastasia, an elderly armenian double refugee who had first fled armenia to turkey and then in turn fled turkey. she spoke little english. miss talbot had somehow acquired her from the red cross after the war, and here at malahide she had remained, cooking and ironing ever since – one of those seemingly stateless people who can neither go on, nor go back. she could never give notice.

now that i write this, i am unsure of my facts about anastasia, but have no way of checking them. looking back, it seems an unlikely tale. but it is often these mysteries, these things that do not quite hang together, which are the truth. it is the neat and convincing stories that turn out to be a web of deception.

it was at malahide that i made another great gaffe. it was at lunch and i was proceeding around the dining table, backwards, clockwise, offering the mashed potatoes from the correct left side with my left hand (footmen, and the port decanter, always move around a table clockwise, like the shadow of the sundial). i was doing something that nugent never did. i was listening to – or at least overhearing bits of – the conversation. a man who seemed to be an english politician, and who seemed to have been trying very hard to impress 'the lord' all through lunch, was struggling to remember a word which meant something like 'a self-contradictory expression'. he was concentrating so hard on this train of thought, that he was in danger of upsetting the silver vegetable dish out of my hand from not watching what he was doing. i steadied the mashed potatoes with my other hand and without thinking said quietly –

'oxymoron.'

if i had cursed or farted, or dumped the entire dish of mashed spud upon the head of the unfortunate member of parliament, the silence which followed could not have been more profound. as i hurriedly retreated back to my post at the side serving table, lord talbot resumed talking – as if he had not heard anything – about gardening …

lord talbot was a reserved but thoughtful man, probably by breeding, and not just from service with the british foreign office. once an african prince came alone, to lunch. it was winter, and lunch was being served in the old library, which was easier to heat. clearly out of his depth in a lunchtime format that was not only foreign, and formal, but already very dated even then, the prince washed his orange in the finger bowl. coming back with the coffee, i vaguely wondered if 'the lord' would gently explain to him what the finger bowl was for – washing your fingers in after eating the orange – only to see lord talbot diplomatically washing his own orange in the finger bowl …

i was content at malahide. this was before the thirty years of troubles disturbed the country, and ireland was peaceful. i often slept in the castle alone. nugent and other servants, most of them married, lived out in lodges and other houses scattered around the estate. when i say 'alone' i realize that i am not counting anastasia the armenian refugee, or miss talbot's big poodle dog. they both slept in the dark mediaeval basement three long flights of stairs, eighty-three steps in total, below me. i slept up in a georgian attic. sitting in my bath, located in a corner turret, i could see straight across the city and, on a clear day, twenty-five miles to the wicklow mountains.

when the lord or his sister were returning from england or further abroad, nugent the butler would have me lay the big drawing room fire, and would stand sentinel at the window. when the afternoon plane from heathrow came in over the trees (malahide is not very far from dublin airport), nugent would say –

'light the fire.'

he knew that by the time the car came over from the airport, within the hour, the logs would be blazing up well, in time for tea.

the large and small drawing rooms at malahide were decorated a colour that can best be called 'deep blood orange'. i saw several attempts in smaller or newer houses to imitate the colour, but for some reason it never quite came off. perhaps it was something to do with the fact that at malahide the very strong colour was only seen between pictures above pictures above pictures, many of them in carved and gilded frames. the windows at malahide were large georgian sash windows, for malahide was at one and the same time a genuine mediaeval fortress, and a gothic georgian fake. the much-admired low front door had metal studs in the panels. it was for effect. a real mediaeval door would have had oak pegs to hold it together, and these at the points where the timbers cross each other, not in the middle of the panels where there is nothing to secure.

it is very difficult to clean the last bit of a sash window. the castle was too tall for ladders. when the lord was away and the weather was fine, nugent would put me out of the window with a wet cloth, and close it. the window sills were stone and about a foot wide. there i held on with the fingers of one hand, and cleaned the last inaccessible bit of the window where the sashes overlapped, with the other, trying not to look down at the flowerbeds forty feet below. then he would open up and let me in again.

several gardens and nearly three hundred acres of a farm surrounded the house, and a substantial wall and a belt of trees divided it from the endless suburbs outside, places where i had little reason to venture. to walk the dog, in miss talbot's absence, i would take a route from cedar to cedar across the fields, or go through the back gates to the village and down past the hotel and along the beach.

malahide castle and the immaculate gardens were at the centre of a wider demesne of still unkempt fields and woods – an enchanted circle which the awakening city dare not yet approach or enter. a great house entered by a low door. a secret garden separated from the modern world.

by the time taoiseach charles j haughey used dublin county council's malahide as a lunch venue to impress prime minister margaret thatcher, with the ardagh chalice stuck up on the sideboard like some golfing trophy, the real essence of malahide had already seeped away. an auction had scattered many of its lesser treasures. the house was opened to the public, and professional guides who had never known the talbots began to disclose mildly inaccurate titbits of information about them to awestruck bus-tour parties.

the eight hundred years of the talbots of malahide were by then finally, and irreversibly, over.

the wide world, 1966

the summer after i first went to malahide my memory started to let me down again. a footman needs his memory. if your table setting is short of only one soup spoon, you must remember to bring one from your next trip to the pantry …

if your mind is away thinking about something else, and you forget that spoon, the candlelit table will still look just as impressive, and no one will notice the absence, but as dinner begins, there will be a break in the rhythm … someone, somewhere on the table will not begin their soup, because they have no spoon. someone beside them may wait politely, unwilling to start before them. two people fall behind. two soups begin to go cold. a spoon has to be asked for, and fetched from afar.

my mind was sharp and quick to pick things up, but after a while my memory seemed to discard stuff, things i was supposed to know. simple omissions – a bar of soap here, an unopened shutter there – it was as though my memory was wired back to front, handling the unfamiliar with ease, while discarding and forgetting things as soon as they became routine.

the upshot of this, one morning, was that the lord asked me, as i removed an overlooked full wastepaper basket from his study, whether i had ever considered becoming a male model. now there was nothing that i could imagine hating more, or being more unsuited to, but i knew that he was asking me, gently, not to see myself as a permanent fixture at malahide, but to consider the possibility of some other career.

this i gave thought to. i was now twenty-three, and knew that i had a legacy from my late mother, untouched, of two thousand five hundred pounds. i decided that if employment at malahide was no longer going to provide me with a home and security, which was the thing that i valued most, i would have to buy a home of my own.

i began to follow the weekly property columns in mr nugent's *irish times*, and soon had my eye upon a two-storey thatched house, 'bayfield', for sale on the edge of the burren, the county clare side of galway bay.

first, i wrote to the solicitors in england who had handled my late mother's estate. they wrote back to inform me that the sum that i had inherited was not two thousand five hundred pounds as i supposed, but *five thousand two hundred* pounds. memory had let me down again. but it now looked as if the cottage was within my reach.

i had not yet used up all of my annual fortnight's holiday, so, as it was still summer, i asked for a break, and set off on my bicycle up to dublin to catch the galway train. i got off one stop short of galway, at athenry, and cycled all the way over to new quay, in the burren. the north clare coast faces connemara across galway bay, but is limestone and dry, not at all like connemara's granite and bog. 'bayfield' cottage stood in a large flower-filled field that sloped towards an inlet of the sea. the storm-battered elms on the driveway showed clearly from which direction came the prevailing wind. the thatch looked a little moss-grown. inside on the only corner of a sofa left vacant by two large labradors, sat the owner. he smelt slightly of whiskey, but offered none.

he had all the faded tweedy appearance of a man who had known better days. it was more of an interview than a negotiation. i did get a cup of tea. after twenty minutes of warily answering his questions i offered him two thousand seven hundred pounds for his house. his answer to this was no more than a noise, a kind of 'hmmph.'

we sat for a little longer in silence. the dogs looked patient but bored, cheated of a walk, perhaps.

i did not know how to reopen the conversation. I had been warned that a man of the west would ask at least twice what he was expecting. i would have gone further, but in my inexperience i could not distinguish between mere horse-trading tactics and final, total rejection. i sat in silent misery. before i had fully resolved this dilemma he had lost patience, and i found that we were already walking back down the short avenue of wind-bent ash trees, to my bicycle at the gate.

half days in dublin

although i have given a brief account of each of my employments, there was another side to my life at this time, the half day off. all three houses that i had worked in were within bicycling distance of dublin.

at 'the bailey', a well-known but ramshackle bar off grafton street, there was a green-liveried doorman, 'luke'. no one would dare to ask luke to look after a bicycle, but if you left it in the hall passage, right under his eye, you could be sure that by his presence alone and disapproving gaze he would deter any trinity student who thought of 'borrowing' it. at this time i was still intending to find permanent work as a butler, and it occurred to me that there might be butlers in trinity college, as there definitely were in oxford and cambridge. how to find out?

one afternoon in the bailey i simply went up to a long-haired youth who looked amiable and fairly approachable and asked him if he were at trinity college?

'no,' he said, 'are you?'

i confessed that i was not.

'then you and i,' he said, 'are probably the only two people in this bar who are not.'

this was the artist, sketchley. this brief exchange was to be the beginning of a new friendship – unusual for me, but part of the day's routine for him. by virtue of spending as much of his life as he could afford in the bars frequented by the students, he knew a large number of them. he was a very recognizable figure. he had thick black hair, tied back in a small ponytail for formal occasions. he wore a long military-style coat, making it into a cloak by leaving his arms out of the sleeves, and he always wore leather boots, black like riding boots, and handmade at *twenty pounds a pair*. was he a good artist? we will not enquire too far into that. at that time dublin was a recognized haven for novelists unpublished, and artists unhung.

my own social life was of necessity fragmented, consisting largely of tuesday afternoons. sketchley on the other hand was someone who could easily be adopted as a companion by anyone, on any day of the week, and was always ready to idle away an hour or so over a pint of stout or a glass. once in his company you were introduced to numerous friends and acquaintances among the passing stream of people.

sketchley suggested that i apply for an advertised vacancy at trinity college for a porter on the entrance gate. these porters, who were several in number, wore a vaguely eighteenth-century style of uniform which included a velvet-covered riding hat. this appealed to me. looking back i can see that sketchley possibly saw advantages in this for himself. he would have an ally in a key position who might, for instance, let him in to the annual trinity ball without a ticket, and save him the indignity and exertion of his usual entrance over the college railings.

anyway, i applied.

– and in due course was turned down. this was more painful to me than earlier being turned down for a place at the college to read philosophy.

before i had left england i had had only the vaguest idea of what i wanted to do. the idea of reading philosophy was not in any sense a career move. it was simply a desire to find out more about the meaning of life. in this respect the trinity college course might well have disappointed me, had my results not first disappointed trinity college.

some weeks before finally leaving england, i had had an odd moment of clairvoyance. i was drinking with journalist friends in a run-down pub in an inner suburb of sheffield, yorkshire. a journalist's sister, by name penny cuthbertson, asked me what i was going to do in dublin, which she said she knew well. i told her about my application to trinity, and being a direct kind of a person, she then asked what would i do if i failed to get in?

'i suppose i'll have to get a job. i'll be the guinnesses' butler, or something.'

while i never became the guinnesses' butler, to be lady honor's single-handed houseman came very close indeed.

penny knew some of the guinnesses – particularly the ones at leixlip castle – and had met other connections of that family.

'if you go to Dublin,' she advised, 'gareth brown gives all the best parties.'

– at least, that is what i understood her to say. i had no notion at that time of the spelling of irish names.

there is a saying about the nineteen sixties – 'if you can remember the sixties – you probably weren't part of it.'

perhaps there are some parts of the sixties that garech browne had forgotten? i had been 'lent' to woodstream one week, to help out at parties. he arrived late, and drunk, for the formal dinner. i went out to the hall to find him in a dinner jacket, but carrying an aran sweater in one hand and a black bow tie in the other. the task which had defeated sir dermot's sons was to tie this bow tie for him, because he was in no condition to do it for himself. to tie a bow tie on someone else is not easy. you are doing it backways. some married women can do it, but no one had thought of asking a woman. i finally managed to tie it for him, with careful concentration.

dinner, though it started late, passed off smoothly.

(if you are ever asked to tie another person's bow tie, you might find it tricky, as i did, to tie one the wrong way around. the easier way is to find a mirror, and by standing behind the person you can then tie their tie the same way round that you tie your own.)

when dinner was over i found a fiddler and a flute player and a chauffeur in the staff kitchen, drinking black coffee. these men were apparently garech browne's travelling entourage. he had a company that made irish traditional music recordings. the chauffeur was patient and sober, and the other two were doing their best.

this must have been on a monday, because the next day was my day off, which was usually on a tuesday. i had bicycled into dublin and met sketchley for a drink in jammet's restaurant back bar. my bicycle was a 'moulton' – a strange invention with rubber suspension and small wheels. i had left it for safekeeping in the side passage of the bailey around the corner in duke street.

as we fell in through the door of jammet's, who was coming out – but garech browne. knowing full well who he was, having tied his tie for dinner the night before, i said:

'are you gareth brown?'

(i had still not yet encountered his name in print.)

he turned, naturally, and said that he was, and that is all (this being the sixties) that i can remember of that day's conversation, which continued in jammet's back bar, davy byrne's, the bailey, and neary's, and ended in mcdaid's. a long day's journey within a confined geographical area!

one thing garech browne never forgot was to correct someone if they misspelled his name. supremely confident in all other matters, he seemed to feel naked without that final 'e'. sketchley, of course knew him. sketchley knew him in the same way that sketchley had known brendan behan and patrick kavanagh – never actually being introduced to them, but often drunk in the same room that they were drunk in. garech browne's aran sweater and crios (multicoloured aran woven woollen belt) were as personal and distinctive as sketchley's own riding boots and greatcoat.

it had not been until several pints later that garech browne understood that he was drinking with one of sir dermot's servants. this did not bother him at all. he apparently had no clear memory of the dinner the night before, but in any case, people do not observe servants closely (unless something is late or missing). people who are used to living their lives in front of servants are more interested in what is on the silver salver, than whose hand is supporting it. as for garech himself – amiable though he was – it would have to be a very boring party indeed if one had nothing better to do than stare at the footmen?

the only bit of that afternoon and evening that i do remember is being delivered back to woodstream by garech browne and his uniformed chauffeur, in a small morris 1100 car. the bicycle, because of its small wheels, fitted in the back, just about. garech browne was intrigued by the revolutionary design, and when we unloaded the thing at woodstream, he requested a turn on it. the wheels were very small, and sir dermot's freshly-raked gravel was very deep, and for this or for other reasons he proved unable to ride it.

the acquaintances that i made on that, and subsequent tuesdays, were wide-ranging, but inevitably shallow. sketchley was uncritical of his many and varied friends, except the few to whom he owed money – and even these he did not really bother to avoid. in comparison to myself he was a man of the world, and at twenty-six, seemed to me to have the wisdom of advanced years. he did not see the approaching end of my employment at malahide as a problem. he himself had no regular source of income, but survived. he offered to introduce me to his landlady, around the corner in parliament street.

the knitting factory

sketchley lived in a one-room flat over a knitting factory, in a decaying georgian property in parliament street. for this he paid – or rather, owed – one pound per week. his room was in the attic under the slates. you reached it up an elegant georgian stairs which leaned outwards, towards the stairwell. it was advisable to keep to the side nearer to the wall.

on the way up you passed a toilet on a landing, and a solitary tap which was the only other amenity. in the room itself the occasional gap in the slating admitted fresh air, a little rain in certain weather conditions, and the sounds of the seagulls quarrelling on the rooftop. sketchley was mildly indignant when the manageress of the knitting factory agreed to let me have the vacant back room for only ten shillings weekly. the fact that he invariably owed her, while i paid up promptly, made no difference. to him, it was a question of principle.

sketchley lived as elegantly as his circumstances allowed. his day began when he heard the metal shutters of the 'county bar' on the other side of parliament street being opened up. he shaved with the help of an open cut-throat razor, a car wing mirror, and with a little water heated in a small omelette pan over a primus stove.

the gaps in the slates prevented the air in his studio becoming stale or fusty, but this was also helped by the overall distinctive smell of oil paints and turpentine. his possessions were mostly elegant, but useless – mounted antlers, volumes of military history. his sofa was a dismantled car back seat.

i can no longer remember the actual day when i left malahide castle and moved into the attic in parliament street, which is odd, because it must have been one of the pivotal turning points of my life. what i do remember is sketchley's morning routine. he rose at opening time, heralded by the rattle of metal shutters, greeted our landlady and the teenage knitters on his way down the stairs, and minutes after waking was out and into the street.

sketchley taught me how to walk confidently past the porters on trinity college gate, across the cobbled front square, and into the bathhouse donated and erected by one of the earls of iveagh for the benefit of the students. once safely behind the bolted door of the cubicles, it was possible to wallow in a bath both long and deep. sketchley, who was a little shorter in stature than i was, claimed to be able to float on his back in the bath. the endless hot water, as well as the cold, gushed from the brass taps with amazing force.

before noon we made our way to the bailey where the less studious of the trinity students, many of them oxford or cambridge rejects whose snobbish english parents only recognized three 'real' universities in these islands, also tackled the first pint of the day. for some – 'latin, or leopardstown?' was the most pressing question of the morning session – how they should spend the afternoon. these english and anglo-irish students sported tweed jackets, appropriate wear for either the lecture hall or the race track.

for many years there had been a 'ban' on catholic students attending trinity college, and thus by a simple process of elimination many students were from england or northern ireland. i remember a televised student debate on the subject: 'that this house believes that ireland should rejoin the british commonwealth'. the speaker from trinity got the biggest cheer of the evening by beginning his speech by saying that trinity college had never left it.

now in the mid-sixties times were changing, but at a snail's pace.

one day sketchley 'invited' me to a trinity college garden party, and there on a lawn in front square i saw president eamon de valera. he was nearly blind by this time, and for this reason closely attended by an aide-de-camp who acted as a kind of guide dog. by his mere presence on the lawns of trinity the president was making a deliberate and symbolic gesture concerning attendance at the college. i often boasted afterwards that i had taken tea with eamon de valera, carefully omitting to mention the five hundred other people present on the college lawns.

i spent several weeks looking at houses in the south dublin suburbs, but a recent rise in property prices meant that there was no house (or not one that i wanted to live in), from ballsbridge down as far as blackrock seafront, for much less than five thousand pounds. days spent waiting for auctions to come around passed very pleasantly in sketchley's company, but i was consuming my capital at the rate of fifteen pounds per week. i was anxious to get what remained of it invested in a house as soon as i could, to defend my fortune against the very real danger of frittering it away.

a cocktail party

one morning in late autumn i accompanied sketchley to the 66 bus stop. he was going to see 'a little girl in maynooth.' his manner was vaguely mysterious and i wondered what he was up to. had he fallen for a girl who was underage, or something? most of his alliances with girls were short and shallow. he fell for girls quite heavily, often on aesthetic grounds. some of these affairs ran aground later on the same day that they had begun, as a result of a lack of funds.

sketchley was an amiable afternoon escort for a sociable girl, but not a great marriage prospect. i saw him off and went to look in the estate agents' windows in westmoreland street.

after a week or two, having gone off to catch the 66 bus on several occasions, sketchley confided in me that the 'little girl' in whom he had begun to take a serious interest, was not yet fully detached from her husband. discretion was therefore called for.

he had met her like this: every year it was sketchley's habit to spend part of the summer painting in connemara, living rough or staying with any friends who would tolerate him. on one of these painting trips sketchley and an english friend of his, gilbert tode-kerr, had been out drinking very late. the following morning they were washing their heads in cold water under a roadside pump to freshen up, having removed their shirts for the purpose, when a woman in a jaguar car pulled up to ask directions.

tode-kerr, whom i was to meet later, was an opportunist, and not averse to pretty women driving jaguar cars. he immediately and typically assured her that the place she sought was nearly impossible to find, but offered to act as guide if he and sketchley were given a lift.

they put their shirts on.

this was the start of an alliance which began innocently enough, as most alliances, presumably, do …

so this was sketchley's story, and indeed i might have been one of that connemara holiday party myself, if i had not stayed in dublin tramping all over the south side suburbs looking at unsuitable houses with my five thousand pounds. i had never been to connemara, but had a clear mental picture of it. one morning on the yacht *clonsilla*, off the island of cythera in the greek peloponnese, one of the guests had cried,

'look. come and look at this. it's just like connemara!'

– which it was.

the rest of sketchley's story gradually unfolded. the girl, whose name was ursula, had left her husband and taken refuge with her brother in maynooth. this was also tricky, because the brother was an old friend of the rather distinguished husband and furthermore, not in favour of the split. she also took refuge at intervals in her own seaside holiday house in connemara. ursula suffered from a mild form of paranoia, convinced that she was being followed everywhere by her husband's private detectives, but otherwise was healthy and normal.

the journeys on the 66 bus continued.

meanwhile i was following another plan of my own. i now reluctantly accepted that i might always be more or less unemployable. although i might progress from job to job, i might never have any prospect of a regular career. this is not a great help in attracting a mate.

i had a second major disadvantage which was this – my intense love of ireland, which had deepened, was hampered by the fact that it was at the time still a very catholic country, and i happened to have been christened and brought up in the church of england. this was a major drawback in the eyes of nineteen out of twenty irish girls.

and so, for not particularly noble or spiritual motives, i had decided to become a catholic. i had no ambition to be a hermit or a martyr – just to become a lapsed catholic would have satisfied me.

while sketchley was occupied with clandestine meetings in a café in maynooth, i used the evenings to take weekly instruction from the jesuit fathers in milltown park. i did not see this at the time as a conversion, more as the removal of an unnecessary barrier that lay between me and the ireland that i loved.

sometime in november sketchley announced that he wanted me to accompany him on his next expedition on the 66 bus, as he needed my moral support at a cocktail party to which he had been invited. his girlfriend ursula, for such she had undoubtedly become, was asking us out to her brother's enormous house, outside maynooth.

it would take some time to describe this house, but the curious can look it up in any book of irish houses. it has since become a hotel. it is a large oblong georgian block, linked to two other blocks on either side by straight colonnades. it was a house far too large for family convenience in the twentieth century.

ursula's father seemed to own several large houses in england and ireland, and a couple of much smaller irish hotels. he travelled between these without luggage, keeping a toothbrush, a dinner jacket – in fact one of everything – in each house. this meant that his suits lasted for years, being made in batches of several identical ones at a time. sketchley likewise travelled around unencumbered by luggage, in his case because he owned only the one set of clothes …

the cocktail party turned out to be in one of the wings, in a large room which was – if you follow me – one of the smaller rooms. the people already in the room when we arrived seemed rather short haired and fresh faced. most were men. i suspected that we had been mixed in with a drinks party consisting mostly of farm managers, land agents, or people connected with the running of estates.

ursula came straight over to us, conspiratorially, and organized us a drink, but went off again without introducing us to anyone at all. thus it was that i was still with sketchley twenty minutes later when she came back, closed the double doors behind her, said –

'change of plan.'

– and unceremoniously hustled us both out to her car, in the stable yard.

in much less time than it had taken on the 66 bus, we were back in 'the county bar' in the city centre. ursula was then a confident woman of twenty-seven or twenty-eight, and this was the only time that i saw her really flustered. she was sure that we would be mortally offended – but i, for one, had not been invited to the party in the first place, and as for sketchley, being thrown out of places was all part of the normal course of his day …

although she apologized, she never did reveal to us what had been said, but her pink face, as she had come through the double doors, had been exactly how you might look if your brother had just said to you something along the lines of –

'get that awful man out of my house, *immediately*.'

the chaperone

before long, sketchley approached me with another proposal. he needed a 'chaperone'. ursula wanted to escape the tensions of her family situation for a while, and get away to some cottage by the sea, other than her own holiday house where she was too well-known and felt under local scrutiny. they had been offered a cottage to rent in a pretty village in west cork. sketchley would travel down and take the opportunity to do some serious painting. this too was part of her plan. ursula would follow down separately. ursula's husband was thought to be impulsive, known to carry a gun, and believed, rightly or wrongly, to employ private detectives. thus we were to appear in public at all times, either separately, or as a threesome. i was to be on the lookout against our being followed by unexplained persons in cars or on foot.

who could resist an invitation like that?

i made my own meandering way down to west cork, first by train to limerick junction, then by bicycle through county tipperary and over the mountain pass called 'the vee' into county waterford. before becoming an accessory to adultery, i was to be christened a catholic at mount melleray. sketchley had no sympathy with my plan. he had suffered a benedictine education at glenstal abbey school – and had no wish to have anything to do with the catholic church ever again.

it was glorious winter sunshine. in my enthusiasm i rode over 'the vee' – very slowly, but without once dismounting from the bicycle. the essential ireland, to me, is not a green country, but brown and amber and slate grey. these are the colours of autumn and winter, of bracken and rock and cloud. the monastery of mount melleray is set in beautiful half-wild country, but this time i was only to stay for as long as it would take to carry out the christening ceremony.

in those days, even though they seem so recent, the protestant version of the christian faith was classed as a heresy. the service of baptism and reception of a convert (which aroused a lot of interest among the melleray novices), began with an unambiguous renunciation of heresy.

since then, this has changed. the validity of the earlier christian baptism of a catholic convert is acknowledged now, but you will not easily get any churchman to admit that catholic doctrines change, even though it is now the position in these more ecumenical days that protestant baptism is acceptable, and so re-baptism is no longer required in later years i tried to get hold of a copy of this earlier form of service (for the reception of a convert) – but none was to be found.

in my case a legalistic anomaly now exists. i was christened as an uncomplaining infant in the church of england, and then as a willing adult in the catholic church – but the catholic church now recognizes the validity of the first christening. so am i twice christened? i like to think so. or was the first christening invalid at the time of the second christening? whereas the second christening would be invalid – or surplus to requirements – if performed now?

but i have already confessed that my motive, as i analyzed it to myself at the time, was not primarily doctrinal or religious. people are more complicated than the strict dogmas of sectarian religion allow. perhaps my attitude at this time could be described by the epigram once used to explain the mentality of certain northern republicans –

'ireland is their religion. catholicism is merely their nationality.'

thus i came to be christened, alone, in the abbey church of mount melleray, with two english novices for 'sponsors', or godparents. this was meant as a thoughtful gesture by the guestmaster – that the chosen two were specifically english. he had obviously failed to pick up on the element of renunciation in my decision to convert. my face must have fallen as i was introduced to these two yorkshire youths, slightly younger than myself, minutes before the service began.

two lads. my godparents! i never saw them again.

confirmation, unlike baptism, requires a bishop. this was the next step. that night i stayed at the monastery and early the next morning, my business being complete, rode down the wooded valley to put my bicycle on the waterford train, at cappoquin station.

in waterford city, from a telephone box outside the railway station, i rang doctor russell, the bishop of waterford and lismore, and was told to come straight on up to the palace. there half an hour later in his private chapel i was confirmed. this too was accomplished by the bishop with the minimum of delay, ably assisted by his chaplain.

'quicker than a haircut!' joked the bishop afterwards, to put me at my ease. then – 'nice bicycle,' he said, seeing my bike leaning up against the chapel wall.

'oh i thought that was yours, bishop,' – quipped the chaplain.

i may have belittled my own religious impulses at this time, but then again, who knows what mysterious forces were at work? what, after all, had brought me from another country to mount melleray, in the depths of the severe winter of 1963, in the first place?

christened, and now confirmed, i made my farewells, and throwing a leg over the bicycle, rode away into the evening.

when i got to waterford station the last train of the day for cork was just leaving. unwilling to hang around any longer, i returned to the main road and headed south and west. i rode until dusk, rode on through the night, and on into the dawn of the following day. in the end i rode all the way to castletownsend at the further end of county cork, a distance of one hundred and forty miles.

i had never ridden as far before, nor have i since. in kinsale in a drizzly dawn i tried to give up and sleep in a telephone box until i could find a bed and breakfast open, but it was almost more comfortable to be wet riding out in the open, than wet under cover and trying to sleep sitting up. i got up and went on.

as soon as ten thirty opening time came i stopped at a crossroads pub to look for hot whiskey. walking into the bar i left a trail of watery footsteps on the linoleum.

attempting humour i asked the barman in the empty pub –

'do you serve drowned men?'

he took me up wrongly –

'no,' he said, 'i can do you a tom collins, a bloody mary, or a whiskey sour …'

at last in a steep side street of castletownsend village, in the rented cottage, i again found sketchley.

a hundred and forty miles, about a hundred in the dark, the last forty in the rain. december. i was utterly exhausted. i tried to talk and failed, had another drink, fell into a hot bath, fell into bed, and slept right around the clock and well into the following day.

sketchley was expecting ursula to arrive in a day or so. in the meantime he was suspicious of a man in a black ford anglia, sitting in a car parked in the village street. we immediately decided to christen this person with the code name 'murphy.'

'murphy' stayed around the place to share our entire holiday. murphy seemed to know where we were at all times. during the day he drank in a bar at the top of the street, while we drank in a bar halfway down. when we walked along the sea's stony edge, he parked his car along the harbour quay. when we went home for tea, he read his paper in his car at the end of the lane.

when ursula arrived we were able to confirm her earlier suspicions. she quickly took sketchley aside and gave him his orders: on no occasion would they appear out together, at all. he could spend the evenings with me in 'mary jane's bar' behind our cottage. in the mornings he could paint. in the afternoons i could go for a long walk along the rocks on my own, while he stayed with her in the cottage.

she had calculated, i think, that the possibility of sex in daylight hours on a mid-winter afternoon was beyond the imagination of a straight-laced irish detective, who was probably a rural ex-garda. she may have been right. months later she laughed a lot over affidavits in her divorce proceedings which referred to this period, but she never showed them to us.

the aristocracy

as christmas approached, neither parliament street, nor sketchley's parents, nor ursula's brother in maynooth, seemed remotely possible as places for any of us to spend christmas, so we were pleased to get an invitation from gilbert tode-kerr to spend it in connemara. ursula could then stay in her own seaside bungalow some miles away. ursula also had three small children. these moved between various houses with their full-time nanny, who was in these uncertain times their rock of stability.

gilbert tode-kerr threw a house party in the following manner, which i only fully worked out much later. renting a spacious farmhouse in the much cheaper off-season, he invited down the maximum number of friends. as soon as they had all arrived and been seen around the place, he would stroll into the village and open accounts in a shop or two, and a bar. this he managed partly by persuasiveness, and a form of insistent charm-laced bullying, but also by making the proprietors fear that if refused he might take his business to their rivals down the street.

tode-kerr then treated his guests lavishly from these accounts, and modestly accepted contributions to what (he would let slip), was the considerable cost of renting the farm. thus supplied with shelter, food, drink, cash in hand, and the gratitude of his friends, he lived off the land. meanwhile, the rent accumulated and the balance remained unpaid.

tode-kerr also had under his care an eccentric young cousin, whom he claimed to be looking after. this cousin, called peregrine, had run away from eton to become a stable boy, but the job had not lasted for long. lord peregrine bore a courtesy title, was now about nineteen, and good-looking. he had, to me, the distant manner of someone who might have been drugged, but we knew little of drugs in the ireland of that time. on first encountering him, most girls could not believe their luck. (they were also encouraged by tode-kerr's hints of his own great wealth, tied up in trust funds, and temporarily inaccessible …) but they all soon met with a glazed eye, and a disappointingly absent-mannered response. the last member of the house party was also english, a student from trinity college.

i knew little about any of my companions, it was as though a careless indifference to each other's lives, loves, and finances, was part of a shared ethos.

ursula stayed intermittently at her own bungalow, and the afternoon siestas continued. in the connemara landscape, devoid of tourists for the winter, and also stripped of many of its own young people through emigration, we were very conspicuous. 'murphy' did not follow us down for the festive season, but perhaps he did not need to. perhaps news, if there had been any, would have made its way to him.

the native people of connemara, with wit and barely concealed sarcasm, christened our house party 'the aristocracy'. our ill-assorted company was quite happy to believe this myth about itself, and began an almost methodical breaking of local taboos. for those of my companions who had come from england, 'the sixties' were in full swing, and there was much questioning of established norms. this made yet a further gulf between them and 'the plain people of ireland'. in ireland, the nineteen sixties social revolution was much diluted, and even then it had to wait until the nineteen seventies.

tode-kerr drove a battered mercedes, which broke down every few miles. whatever the fault was, he was able to fix it with baler twine. a cigarette perpetually hung from his lip. his negotiations for a christmas turkey, and then despairingly for a lamb (which he claimed to be able to butcher himself), had broken down. this may have been over some small matter to do with immediate payment.

on the morning of christmas eve, all else having failed, peregrine took down the shotgun which lay on the kitchen mantlepiece. unannounced and alone, he went down to the small lough below the farm, and shot a swan. tode-kerr, normally unflappable, not to say utterly shameless, seemed disturbed by this. legality seldom concerned him, so was it superstition, or just some breach of his late father's rules of shooting etiquette, to shoot a swan up the backside?

tode-kerr went off to make rendezvous with the conspicuous white corpse, which drifted slowly downwind to the far shore of the lough. so the swan was recovered, and hung from a hook in the farmhouse ceiling, over the old kitchen table.

christmas eve of 1966 found us, crushed into the mercedes, turning into the driveway of 'the hermitage', a small hotel closed up for the winter. we had been invited for drinks. for some reason, the families of connemara, or at least those anglo-irish families likely to take any interest in us at all, had produced many daughters in this particular generation, but few sons. with ursula not yet back from dublin, we were, for the moment, five unattached males, too socially useful to be ignored.

the hermitage perched on a precarious site between the narrow road and the seaweed-bedraggled rocks of the bay. life was about to change, again, but try as i might i cannot remember the precise moment of its changing …

we come into a lighted hall. we are given sherry by our hostess, but this is far from being the first drink of the day. in the carpeted hall there is a log and turf fire, and with their backs to the fire stand three girls – all young, all tall – three sisters.

the third of these has red hair. lots of it. striking pre-raphaelite red hair …

i am going to fall in love with this girl. you knew? i had not said anything yet, so how did you know? this is only a book, but put it this way – if this had been a film and the camera turned to her for the first time, slightly out of focus, you would have known it at once.

'uh-oh, here's the heroine.'

claudia

that night gilbert tode-kerr passed out on the hearthstone in front of the farmhouse kitchen fire, anaesthetized by a combination of sea air, exercise, and the effects of the day's drinking. he was still there when i came into the kitchen late on christmas morning. even a kick could not waken him. the fire had gone out, the house was cold, a light frost whitened the hills and sparkled on the kitchen table – and tode-kerr's boasted ability to pluck, gut, and roast a swan, remained as yet unproven.

as lunchtime came and went, faced with a mutiny, he retreated to his car and was soon on the telephone from the village to the hermitage what he said, we did not hear, but after half an hour he had excelled himself by persuading the closed hotel to open up, just for us, on christmas afternoon.

the small hotel's owner 'bubbles', as she was nicknamed, our hostess of the night before and the mother of the three girls, liked adventures. although apparently surrounded by her entire household making faces that said 'you're mad to even think of it' – she had agreed to open up her dining room and serve us the cold and reheated remains of her own family's christmas dinner. this she did. washed down by a quantity of white wine, it was delicious, not least because it was now early evening and we were famished with hunger. bubbles questioned us as we ate, in-between producing puddings and serving wine – asking, telling, teasing, flirting outrageously, and pouring forth her opinions upon every topic under the sun, and upon local people that she knew, in particular. her daughters and their cousin came and went in the background, and watched.

for the moment the victorious tode-kerr was our spokesman. he never failed to get in well-practised hints at the enormous inheritance, yet to come, or trust funds somehow mysteriously and temporarily inaccessible. he mentioned a castle on a hebridean island, but with such modesty that his exact relationship to this property was never fully established. when you began to doubt if any of this patrimony actually existed, he weighed in with the old connemara story of his great-uncle cyril and the IRA.

this tale was local knowledge, folklore almost, and no doubt the story could be told somewhat differently from the other side. this tode-kerr uncle had a yacht and a rolls royce. in the days of the war of independence, before motor cars were generally available, the rolls royce was naturally coveted by the local IRA. one evening the great-uncle was tipped off that his car was going to be commandeered that night. he may even have been sent the tip-off by the local IRA themselves, in the hope that he would see the sense of giving it up without struggle …

instead the great-uncle took the car out on to the coast road, parked it in a conspicuous spot, and concealed himself with his deer-hunting rifle in the rocks high above the road. this tode-kerr was a crack shot. the locals, who at best had one or two handguns, declined to take on the unequal contest, and the car stayed where it was. so cyril tode-kerr won the battle of wits, but shortly afterwards he got a couple of messages that were impossible to ignore, and very soon had to take himself off to england at short notice for the duration of the troubles.

gilbert tode-kerr, had we known it, was likewise running up accounts that would shortly cause him to take off in a similar direction, but for the time being his connection with local history only gave him added glamour. tode-kerr was living in a fantasy world, and to some extent i joined him there. i began to believe that i was an interesting person, with intriguing background and experiences. in my case, simply believing this may have helped it to begin to be true. bubbles, who had a way with people, was always ready to conspire with a man's opinion of himself, being a flatterer, and a charmer. i had no experience of being the object of so much attention.

claudia, the third and flame-haired daughter, said nothing on this occasion (and in fact said little for the next five years). perhaps i did seem sophisticated, to her? i was after all, nearly twenty-four.

claudia kenny was not yet sixteen.

i am trying to tell this story in sequence, and yet to paint the full picture i need to give a glimpse of what is to come. a great love story needs, firstly, two people who intuitively recognize that they are fated to come together – and secondly, an obstacle to prevent that happening. 'miss bubbles' as sketchley christened claudia, after her mother's nickname, was still at boarding school. there were to be other more serious obstacles later, but this, for the moment, was enough.

claudia was tall but slightly plump. a bulge of teenage puppy fat showed under the shirt above her tight jeans. she was only just beginning to show the signs of what she was to become over the next five or ten years – one of the most beautiful women in ireland, north or south, east or west. as it was – in the jurisdictions of both the (united) kingdom and the (divided) republic – she was still a child.

had we been of the same age, she would have been far beyond my reach. as it was, the eight years between us made up for any maturity deficit on my side – at least it did at the beginning ...

christmas day passed, but the christmas holiday went on. for me, the memory of love is inextricably mingled with the smell of the sea and of turf smoke, the taste of mussels eaten raw straight off the rocks, and the music of certain records from the hermitage's limited collection, played over and over again.

while tode-kerr's credit lasted, we lived a charmed life. the anglo-irish winter residents of connemara, separated from the rest of ireland by miles of twisting and single track roads over bogs and rocks and beside the sea, were curious to meet 'the aristocracy'. sketchley in boots and ponytail, tode-kerr in crumpled tweed, myself in a green coat purchased from luke the doorman in grafton street – with 'the bailey' in gold thread on each collar. peregrine, having run away from school directly and done no shopping since, borrowed whatever anyone else could spare, while ursula, when she came, always wore the kind of clothes some young county meath women wore to point-to-points.

tode-kerr's visit to any hospitable house was more like a raid. first of all, was there food? he had an endless repertoire of plausible reasons why our own elaborate supper plans had suddenly and unavoidably fallen through. the last thing he did on leaving any house was to make a couple of long-distance telephone calls, offer a cheque in payment (naturally invariably declined), and 'borrow' a bottle of whiskey.

we drank each day, not heavily, but steadily, and one late december afternoon, wanting to clear away the cobwebs from the night before, and in preparation for the night to come, i asked claudia out for a walk.

that's not true. in fact, i asked her mother.

bubbles did everything – claudia seeming hesitant – except actually push her daughter out of the door. eventually when i suggested going on my own, claudia was conscripted to go with me, in order to show me the way. this was not over subtle, as there is only one road above that long inlet of the sea, and that runs straight, between stone walls, with few turnings.

claudia matched my stride down the long road above the sea, but said nothing.

grey walls, grey sky, white lichens on the stones, yellow lichens. bracken amber, sea grey-green, sand white, wellies black, sweater navy, hair red, red, red …

her hair blood orange red, luxuriant, coarse, atlantic wind-blown, freckle-hiding, coy, unruly, challenging, ticklish …

she did not say a word to me, all the way back.

CHAPTER THREE 1967

islands

in the new year, i took leave of my companions and went by bicycle to roonah quay in north mayo, the point of departure for clare island. the ferryman seemed most reluctant to take me on board. this turned out to be not because of my bicycle, which travelled with the gas cylinders and other stores in the middle of the boat, but because he was also the owner of the only hotel on the island, and it was closed up for the winter. with a lot of persuading he agreed that i could stay in the hotel, alone. he lived in his own house at some distance. it then turned out that the hotel electricity was turned off until the new season began, around easter, so i also stayed without water, and by the light of a single candle.

i was welcomed into the hotel owner's family's cottage, and i ate out of the island shop beside the harbour. i was a pure romantic. the islanders were practical men. i was looking for a past which i expected to resemble the aran islands of john millington synge. they gathered around a small black and white television in a cottage near the harbour to watch 'wagon train' – a weekly series about the wild west. the television, and the money that they made working on the buildings in nottingham, england, were for them the new bounds of their expanding horizons.

on my twenty-fourth birthday i returned to the hermitage, this time to stay, as the rented farm had been hurriedly vacated. before i went back to dublin to resume my house hunting, one further temptation came my way: off the western extremity of connemara are a number of islands, some like inishbofin, inhabited – but many others smaller and uninhabited.

one of the latter, 'high island', was the property of a galway butcher. it had no beach, but faced the sea with high cliffs on every side, hence its name. the only way that it could be farmed was by putting sheep onto it from a boat, by bodily throwing them on to a ledge of rock. the sheep were then left to graze until the autumn. one or two might fall over the cliffs and be lost, but those which survived fattened well on the island grass, free from the threat of foxes, disease, or the expenses of fencing or shepherding. the journey back, like the journey out, could only be made with difficulty and in calm weather.

the butcher now had the island up for sale. i proposed going to galway, to buy it. bubbles was aghast. what would i do with it? i tried to explain to her that that was not the point, that the island was in its own right a thing of beauty, but failed. perhaps bubbles saved me from making a disastrous decision?

the price was a thousand pounds.

laragh house

it was early february when i stopped to look into the window of battersby's estate agency in westmoreland street, dublin. in the window was a photograph of a large country house, and underneath the legend £, 5, 0, 0, 0 in tiny plastic stickers. i went in to the musty front office, which had a wooden counter like an old-style grocery shop. a man behind the counter reading *the irish times* looked over his spectacles at me. i began diffidently –

'there's a house in your window …'

he came out into the street for me to point it out.

'… it says £5,000, i suppose it really means £15,000?'

he hurried back in and started to root about in a drawer full of papers.

'no,' he muttered, 'county monaghan. £5,000.'

i began to think that if i could afford to buy a house like that, i would happily live on potatoes ever after.

the assistant became more flustered as he still failed to find the particulars. he kept on rooting. i guessed that no one had asked about the house for months. finally he gave up, and presented me with the particulars of a different property.

'here's another one we have in county monaghan,' he said.

he gave me a typed sheet. disappointed, i folded it into my pocket, and left. it was the house, not the location, which had brought me in to the shop. i knew nothing about county monaghan and had never been there.

it was not until i was emptying my pockets that evening that i found the crumpled piece of paper and studied it. it said –

auction on wednesday 1st of march 1967
at 2.30 on the lands
laragh house
45 acres approximately.

– and the details went on through a list of reception rooms, kitchen, pantry, scullery, dairy, breakfast room, bedrooms, bathroom, outoffices, garages, stables, gate lodge, orchard, rhododendron walks, lands well-fenced and watered, etc.

a georgian house with twenty rooms and forty acres, for five thousand pounds or so, seemed good value. this time bubbles was not at hand to ask me what i could possibly intend to do with it.

the following day i showed the details to sketchley, who at once proposed an expedition. he would persuade ursula to drive us down. apparently she needed, again, already, to get away.

i rang the owner and arranged to see the house, then sketchley telephoned ursula from the bailey and proposed the plan. over the noise of the bar i could hear her voice (the one she used for disobedient labradors) saying 'put him on'. she was not very encouraging.

'monaghan?' she shrieked down the bad line. '*nobody* lives in county monaghan.'

what she meant was that none of her own many friends lived in county monaghan. it was only thirty miles down the road from her own county meath, but as remote to her as outer mongolia. 'nobody' would consider living in county monaghan. 'everybody' knew that. the expedition was off.

regretfully, i rang the owner and told him that because of certain unavoidable circumstances i would not be able to get down to county monaghan.

'what's that?' he barked, on another bad line. i explained again.

'no bother,' he said, 'meet you off the morning train at dundalk. g'bye.'

– and hung up.

the auction

when i first met claudia kenny, i had no idea of the role she was to play in my life. when i saw laragh house, on the other hand, limewashed in yellow ochre, surrounded by damp dead leaves among the bare trees, i thought at once –

'that's my house.'

that is how i came to be standing on the gravel in front of laragh three weeks later, with one or two men in suits, and twenty or thirty farmers in muddy boots and ragged coats. i had come to bid for the house and twenty acres, the rest of the land would be offered as a separate lot. i stood at the front of the crowd, fearful of being overlooked. the auction was late starting. at twenty to three the auctioneer came over to me.

'we will be selling in one lot. the entire will go in one lot to the highest bidder.'

then he smacked his pen against his book and called the crowd to order. there was no time to consider what to do.

looking back now, i can see that i was the only genuine bidder present. and looking back, i can sense that everyone else there that day probably already knew well or had guessed, that i was the only interested party.

but now i had to make my mind up …

the bidding opened at four thousand five hundred pounds. if you had asked me that day what a 'sweetener' was, i would probably have guessed saccharine, on the grounds that it is a substitute for sugar …

quite quickly the bidding, rising a hundred pounds at a time, stalled at my bid of four thousand eight hundred pounds. then there was a pause. the auctioneer and his clerk took the owner inside the house to confer. the front door was shut and they were gone for quite a long time. they re-emerged solemn-faced and the auctioneer announced that they could not possibly sell the property at that price. he would take further bids of fifty pounds.

the bidding resumed. a man in a hat at the back bid four thousand eight hundred and fifty.

we bid on in fifties. i only had five thousand pounds.

but it was my house, i knew it.

at my bid of five thousand three hundred and fifty pounds the whole attendance must have been able to detect the tension in my agonized face, which was not just an effect of the bitter march wind –

the bidding ground to a halt.

'sold for the first time,' said the auctioneer and paused.

'sold for the second time.'

pause.

'sold.'

and he rapped his book with his pen.

the crowd broke up into groups. there were ritual handshakes for me from the owner and the auctioneer and the clerk. two men detached themselves from a huddle and came over to us.

'is he english?'

'not really ...' i began. but this was no moment to be claiming my distant scots gaelic ancestry.

'more money than sense' was the comment of the other, in an accent that i could barely decipher. although he had not himself bid at the auction, there was fierce disappointment in every line of his unshaven face, as though i had cheated him of something.

the result of the auction was that i had agreed to buy the house, and the land, and i had also become the owner of the remains of the village of laragh which included one or two sitting tenants at a rent of ten shillings a week each.

as a foreigner, technically, i now would have to wait an indefinite period to get clearance from the irish land commission to purchase irish land. even if this were just a formality (and this i was not sure of), there was no point in going on looking at any more dublin houses for sale. i was left in limbo, at the pleasure of the irish land commission.

fortunately for me, sketchley's life took a turn for the dramatic. ursula was moving out her children, her nanny, her furniture, and her belongings, and finally leaving her husband.

one morning soon afterwards ursula arrived at the front door of the knitting factory in parliament street in her jaguar car, towing a large horsebox.

she pulled into the bus stop, and blew the horn. the bus queue looked on curiously and as i helped sketchley load all of his oddly assorted worldly goods into the horsebox, some of the spectators may have even missed a bus or two. out came the stag's antlers, the volumes of military history, and a mountain of half-finished or unsold canvases that constituted his recent life's work. down the stairs they came and out into the street. the old car seat was left behind, but the omelette pan, the primus stove, and the cut-throat razor, all came with us down the country.

the glebe

ursula was going back to live in county meath. she had rented, on impulse, an absent italian diplomat's holiday home, an empty glebe house on five acres. this was near enough to her husband's home, but also far enough away. she had children and schools to think about.

with a brief farewell to the lady manageress of the knitting factory, and her wide-eyed teenage knitters, sketchley and i had evacuated dublin. now, some twenty miles down the road we pulled into the forecourt of a hotel, where ursula extracted from the coffee lounge one small boy and two smaller girls, in the care of an aged nanny.

a church of ireland glebe house is a rectory with a small acreage for the support of the clergyman and his family. this one, like many, was redundant, even though the church still stood opposite the gate and was in occasional use. church of ireland rectors often drive like lunatics, from ten o'clock sunday service in one church to eleven thirty in some other (amalgamated) parish many miles away.

ursula had now reassembled her family, her car, her horsebox and her two horses, and had her estranged husband at a convenient distance.

things could have been worse, but she faced a number of problems, foreseen and unforeseen.

firstly, it seemed that half of anglo-irish county meath was not talking to her, but there was no doubt that the whole of the county was talking *about* her.

secondly, her husband, who seemed to have the sympathy of many, was not reconciled to her departure, and was reputed, as stated, to carry a gun.

thirdly, sketchley started to drink. 'started' is perhaps the wrong word. sketchley had been drinking for years, but had been limited to what he could afford or could scrounge. now, instead of the slow pint of stout that had been his accustomed breakfast, he began to drink spirits, ad lib, from ursula's sideboard.

fourthly, the owners of summertown, the big house beyond whose gates the glebe house stood, came down one morning to pay their respects to ursula. i knew at once that they came not only out of neighbourliness, nor merely to satisfy themselves as to what was going on, but also to act as the eyes and ears of the whole county.

what i had no way of knowing, as they left after a brief chat and a morning cup of coffee (and only learned later), was that they had taken one look at the not yet shaven, but already slightly drunk, sketchley – and decided that he could not possibly be the lover. until they found out differently, they reserved their particular coolness for me.

thus began springtime in the glebe.

apart from a certain listlessness, caused by not being sure as to whether or not i was to be the owner of a house, this was a pleasant few weeks for me. ursula left my role deliberately vague, half house guest and chaperone, half painter and handyman. in the removal of her furniture and possessions from her former house, i took on the role of a neutral go-between.

mornings would find me in a land rover (whether this was his or hers was not clear), driving the twenty miles over to her marital home. this was a grand georgian house with extensive wings, not dissimilar to her brother's house in maynooth. turning into the broad gravel sweep in front of the house i would back up to a side entrance. there in the wing i would find china and knick-knacks already laid out for me on a hall table, as if for an auction. there were boxes provided to pack them in.

ursula came as well but usually drove over separately, and it was generally assumed that i was her employee, or a neighbour, so i was able to make myself useful without becoming involved in the difficult debates with her mother-in-law over wedding presents and ashtrays. her husband never appeared. the word was that he would find all of this 'too distressing.'

i think that i must have some ability to melt into my surroundings when that is what is required. ursula's mother-in-law only once referred to or even acknowledged my presence in the room. she waved a hand in my general direction and addressing ursula, enquired –

'has your man had lunch?'

(servants are traditionally fed first.) ursula knew that i had not.

'yes,' she lied, in case i were to be led off to the kitchens. the sooner we got out of there and down to the hotel bar where sketchley waited for us over his pint, the better …

in spite of the continuously replenished drinks tray at the glebe, sketchley now began to drink in the village. had ursula begun to monitor his intake? i felt that he simply needed a break from the new domestic scene. drinking for him was not just an intake of alcohol, it was a ritual. the walk to the bar, the few words of greeting to all present, the slow pulling of the pint, even the walk home down the road later, these were all part of it.

on mornings when ursula had driven off to dublin for consultations with her lawyers, i would often follow him down to the bar at the crossroads.

one morning i was met, just outside the gate, by a man looking over our wall into the garden. i watched him, curiously. he eventually asked me if i had seen a couple of weanling bullocks straying on the road, a black whitehead and a red whitehead …

i had not. he thanked me, and got into a small black car, and drove off.

there was something funny about this man … before i got to the end of the road, i realized what it was. farmers looking for a couple of stray cattle do not usually wear highly polished black shoes. some habit left over from a past life, perhaps? a retired garda?

temporarily at odds with sketchley – who not only failed to offer me a pint, but expected me to pay for the one he had already half downed. i kept news of this latest development to myself.

– i had met 'murphy'.

over the week or two that followed i learned to look out for the little black ford anglia in the pub car park. murphy, who turned out to be unfailingly generous in the matter of buying pints, seemed delighted to strike up conversation with anyone in the bar, but particularly with me.

clearly better briefed than the vast majority of county meath society as to who was the lover, and who was the handyman, he skilfully sought for scraps of information, in the midst of talking about a range of local matters. aware that i was taking risks by drinking with the enemy, i carefully confined my information to the harmless and to matters already locally known.

back at the glebe when sketchley returned, i could no longer resist telling him at whose expense i was now enjoying free pints. to my dismay, instead of praising my cleverness, he seemed to think that it was easy. perhaps he too could manage to drink – at one or two removes – on ursula's husband's account? in fact he insisted upon us both returning to the village, there and then.

the black ford anglia was still parked in its place, but so was the dusty van of brennan the builder, who was engaged in minor repairs at the glebe and had by now finished work for the day. we were hardly inside the door of the bar when my new friend murphy came over. all i had to do was to hesitate for a moment, knowing that he would offer to stand a round.

this murphy did. but he had barely time to enquire if sketchley would join us, and give the order, when brennan the builder, a towering man with a thick neck, barged into our company, already slightly the worse for wear, and started to harangue us. eventually, he stuck a finger in murphy's face –

'we don't think this man is a cattle dealer at all. looks more like a detective to me!'

we tried to shush him but it was too late. the pints were coming up on the counter, but murphy was already on his way to the passage that led to the 'gents' – and also to the side door out of the pub.

– and that was the last we ever saw of him.

thinking about these times years afterwards, i realized that we only ever heard one side of ursula's story. sometimes she got voluminous post – but never shared it with us.

'affidavits,' was all she said in explanation. or, 'more affidavits.'

one night sketchley got gloriously drunk at a hunt ball. he ended up back at home insisting upon playing his (scottish) bagpipes, but banished from the house, he retreated to play them in the graveyard opposite. i could see him in the moonlight, naked except for the handmade leather boots. although the worse for wear myself, i could just imagine what this would look like in an affidavit, and pulling a blanket off my own bed, to cover him with, i rushed over to get him back into the house.

another day, at the same graveyard wall, we met a distinguished-looking man accompanied by a well-dressed woman.

'is this the church that contains a thirteenth-century altar tomb?' the man enquired, staring over the gates at the locked building. we did not know. we had never been inside. but when we got back into the house, ursula had seen the encounter from the drawing room window.

'was that a murphy?' she asked.

we began to wonder just how an early nineteenth-century church could contain a thirteenth-century altar tomb. i thought this over and gave her my opinion –

i said, 'if that was a murphy, it was a very senior one.'

from this point on, our lives became more in earnest. nanny and the children came and went, happily oblivious of any drama. meanwhile we three became nervous of many things – black ford cars, shiny shoes, chance greetings or enquiries, even a light plane from the flying club apparently circling the house. sketchley began the pointless exercise of walking to the pub across the fields, instead of down the road. in our half sober nocturnal imaginings, the affronted husband became an unstable stalker, scheming, heavily armed, and seven feet tall. our lives became a game, half charade, half deadly serious. i began to take over sitting in the front of the car, with sketchley transported lying on the floor in the back, to make it seem as though he had not left the house at all. this served little purpose, but i could see that the heart-stopping tension and excitement of these escapades did wonders for their affair.

in the end the man we had come to imagine capable of anything, did the thing we least expected. he knocked in person on the front door of the glebe in the early hours of the morning while it was still dark.

i had woken at the headlights of a car, and almost at the first ring of the doorbell i was into my shirt and trousers, and slipping my feet into my shoes. an ashen-faced ursula met me on the landing, wearing sketchley's overcoat as a dressing gown.

'it's him,' she said.

what did we do now? ring for help? the telephone had not yet been connected. flee out of the back door over the fields? to where? this was a ridiculous situation, but anyway, it was not me he wanted to shoot. in a moment i saw the potential for us all becoming the laughing stock of the county. better to answer the door.

leaving ursula to conceal sketchley as best she could, i went down to the front door and opened it as far as its chain would allow.

on the doorstep stood a man, tense but calm, tall but some six inches shorter than i had imagined.

'is ursula here?' he said —

i waited. the door was still on its chain.

'– her father has died.'

i took the door off the chain, but ursula was already behind me at the foot of the stairs, in sketchley's coat, and had overheard.

a tense fifteen minutes later the two of them emerged from the dining room, and he left. i had stayed hovering in the hall throughout, but the voices were not raised, and gave no cause for alarm. there was a funeral to be planned.

as the front door closed behind him, ursula said —

'i have to go to england.'

it was around easter. this was the day we were to have gone to the west for a long weekend, but now the plan had to change.

'hell,' said ursula, 'hell. do you think he recognized the coat?'

then, reminded of sketchley, whom she had locked in the bathroom, she headed up the stairs. i went into the dining room, got a small tumbler and half filled it with brandy. when she unlocked the door. sketchley emerged wearing just a long shirt, and the inevitable riding boots.

without a word, at the foot of the stairs, he took the proffered tumbler from my hand. ursula said —

'i have to fly to england this morning. you two will need to lie low for a bit. i can get a taxi to the airport. you take the car and go to the west. you can't hang around here.'

at least we didn't have nanny and the children to worry about, it was their father's turn for access.

'it's going to be a long day,' i said. 'better put on some porridge.'

back to connemara

it was not until mid-morning, with some fifty miles behind us down the main galway road, that sketchley and i began to relax. although the road was dry and clear of traffic, we had been making slow progress.

'can you drive this thing?' he asked.

sketchley had no affinity for mechanical contrivances. he pulled in to the side of the road, and we changed over. he hauled himself into the back, where he could lie down. the brandy had taken its effect. he quietly passed out.

with motor cars, as with much else, i was a romantic. i was happy to ease myself in behind the steering wheel and the walnut facia with its row of precise dials. i was in the middle of an adventure, the kind that provides the raw material for autobiographies or cheap romantic novels. i had taken control of my inheritance, chosen my house, adopted a country and a religion, and found a girl in a hermitage in furthest connemara on the edge of the atlantic ocean. now fate had put a three litre jaguar car into my hands …

this was somewhat better than a life of waiting at table and i began to wonder – 'what next?'

the road was largely empty. with sketchley unconscious and uncomplaining in the back, i put my foot down, and wooshed silently down the highway to the west, sailing along – in those places where the road allowed – at ninety miles per hour.

the interlude that followed was more sober than most. for a start the two large petrol tanks of the car drank much of our spare cash before we even set out each day. secondly, we were not as sure of a welcome in connemara this time, in houses where tode-kerr had either outstayed his welcome or failed to repay what he had borrowed, nor in the two bars where he had yet to clear his account. we were now living on borrowed time, and in a fool's paradise. our reputation had gone abroad. this time the families in the west knew who we were – and girls who might have piled happily into tode-kerr's battered mercedes were acutely aware to whom this new gleaming chariot belonged. so were their parents, for although we were in our twenties, the girls that we knew socially were often of an age at which permission from the parents was still a part of arranging an evening's outing. that sketchley even considered asking any girl out, even for an afternoon walk on the beach, did not immediately strike me as a danger sign for the future of his affair.

as for me, i went, of course, to visit claudia – but claudia had in some sense liberated me. for the first time i saw myself through her eyes, as something dashing and desirable. i wanted nothing more than to try out this new-found power on every girl that we met.

all of that is an explanation – but not an excuse – for why sketchley and i found ourselves walking on a pebbly beach at dusk with two daughters of the major from errismore lodge.

the beach was a steep shingle of pebbles, rattled and sucked by a rough sea. there were upturned currachs – tarred works of art. i had never seen one before at close quarters.

sketchley and i now tested the goodwill of the gods to the very limit. while the girls retreated to the grassy bank high above the beach, we launched one light currach into the breakers and confidently stepped aboard, wet only to the knees. the next task was to sit in the centre, balance her, and get the oars quickly on to the rowlock pegs before the waves spun us sideways. then to keep her faced into each breaker. if you did that she rose like a living cork and took each wave like a loose horse clearing hurdles. it was necessary to pull steadily seawards, as each wave threatened to carry us back towards the shingle. this we did. it was exhilarating.

then came shouts from the beach, in unintelligible gaelic. a girl screaming –

'michéal, michéal, michéal!'

michéal appeared from somewhere running, hobbling along the pebbles, and stood staring at us open mouthed, unsure what to do. the girl screamed at him louder and more passionately. like a celtic warrior of old, driven into battle by the stinging tongue of the womenfolk, michael picked up a rock and fired it in our direction. we had no desire either to give battle or to be sunk. we instinctively stood up to surrender. at this moment a second rock hit sketchley right in his middle, and even though the force of it was softened by his heavy coat, he sat down again abruptly.

so did i. you cannot stand up, even briefly, in a currach in a swell. we wanted to raise our hands to surrender, like soldiers, but even this was not possible as constant attention to the oars was necessary to avoid meeting the next breaker crosswise and being capsized. michael reached for more rocks.

'alright, alright, alright!' sketchley roared from a sitting position, and michael withheld the next rock.

the waves brought the currach in again and the owner seized the stern with one strong hand while we stepped out again into the surf. our body language spoke of surrender.

honour was partly satisfied, but the girl had not fallen silent. now some compensation would have to be made. the passionate prompting of michael by the girl continued.

michael upturned the currach on the beach, without our help, and it displayed fresh scratches on the canvas bottom where it had scraped across the pebbles. they were not very serious scratches, but we were at a disadvantage. i searched my pockets and came up with three pound notes, which were accepted as compensation.

the girls from ennismore lodge had already retreated to the parked car. sketchley was disgusted at the easy way i had been persuaded to part with money.

'bloody peasants,' he said, of his countrymen.

but i was not listening. i had been totally captivated by the stream of gaelic imprecations – so unlike the irish that i was familiar with from the television, or 'school irish.'

my head was aflame with the poetry of it. meeting the gaelic spirit at last i was astounded to realize just how tame and diluted most of ireland had become, but this was something different. this other wild ireland still existed.

i tried to explain the fascination of my first encounter with passionate vernacular irish to the major's daughters.

though english-educated, they had always had a house here in the west and knew connemara since childhood. they replied, surprisingly, that there was no irish spoken in ennismore, the nearest gaeltacht was miles away and most of the people there did not speak it very much either.

what i had heard as unintelligible gaelic was in fact composed of english words – english words grafted on to a passionately angry gaelic intonation and rhythm.

later i understood why there was still such a struggle to get irish people to speak irish, once they had left school. like the man on the television news, most schoolteachers only have the words, not the music. this girl had her native music, and so naturally and perfectly that the words did not matter. She could just as well have denounced us in arabic. the music is what had been passed on to her, and when does the child have to learn it? from birth? no, it comes even before that. that music has to be learned the way that the rhythm of native speech has always been learned – by the unborn child muffled in its mother's womb.

the absentee landlord

thirteen weeks after the auction, permission to purchase laragh house and lands finally came through.

the vendor of the property, mr ramsbottom, was an importer of used farm machinery, and as i was anxious to take up residence, while he had yet to wind up his business, we made an arrangement to share the house for a month or two. it was large enough for all.

ramsbottom was a county westmorland man, who as well as buying used farm machinery bought horse tack in carlisle market and such places, and imported it, legitimately, to the north of ireland. the border was only five miles away, and it did not take me long to catch on that while some of this machinery was sold on to northern ireland farmers, much of it also ended up on the south side of the border – which was long and porous. later in the summer, on a couple of occasions, i accompanied him over the 'unapproved' moorland roads between north county monaghan and county tyrone over which he plied his trade. i had a mental picture of smugglers as people who dealt in diamonds and watches – easily concealed valuables. smuggling ploughs and pony traps was new to me, but these carried an import duty at the time, and this percentage was the margin which ramsbottom shared with his customers and by which he lived.

laragh house had originally been a mill owner's house, and the mill race still ran through it, but the mill had long since been demolished. the extensive, but now incomplete row of mill workers' cottages down at the road formed laragh village, most of which still belonged to the house.

mrs ramsbottom gave me some advice about collecting the rent on these cottages. she did not actually say in so many words that i could try but would not get any, but she did tell me a cautionary tale that on going to collect from one tenant, she had been invited in to the tiny cottage and served a cup of tea out of one of her own tea cups …

my own knowledge of being an irish landlord was almost entirely derived from history books and literature. i thought that a knowledge of history would stand me in good stead, and i felt that i could have passed any examination question in irish history from saint patrick to eamon de valera, via dermot macmurrough and captain boycott. i was, after all, on the romantic and 'green' side of the ancient quarrel, or thought i was. but now i was about to sit the practical exam in landlordism – for which i was ill-prepared. when first seeing a large county monaghan house in the estate agent's window, my immediate thought had been – 'if i could own a house like that, i would be happy to live on potatoes.' having no income, and no remaining capital, things had very nearly come to that pass – but it was now late summer. planting a garden was still many months away, let alone harvesting anything from it. 'living on potatoes' is just not that easy.

i also had in mind to let the outer fields, but late summer was not the proper time for doing this either. the land was only fenced in places, and open to wandering livestock. much of county monaghan is drumlin country. drumlins are little domed hills formed in the ice age, with a sunny side, a shady side, and little fields where lots of rushes will grow if the land is neglected for even a season.

the first job was to defend the territory. goats which seemed to belong to one of the cottages below spent a lot of time in my biggest and best five-acre field. i drove them out once or twice, but in the end lost patience, seized each by its collar (they were linked together at the neck by old metal bucket handles), and took them home to their owner.

sidney corrigan, my tenant, was full of apologies. he took the two goats off in the direction of a shed at the back of his house, invited me into the cottage, and gestured to his wife to shift the kettle on to the hot part of the range, to make us a cup of tea. he was charming. we talked for an hour, maybe more, during which he made trips outside to get sticks for the fire in the range. i did not stop to think where a man without any land or trees found sticks, but mam corrigan was busy filling up my cup with tea while her children played around at my feet, and, before i left, a small glass of poteen was put in front of me. it did not take too long to pacify me.

eventually i went home, congratulating myself that the first visit to the village had passed off so diplomatically, so smoothly. it was then that i realized i had forgotten to bring up the matter of the rent.

as i passed the empty gate lodge on the avenue up to the house, i met the two goats, once again grazing contentedly in my big field of flattened, unharvested hay.

i had a try at collecting rent later from another tenant, this time from mary anne corrigan. mary anne also asked me in to her cottage, took a ten shilling note from behind the clock, but before she could put it into my hand, burst into tears. between sniffs she told me a tale that i could not follow, but i began to get the general theme of it – she was willing to hand over what she owed, but in doing so she would reduce herself to unbearable poverty and starvation, because of desperate but unavoidable personal circumstances. i retreated backwards out of her cottage, mumbling reassurances.

the next thing i did – i was not far from poverty and starvation myself – was to let the fields. the hay had not been harvested, but it was too late in the year to do anything about it. i let the land privately through the auctioneer who had sold me the house. soon a dozen large bullocks came to eat down the grass, but when there is too much of it, bullocks can trample almost as much as they eat. the fences had not been seen to, and the bullocks soon found their way into the 'lawns', and discovered more interesting things to eat among the trees and rhododendrons around the house.

i used the proceeds of the letting to send for what remained of my late mother's furniture, still in storage in england. this arrived, but although well-suited, only filled two or three of the house's many rooms.

perhaps i should describe laragh. it was a house of about 1790, or perhaps 1810. old photographs showed it with a full complement of terraced croquet lawns, tennis court, greenhouses, clipped box hedges and vegetable gardens. since the going out of business and demolition of the mill, it had gone to seed. it had a fanlighted front door, three windows above and one to each side of the door. it was lime washed deep yellow. it had a long low wing to the rear of one side which may have formed an earlier house. the buildings then went around a further side of the yard with stables and garages, the square finally completed by a high wall entered by a handsome pillared gate.

the glory of the house was its trees. after a hundred and fifty years these were all still in their prime, but closed in with overgrown laurels and rhododendrons underneath. over the tops of the trees the hillside to the south was visible, but while our side of the narrow valley was large fields, the other side was a maze of straggly hedges, rocks, stone walls, heather, and tiny fields like rooms.

i thought of selling off the good fields, but was advised not to do so while they were let. i thought of looking for employment in the locality, but there was already a network of uncles and cousins forced to emigrate to england, and only waiting to get word to come back at the first sign of any vacancy. i did not have the inside track. i even thought of renting out the house, but the advert in *the irish times* was expensive, and no one replied, except claudia kenny, for a joke.

several weeks of damp weather followed, i began to get depressed, looking out on the dripping trees and the foraging bullocks making new tracks in the muddy grass. when one of them ate a yew tree and died, i was almost pleased. now someone might make a little effort to fence them in to their own rented fields.

i was rescued by a flashy gold-printed invitation, to attend, in grafton street, dublin 'an exhibition of recent paintings – by francis sketchley.'

the exhibition

temporarily freed from the new responsibilities of being a landlord, i set off down the road, hitch-hiking towards dublin. i left laragh unlocked – at least i bolted the front door and left by way of the back – the iron front door key was too big to carry around. i left the bullocks to ramble at will over the lawns. i spent the night at the glebe on the way down to dublin.

sketchley's exhibition, in the gallery of a large department store, brown thomas's, was a great social success. everyone enjoyed it. whether many pictures were sold, i am not sure, as ursula had been around the room beforehand with a few red 'sold' stickers to take the bare look off the thing and help the show along. of the three of us, she was the only one with any business sense.

i was the real winner of the evening. sketchley had invited an art historian, amelia, who came from his own native county of carlow. she half complained, half boasted to me, that she was being left on her own to mind the largest house in the south of ireland, for the rest of the summer. this was in celbridge, county kildare. her fellow caretaker had committed himself to taking examinations, and was thus about to leave her high and dry. before the evening was over i had allowed myself to be talked into a job.

sketchley and ursula took me home, first to the glebe, and next morning, the last thirty miles to laragh. they were curious to see the house, naturally, but did not have time to stay. they argued about this. i could see tensions creeping into their relationship. sketchley, i knew well, had always been poor, but free. he was used to being able to go, at any hour of the day, wherever the impulse took him.

ursula was also now at last in control of her own life, but it had to take into account the schedules of children, nanny, dogs, builders, and lawyers. horses were another responsibility, and then, like many people with two houses, to be resident in one often meant that she was worrying about the other.

sketchley's way of drinking had continued to change — from a public and sociable pastime, to a different, private, slightly furtive and desperate activity.

before they left, ursula looked around the half empty house, and observed abruptly in her usual forthright way —

'you need a wife – or a dog.'

within the fortnight, impractical as ever, i spent my last fifty pounds on a young but full-grown wolfhound dog. the dog, my sole companion around my derelict estate, soon got to know me and to follow me everywhere, like a shadow. it was not hard to find a name for him. i called him 'murphy'.

before going to take up my new job, i tried once more to collect a little rent. at the first cottage there was a bicycle leaning up against the window. i knocked. a curtain moved slightly, but no one came to the door.

mary anne's i did not bother with.

sidney corrigan was absolutely straight with me about his financial affairs —

five pounds dole money. had drunk two. had given three to the wife to go to the shop. so, begob, no money. still two days left in the week before next dole day. this straight refusal to pay so bemused me, that i forgot to say anything about the goats, which had begun to eat the ornamental shrubs under my front windows.

castletown house

the job that i had been offered near dublin, was as a temporary caretaker and guide at castletown connolly, in celbridge, reputed to be the largest house in ireland. i had been there once before. i had gone, out of curiosity, to the auction of its contents, when the connolly-carew family who had built it in 1722 were moving out. now it belonged to desmond guinness, founder of the irish georgian society, a distant cousin of some kind to my former employer lady honor. he had bought it and all its land for one hundred and sixty-six thousand pounds.

mr guinness had also made a brief appearance at sketchley's exhibition.

'you *must* come,' he had said, with enormous emphasis, 'and help us open up a *vista.*'

'i am not sure about that,' i had replied, mindful of the overgrown laurel shrubberies under the trees at laragh, 'i have unopened vistas of my own.'

at this he laughed uproariously, and was gone in an instant, leaving me both flattered and snubbed at the same time. that was his way.

amelia the art historian had told me what day i was to begin, and given me permission to bring the dog, but how to get there was my own problem. in the end i went by taxi, dressed in my best and only tweed suit, and taking my bedding, a suitcase, a folding card table (castletown was largely unfurnished since the auction), and the dog. my fellow workers would be student volunteers, but i had demanded, and been given, the unprecedented deal of eight pounds per week, and my keep.

the avenue at castletown approaches the house from the side, unlike the usual georgian device of having the drive up to a house in an 's' shape so that those on either side of a carriage are afforded, in turn, the chance to be impressed by a facade. i had intended to arrive in style, but even so, as the taxi turned from the avenue of lime trees into the gravel forecourt, i was taken aback to be met by two photographers and two other men who looked like reporters.

as the taxi disgorged the dog, the green baize table, the battered suitcase and the bundle of bedding, one of these came up to me.

'excuse me sir, but are you one of the rolling stones?'

i hesitated at this unexpected question ...

'no,' i said at last.

the hesitation proved fatal. perhaps i sometimes speak with a slight lack of conviction? out of the corner of my eye i saw the questioner nod to the cameraman. i was not believed. they had seen straight through my pretence. i tried the front door, which was barred, and rang the bell, and waited, and waited. from behind me there was a noticeable 'click'.

eventually amelia came to the door, and out on to the steps. she did not open the door to let me in, but came out instead and shut it behind her. she said to the hovering four –

'you'll get one photograph, and that will be all.'

they signified grateful assent.

at this point there emerged out of the front door, desmond guinness's wife marie-gabrielle ('mariga') in an edwardian tennis dress, mick jagger of the rolling stones in a cloak and a browband, and marianne faithfull, in head-to-toe black leather (hell's angels biker gear).

mrs guinness moved purposefully, while the other two followed in a sort of glide, as if in a dream, or not quite conscious of touching the ground as they went. we all stood to one side, while the dreamers arranged themselves in a pose on the steps, looking straight ahead as though unaware of the hovering photographers.

disregarding their agreement with amelia, the photographers then went click click click flash flash flash in a greedy fusillade.

'the dog,' urged the older reporter of the two, 'get the dog in the picture.'

everyone looked at me and i brought the dog up to the step on which the musicians were sitting and said –

'sit.'

murphy sat. but as soon as i went away again, he naturally came with me. three times i took him to the step and said 'sit.' three times the same thing happened. wolfhounds can be very stupid.

mick jagger came out of his daze and looked fondly at the dog.

'hold his collar then,' the reporter suggested.

so i sat down with murphy, on the step above, as the photographers tried to compose a convincing picture of jagger as 'an irish chieftain' – together with leather-clad biker girlfriend and slightly more appropriate wolfhound.

the session ended as suddenly and unexpectedly as it had begun, as the party got up and went to the car, which then reversed away. the photographers ran after the car still shooting and flashing, while mrs guinness, poking her own little camera through the open front window as she drove with the other hand, shot back.

mick jagger had just that week flown out of england after a successful appeal against a sentence for possession of drugs. he had dramatized his departure by leaving in a helicopter from the south coast of england without saying where he was going. this drove the press wild. in fact he had taken refuge with the guinnesses at leixlip castle.

in the photograph on the front page of that evening's dublin paper i appeared centre front staring into the middle distance, with murphy fondly paying attention to me, while mick jagger and marianne faithfull were gazing fondly at the dog.

sketchley was impressed, and said he nearly fell off his bar stool when it was shown to him. in the caption i was named as 'art historian', but i knew as little about art history as i did of the goings on in the england of the late sixties.

the idea that jagger was completely 'stoned' would not for a moment have occurred to me.

the consummation

amelia, the real art historian, had been entrusted with opening up castletown house to the public. the restoration was still far from complete, but was being helped by a small group of student volunteers. i became a caretaker and guide.

mrs guinness led by example. she had mastered every detail of the house's history, and we in turn learned it from her. she was also ready to roll up her sleeves, put on a smock, and pitch into painting the back stairs, or any other job that the volunteers were being asked to undertake.

castletown was built in 1722, by connolly, a politician and land speculator. the fact that connolly was an irishman made no difference to the attitude towards such houses among the irish general public, who as late as the 1960s still saw everything associated with the anglo-irish ascendency as symbols of alien oppression. what had escaped being burned in the 1920s should now politely be left to decay.

the castletown house plan, of a central block joined to two lower wings by colonnades, was the model for many irish houses that followed – such as carton, headfort, and rathbeale.

mrs guinness was an oxford-educated aesthete. people will tell you that she was a german princess, and that is also true – but that particular fact obscures rather than contributes to an understanding of what she was like. she had a particular and consistent style of dressing, which owed something to the irish georgian period, and more to edwardian england. she had a theatrical presence. where others raise their voice to gain attention, she gestured with her hands (in a most un-german way) and spoke ever more softly, obliging listeners to gather closer to her. she called all men and even youths 'mr' and by their surnames – by means of which she seemed able to flatter people and simultaneously keep them at arm's length. this did have the merit of treating everyone exactly the same. she was a 'republican', in the sense that she was a committed irish citizen, as opposed to being a unionist or a royalist.

her style of conversation was already familiar to me, as she had been a guest in more than one of the houses in which i had worked.

i had first seen her at malahide, where she had been asked to lunch to help entertain lord carrington, the first lord of the british admiralty, who was in ireland on a private visit. lord talbot himself was a hereditary admiral, holding the obscure mediaeval title of 'admiral of malahide and the seas adjoining', an ancient office of the english pale. mrs guinness arrived in the uniform of an eighteenth-century english midshipman, which was not as outrageous as it sounds, there being a fashion at the time for antique uniforms, and this one suited her figure very well.

complimented on this, she explained that the choice had seemed appropriate since she was having lunch with 'so many sailors.' this stopped the show.

mrs guinness was also an innovator in interior decoration. she revived the anglo-irish fashion for strong colours, particularly in dining rooms and corridors. this was a good policy in any restored house that had not had time to gather up again the clutter that takes many decades of family life to accumulate. she filled rooms with colour that would otherwise have seemed empty. she also filled empty spaces with vases, not of flowers, but of arrangements of beech leaves six feet across. she liked open turf fires, and her houses often contained dolls' houses and white marble busts wearing hats, scarves, or boaters. this eccentric list does not do full justice to an overall effect that she was able to achieve, and which was much imitated.

mrs guinness and her husband between them, through the georgian society, revived georgian ireland from its dying embers, but they rarely appeared together. each in their own way was a star of the show, and could not easily accommodate the other in the limelight.

amelia commented drily on the difference between them.

'she's very clever at pretending to be a bit mad – almost as clever as he is at pretending to be sane.'

in the evenings the house was left to amelia, myself, and a couple of volunteers. the volunteers slept on the top floor of one wing, while the kitchen in which we ate was on the top floor of the other. one american volunteer who chose to sleep in the further wing measured one hundred and fifty yards from her bedroom to the bathroom. on one occasion she forgot her toothbrush, making a total trek of four hundred and fifty yards – a quarter of a mile.

the sheer remoteness from the front door, when visitors turned up, made life difficult. one day there was a row, when desmond guinness arrived at castletown to find the front door open, people wandering in, and no one to meet them. the house was out of control. amelia, having recruited me as a guide, now needed someone to help out with the cooking, so that she herself was not tied to the kitchen upstairs. i hesitantly suggested the name of claudia kenny as someone who could cook, who might be free until term began in early september, and who might work unpaid.

i was taken up on this suggestion. i rang the far west.

in the middle of that week, 'bubbles' drove her third daughter across the country to join us at castletown. bubbles could not resist an adventure. she was interested in meeting all the people, rather than in the architectural grandeur of the house.

that first night claudia cooked supper for us all, omelettes, as if she had been doing it all her life.

when bubbles had left at last for the long drive back to the west, amelia asked me some complicated question about clean sheets and blankets, which i failed to pick up on. claudia was washing up our plates.

amelia tried again. i still did not get it.

'look,' she said finally, 'i am trying to get this damn palazzo organized. *do you want one room, or two?*'

i opted for one room.

the consummation of the blossoming affair was not however immediate. bubbles, free spirit though she was, would not have abandoned her schoolgoing daughter without some very firm words of warning and advice ...

so in the end we slept in one bed, in a room in the centre block of the house, facing across the drive and the front fields to the river liffey, a tangle of arms and legs.

contraceptives were not readily obtainable in the ireland of the sixties, certainly not in celbridge chemist's shops, so love had to wait for the best part of a week until a plain-cover envelope came from england ...

we worked busily in the mornings, scraping down walls, polishing marble floors and the famous brass bannister rails in the two-storey front hall. in the afternoons there were visitors and occasional tour buses. answering the door alone was a full-time job.

on about our fourth or fifth day claudia gave me a sideways smile at morning coffee break, and asked 'got any letters today?'

she was beginning to develop a certain look. in later years she was able to use this to summon perfect strangers (male) to her, across a crowded room.

'got any letters today?' became our standing joke.

until the plain envelope arrived, we slept each night motionless and entwined, awake or asleep, until the morning light when the mist came up from the river and lay like a blanket over the silent fields.

leixlip castle

one of the rewards for the unpaid volunteers was the chance of being invited to leixlip. leixlip was another and much older house, a castle which the guinnesses had purchased and restored. it stood on a rock at the junction of the liffey and the rye water rivers, shielded by trees from leixlip itself, which was then only a village. as at malahide, its mediaeval shell, most attractively, contained later georgian gothic rooms.

one evening at castletown, mrs guinness (to whom i always give this title, just as she always gave me mine) came to inspect some scrapings. these were experimental scrapings through many layers of old paint, to try and discover the original georgian colours of the rooms. she fulsomely and flatteringly praised the volunteers for their efforts, and left again waving a hand in our direction, declaring vaguely and grandly that we must all come to supper that evening.

we did not need asking twice.

this invitation left me in a slight dilemma which i still had not solved when evening came. desmond guinness had earlier that day, knowing his wife's propensity to issue last-minute invitations to all and sundry, asked me to help out with serving a buffet supper. the leixlip style of entertaining was neither a stand up buffet, nor a formal dinner with placings – but guests helped themselves from a side table, and then sat down wherever they could find a space. this had the virtues of a proper sit-down supper, but with the bonus of being able to circulate between courses if you wished.

the guinnesses mixed people inventively, sometimes almost recklessly – like a human herbaceous border – and were of course the despair of their staff. staff, above all, like to have set mealtimes, with set numbers, and with menus settled upon at least a couple of days in advance.

so now i was asked to help out with a supper, which i had also been invited to. what to do? this did not seem to be the ideal moment to search out either of the hosts for clarification. as so often in life, i drifted.

in the end it was not a problem. i abandoned claudia at the door of leixlip. she at least was one of the castletown volunteers, whereas i was employed and stamping a card. leixlip, which was small as castles go, did not employ a butler. i had worked there once before, for a day, having been 'lent' by lady honor, along with peggy the housemaid, for some special occasion or other. thus, knowing the house, i spent supper coming and going between kitchen and dining room, pouring wine, and snatched tit-bits to eat – as servants sometimes do – in the corridor between. people i knew, and people i did not know, spoke to me. some were as surprised to be there as i was myself. in the candlelight and in the cheerful chaos of a big informal gathering, no one had time to notice anything odd. all the same, some of my fellow guests must have wondered at my excessive politeness, in filling their glasses while neglecting my own (wherever it was), and in offering to fetch them all, in turn, second helpings of puddings.

only claudia guessed what was going on.

claudia had been monopolized for most of the evening by ulick o'connor, a dublin writer (also an accomplished boxer), who was the biographer of oliver st john gogarty. this man was so vain that he had not even asked her for her telephone number, but presented her with his own for her to chase *him* up! i suppose he was about thirty-five.

claudia was not a girl you could leave alone for long …

when the party ended mrs guinness shooed her guests out of the front door and down the stone steps with almost as much enthusiasm as she had gathered them up in the first place. no one seemed to have noticed my dilemma.

when we got back to castletown claudia had a fit of the giggles. she had overheard lord dunsany observing, after i had offered to take his coat to hang on a peg in the back passage, that the manners of the younger generation were not as bad as was being generally portrayed in the london papers.

the dole

at the end of the summer, claudia went back to boarding school. later in september castletown house closed, the student volunteers went back to trinity college and home to america, and desmond guinness gave me my cards. i had hoped to be kept on, but in spite of its size and importance, castletown house was a private project, to be run on a shoestring. it could not afford me and my eight pounds a week.

i went home.

laragh house had grown a fine dusting of green mould on its walls in my absence, and so had any clothes left behind in the wardrobe. my dinner jacket had gone the colour of a mallard drake's head, black in the distance, green when you looked at it in a certain light.

few rural irish houses, large or small, had central heating. the way to keep them dry was this – when the weather is clear and bright but cold, open a window in every room every day. when the weather turns soft and wet, keep all the windows closed and light a fire. this was said to have been the rule of old major connolly at castletown in years gone by, and was one reason why castletown house was so well-preserved. it is damp, not cold, which destroys houses. the damage is done when warm moist air meets cold walls. that is what you have to avoid.

regardless of mould, i was now in a trap. i could neither afford to stay, nor could i afford to go away without someone to mind the house. i decided to take the advice of my nearest neighbour, the 'wee black bookie.'

the county monaghan has a vocabulary and accent of its own. although it is one of the republic's twenty-six counties, it is a part of the old province of ulster, where the common speech is more closely related to old scots english than to english english. most of my neighbours, like the bookie, were named duffy, either that or corrigan, thus they needed further names to distinguish between them. once this became accepted, the original surname confusingly tended to fall into disuse. so 'bookie' was a nickname of one particular duffy family, and 'bookie' in this corner of monaghan meant not a turf accountant, but a small buck goat.

it was over goats, over sidney corrigan's goats in fact, that the bookie first became my ally. the bookie had also suffered in his time as an unwilling host to this rambling pair of browsers, and their many predecessors.

the bookie was small, about five feet tall, very dark, light, and wiry. he used chewing tobacco, and spat a lot.

'take one of them back, just one,' was his advice.

he also made a face which meant – 'and don't let on who told you.'

i did not immediately follow his line of thought. but i managed to catch the two fugitives, unhook the bucket handles that formed their linked metal collars, and shut one in an outhouse with a little leaves and grass to keep it quiet. then i dragged the other, most unhappy to part from its companion, down to the corrigans' cottage. even when livestock are straying, forcibly taking them back to the owner is not usually done in rural ireland. all livestock stray eventually, and to act high-handedly is to invite retaliation in one's turn, and one's turn always comes around quicker than expected. likewise to take the goats off and sell them to the travellers would have solved my problem, but would have been theft, and likewise invited future reprisals.

to take one goat back served to alert the owner that something untoward had happened, because a thief would most likely take both, while if the goats were free and unharmed, they would stay close and one would be found with the other.

i began to appreciate the bookie's thinking. we had set a puzzle. sidney having been returned one goat from my land as evidence of my good intentions, began with a long search of all the rocks and fields of his own side of the valley, searching every farm and outfarm except mine. it was a day and a half later when he eventually found the other goat, which was now bleating, and took it back home, where he tied it up.

from that day on the bookie became my adviser, always giving good counsel, but not above using me (as he had against sidney) to quietly pay off old scores of his own.

there was an election that year. i had become a constant reader of *the irish times* and had followed the campaign closely. as the election neared i was flattered to be approached by three friends of the bookie to ask my advice on how they should vote. i took them into the kitchen for a cup of tea. i willingly gave them my educated and informed rundown of the policies of the parties, fianna fáil, fine gael, and labour, and the merits of each. they thanked me briefly but sincerely and went away.

it took me a while to realize that my comments would now be analysed in mccabe's bar and elsewhere in the locality. in fact the delegation of three had made an assessment of my entire political outlook without revealing a single clue as to their own.

on further consideration, they would almost certainly be voting fine gael, whatever i had to say, the local pronunciation being 'fyne gale.' they would do this because they lived in a little pocket of fine gael territory and they would support the party their fathers had supported, and could never bring themselves to support 'the other crowd' regardless of the policies being put forward.

another well-meaning visitor wished me luck of the house, and reassured me that laragh was a quiet area and 'no one would trouble you down here' – on the grounds that it was not IRA country. this was the first mention that i had heard of the IRA in monaghan. he must have seen me look doubtful, so he elucidated further –

'they all live up in cloonaughamoyne.'

cloonaughamoyne was two and a half miles up the road, so this was less than reassuring.

this man had an old election story, but no doubt the same tale is told of other townlands. a cloonaughamoyne man was going in to town to vote, travelling by donkey and cart. passing a laragh neighbour he offered a lift, which was accepted.

a mile or so passed in silence, the driver sucking on his pipe. elections are serious affairs. then the passenger spoke up, cautiously.

'i suppose ye'll be voting for de valera?'

'aye.'

'well i'm agin him, so the pair of us may as well go home.'

which they did.

laragh at this time was still an isolated place. there was a bus to town on saturdays, but only if you walked the mile to the main road. a few people had cars, but a tractor was usually purchased by a farm family long before the purchase of a car. the typical thirty-acre farm could not support a tractor on its own, and the few farmers that had them survived by also doing work for hire, for the neighbours.

on sundays the roads were black with people walking to mass. here also the occasional tractor was put to use. a farmer with his wife sitting in the transport box behind, would pick up a neighbour's child or two until they were perched all over it like hens in a roost.

the bookie had a pony and cart, this was usually driven by his eldest son pat, then about fourteen. even though the pony's pace was slow, i used to envy pat as he drove standing up at the front of the cart, like cúchulainn in his chariot. the pony and cart were mainly employed in cleaning outhouses (meaning sheds), and spreading the dung back on the land.

pat eventually progressed by stages from this to riding racehorses on the curragh of kildare, and was good at it. later still he even owned a racehorse of his own.

the town was eight miles away from laragh. it was only ten or twenty years since the roads had been 'made up' (with tarmacadam). some of the older men had never even seen the town until they were fourteen or fifteen years old, and thus big enough to walk the eight miles both ways, taking cattle to a fair.

not every house had electricity. some that did, had installed it in the piggery, before the luxury of having it in the house. some cottages still had the open turf fire, the crane, and the blackened kettle that swung over the fire when needed.

the bookie lived up a steep lane in a stone cottage, once thatched, but now slated. there were three rooms in the house, the fourth was a hayloft approached by a stone stair from outside. his lane was a stony track, often a river in winter. his water supply was an iron spout on this lane, fed by an unfailing spring further up the hill. his wife and five or six children (later there were more) were small, dark and bright-eyed, like himself.

in summer he farmed his thirty fractured, rushy acres. he grew oats, barley, grass for seed, and potatoes. he milked four cows and left the milk out in a can at the roadside below. there it was sucked up into the milk lorry through a tube and a meter and taken to the creamery. in winter he worked from dawn until dusk on a threshing machine, earning six pounds a week.

the bookie introduced me to mccabe's bar, the only pub for miles around, which stood a mile further up the millrace bank and a couple of hundred yards off the public road. there was no pub sign, because everyone ever likely to drink there drank there already, and knew where it was.

mrs mccabe was a big woman. she was knowledgeable about pigs and the price of cattle. she did not go to the market herself, but thoroughly cross-questioned everyone who arrived in her bar back from the town. she was invariably known as 'mrs mccabe', a rare distinction in the country. she insisted upon proper decorum in her bar. any customer who attempted to buy drink for people he was not with, was sent back to his 'own company'. women were welcome but were expected to remain in their places, and not to approach the bar to buy drink. troublemakers were put out of the door.

one man ejected on one wet night, had taken shelter in mrs mccabe's henhouse in the yard. there he had taken his revenge by plucking her rooster, live, so that she found it there in the morning shivering on its perch. the bird was naked, but for its head feathers, naked as a goose in a butcher's window.

i was on the dole. once a week i walked the four miles to the garda barracks in shantonagh to sign on, and the four miles back. i think the rate at the time for a single man was three pounds ten shillings. it was a rate that eventually obliged a person to work. it fed you and you even drank a couple of bottles of stout on one night per week, but it did not cover much else.

the stuffed auction

i got one chance to make some money. it was on a visit to ursula and sketchley. ursula was approached by a local dealer, brady the auctioneer. brady was a smooth-talking fellow, an obvious rogue with that gift of smirking and winking to persuade you that he was being roguish in your interest. it was in the drawing room at the glebe. brady wanted ursula to lend him the house, to hold a stuffed auction.

a 'stuffed auction' is one which purports to be the complete clearance auction of a house, but which is 'stuffed' with outside items, often the property of the auctioneer or his pals. it seems that such items make up to twice their usual price if shown off in suitably impressive surroundings. brady explained his requirements, but of course he did not use the word 'stuffed.'

i was only an eavesdropper to this conversation, and busy thinking about something else. i could tell that ursula wasn't interested. it was only when brady said – 'you could make up to four thousand for a couple of days' work,' – that i sat up and took notice.

'i have a house,' i said.

ursula glowered at me. she didn't really want the deal, but she did not want me barging in, either. in fact she had probably forgotten that i was in the room. but four thousand pounds was nearly the price of a farm. money worth having. brady looked at me with new interest. i described laragh for him …

thus a month or so later advertisments appeared in the national and local papers for the complete clearance sale of laragh house. i had wanted brady to sign some kind of agreement but he demurred. my share was to be twenty-five per cent of the profits, but the profits could not be calculated until the auction had been held.

i wanted brady to estimate the takings. four thousand seemed to me a large sum of money to take out of one house auction. brady said we would easily clear four thousand, as long as the people came and the day went well – so i settled down to playing my part in making the day go well.

first i cleaned up the place and sorted out some furniture of my own, and some of the ramsbottoms', that needed to be sold. then a load of furniture and pictures arrived, and brady hung up the pictures here and there more or less at random. there was some very good stuff, some rather ordinary stuff, and some cheap rubbish.

i was interested in houses, and particularly georgian houses, and i knew that this 'complete clearance' story did not ring true. the stuff was neither stacked up as in a crowded shop, nor arranged as in an old family home. that night when brady had gone off for another load, i set to work. if this was my picture, i wondered, where would i hang it? in the library of course, at about eye level. no one hangs a humbert craig over a gas cooker. bit by bit i got the house into shape. the furniture was still pushed back to the walls, but by the time i had finished, it looked like a home. i had no particular intention of 'fooling' the people. i was just embarrassed at the idea of my house being seen with small pictures hung on high hooks and big pictures on low hooks.

when brady came the next day he was delighted. he exclaimed that the 'mansion' really looked as it would have done 'in more gracious times.' he used a sort of exaggerated estate agent language, but still, i was quite pleased with my effort. he had three identical cheap spanish chandeliers, one to hang in the hall, one for a bedroom, and one which got left on a chair in the passage.

when the day of the auction came the sun shone. these days such auctions are held out in marquees, but there is nothing to beat the excitement of a complete clearance with the bidders pushing for space as the auctioneer goes from room to room. brady soon got into his stride. the first lot was hardly pointed out when crack, he hit his little clipboard with his gavel.

'sold to the lady at the back!'

this was met by a chorus of surprised would-be bidders, complaining that they had not realized the bidding had already started, but brady was off and already well into lot two, a plate held up by his assistant. he stood halfway up the stairs, waving his gavel over the heads of the totally mesmerized crowd. it was a show, a pantomime perhaps. he smirked, and winked, and hassled the crowd – he teased, he challenged, he praised them for their eye for a bargain. he did fast lots, and slow pleading, lots. he took bids off the farmers' wives, the well-heeled, the impoverished, the dealers, curious bystanders, and when things flagged – off the curtains at the back of the landing.

he even sold my bureau, for a considerable sum, but when i pushed forward in a panic to stop him because it wasn't meant to be in the sale, he stopped me dead with a glare and a frown. i quickly got the message – it was not sold at all, just part of the show.

a few people had picnics on the long grass of 'the lawns' and all in all it was a grand day. the three identical spanish chandeliers all sold for widely different prices, according to the rooms in which they were displayed.

people must have enquired who i was, because a man stopped me in the front doorway.

'not many of these old places left, now.'

i mumbled something.

'sorry to see the old home go ...'

he suddenly shook my hand with deep emotion, and i did not know where to look. what could i say? – 'actually it all came up in a couple of vans from dublin last tuesday night?'

– of course brady never paid up.

first i got on to him myself. then when i was getting nowhere i went to mr drought my solicitor in dublin to try and sue the little auctioneer. mr drought wrote to him and to the surprise of both of us we got a letter back. there was no problem with the deal – just give him time to calculate the twenty-five per cent of the profits, once all the bidders' accounts were paid, all cheques cleared, and all the bills and the various considerable expenses covered.

'what will his expenses be?' i asked mr drought, doubtfully.

mr drought looked gloomy.

'he can make them whatever he likes ...' he said.

i decided to get serious with brady. i rang the society which controls the auctioneers and valuers of ireland and without even enquiring whom i was talking to i let rip to the person who answered the telephone about honesty, integrity, standards, and unprofessional conduct. the slightly tired voice at the other end waited in silence until i had finished and then enquired –

'was he ever one of our members?'

i was left to promise lamely that i would find out. this official was really quite kind to me. he could well have told me to go and get stuffed, like my auction.

i hitchhiked back penniless to 'the old family home' with my tail between my legs.

a flaming red herring

one day in the autumn term of 1967 stands out in my memory. claudia had gone back for one of her last terms in boarding school. claudia never broke any promise to me – because she never made one. likewise i never broke any promise to her, for the same reason. we corresponded by letter, and if any boarder at that school was suspected of any underhand scheme, or communicating with any undesirable person, the school post was liable to inspection. i always finished my letter *'with love'* and signed it. under my name i would write: *'and love to you too, matron, if you happen to be reading this.'*

a month or so later there was a hunt ball in corbalton hall in county meath, and i went to it. i do not remember getting there, it was after dark when the dance began. perhaps i went along with sketchley and ursula, but i do not remember that either. before hunt balls were held in hotels, they tended to be held in private houses, where presumably they originated.

corbalton hall had become too large for the family that owned it, and was wholly or partly unoccupied. a lot of trouble had been gone to, to make the large ballroom presentable and welcoming for the dance, and it and adjoining rooms were brightly-lit with many candles.

i do not remember being introduced to patra keane, either. most probably we were not introduced. i had bought one ticket only, and gone to the ball without a partner, expecting very little. romantically, in my own head, i belonged to someone, but my time was unavoidably my own. i think that patra keane and i just happened to take a break

97

at the same moment and sit down on opposite ends of a sofa in a passageway, and to fall into conversation. she was tall, she had well-cut red hair – that was possibly not her own shade of red – she had done something elegant and clever with it. it was hard to say what, exactly.

there was dancing, there was drinking, there were things to eat laid out on a buffet in a side room, and there were obviously many people that she knew, but she ignored the whole scene and we just went deeper into conversation. there was something eerily timeless about the atmosphere in the ballroom, perhaps because it lay more or less uninhabited year-round and had been resurrected for one night only, because it contained enough space to house a large crowd of rowdy hunt revellers.

patra keane had pale skin, and a natural west of ireland colouring which was reminding me achingly of someone else. i was also lonely, so between one thing and another, i was her willing captive from the word 'go'. deep conversation between two people within minutes of meeting each other is a rare thing. did i fancy her? those words are too shallow. my mind was engaged with hers and i ceased to notice anything else in the room.

the mind is also an erogenous zone.

after perhaps two hours someone that she knew, probably considering that she was being unfairly monopolized, tried to get her to dance – but she would not. time slows down for the drinker, something that even einstein himself could not explain. she leaned back and stretched out elegantly on the sofa so that her long legs and her long dress half blocked the passage. i moved into the middle of the sofa, leaving no space for any exhausted dancer or gin-dazed hunt follower to flop down between us.

after a while people that she obviously knew well, and who were obliged to step over her feet to get to the buffet or the toilets, began to say things like –

'having a nice time, *mrs keane?*'

'great party isn't it, *mrs keane?*'

i am not utterly stupid. i sensed from the start that i was talking to somebody's wife, and not just to somebody's sister, but it was not my problem. i had not made a move, i had not asked for a telephone number. i had just sat down on a sofa in a passage, for a breather, and fallen into conversation. i had not forced my company onto her. we had by this time been in conversation for over two hours, and i had only just learned her name. patra keane. yes, i had filled her glass several times, and brought her some cold salmon on a plate – but she had only toyed with it.

at the end of the ball she said:

'how are you getting back to dublin?'

'no idea.' (it was laragh i needed to get to.)

'stay there, i have to talk to my driver.'

this puzzled me. a chauffeur? unlikely. a taxi? at this time of night, surely not. friends that she had come with? but i thought she said she had driven herself up the slane road.

perhaps it was someone else she had to get rid of? a compliant husband? i hadn't a clue.

fifteen minutes later we were sailing down the long straight road to dublin, the one that the prince of wales had rebuilt to get to his mistress mrs fitzherbert in the shortest possible time (perhaps i am misquoting the old meath story, but it doesn't matter – i did not believe it, anyway).

it was a large black mercedes. not the sort of car you buy your wife for popping down to dunnes' stores.

this is *his* car, i thought …

you can do ninety or a hundred miles an hour down the slane road, it was almost clear of traffic at half past two in the morning. there was no mist and the road was dry.

i did not ask her about her family, but i did ask her about children, and she had none. i had all the time in the world to study her face in the pale light from the dashboard. she talked about 'we'. 'we were the first to start going to the meath,' she said. i took her to mean that they were the first from outside of the hunt members' circle and their guests to aspire to go to the meath hunt ball.

then something happened to wrench the wheel in her hands, and we were crashing.

we swerved. she managed to pull away from the kerb and over to the oncoming lane, back again to the near side, and back again for a final swerve to the right hand side of the road where we bounced off the verge and came to a sickening halt slewed across the wrong side of the white line.

it took an awful long time to crash. by the time that the car had actually come to a full stop i had had time to twist in my seat, jump clean into the back, and was curled in a ball behind the driving seat.

'hope i didn't scare you,' she said, over her shoulder.

i was so shaken i did not even know if i was injured.

having got into the car at the front i now had to leave it by the rear door on the opposite side. then i stepped onto the road and felt my sock filling with blood.

i looked down gingerly to discover that i had stepped into a puddle. i had exited the front so fast that i had actually left one shoe behind me.

it was only a minute before a van pulled up and two men came over and asked us were we all right. we had had a blowout. the mercedes was buckled but not wrecked, but the two men, who seemed to know about fixing cars, refused to let her drive it. they told her to let off the hand brake and they pushed it into the side of the road.

'i am flying to new york at noon tomorrow and i have to get home,' she said.

there was something about her that made them do just whatever she asked them to. i climbed into the back of their van while she sat in the front and gave directions as they brought us all the way to her front door, deep in south dublin.

where am i now? i wondered.

i was still with patra keane. she was a dress designer – a couturier. she had been a model and had made a successful career change to being a business woman. she had a tiny fashionable shop in dublin called 'cleopatra'. she was working hard to get a toehold in new york. she had the financial backing of her husband, who was, among other things, joint founder of a successful firm of accountants.

she dismissed the van and closed the door behind us and we were in a softly lit stairs hallway in a smart south dublin suburb.

patra keane folded up like a concertina and collapsed into the thick-pile beige carpet.

we were home and dry. alive – and alone.

she raised herself on one elbow. she said:

'i am going to make you want me like crazy then i am going to tell you to fuck off.'

i had no doubt at all that she could do that if she so decided. she seemed to be wearing nothing very much under the floor-length dress, and as for me i was floating somewhere outside of time and space. she was lean and willowy. she was not a woman who required very much undressing – she was not one of those held together by straps and underwiring and industrial-strength corsetry. her underwear was minimalist and unobtrusive, its colour not discernible in the soft subdued light, but probably matching the dress.

she smelled expensive. she was delicious.

if she had been an entrée she would have been a poached salmon hollandaise.

had she been a drink she would have been a straight black bushmills, no ice.

you do not need to understand this last remark – except that i instinctively make a comparison with something that you savour slowly, that you sense first with the nose and then lift to your lips.

a confident woman who had everything

sometime in the darkness between then and the not-too-distant dawn we made a move upstairs, where we resumed our conversation under a duvet, with an open and unguarded intimacy but which stopped short of softness or affection.

'you are very virile,' she said.

i had to laugh.

'not at all. it is just that i haven't been let out for weeks!'

but she was not a flatterer. she was too direct.

'nice to be in bed with someone who hasn't got a tummy.'

for some reason this brought to me an unwanted vision of overweight rag trade millionaires in new york.

nor was everything perfect. she was a cigar smoker, and i was a non-smoker – able to taste tobacco on someone who has had a smoke, even if it were three days ago.

patra keane had everything she wanted, or nearly. her face supremely feminine, but hawklike, she was a magnificent bird of prey. her cheekbones, her height, her thick galway hair, her horsewoman's confidence, her admiring female friends, her husband often away on business, her picture always in the papers, her recognized status as a representative of sixties irish fashion in irish america.

but, like me, she had no children. no tribe to follow on.

gone away

i returned to consciousness in broad daylight, my hostess missing, and voices arguing in the hall, downstairs. my panicky thoughts turned to home and safety, and the problems of catching the next carrickmackross bus while wearing a dinner jacket and a wing collar and black tie.

mrs keane reappeared at the door. she was fully dressed for new york.

'only my sister,' she explained.

'does she know i'm here?'

'yes but she only wants to get a look at you,' she said. 'i told her she's not to come up!'

she had sisters, then, but no children. does having no children matter more, or less, if you yourself come from an extensive family?

she went.

she did not contact me. i did not pursue her, then or later.

if something is almost perfect, and with the luck of the gods you get away with it – and, in this case, get away with your life – why not leave it at that? you may remember it forty years down the tracks, and it will seem as fresh as yesterday ...

or you may be googling something else and stumble across an unmistakable face above an *irish times* obituary:

'a pioneer of irish fashion in america ... at her residence in county meath ... loved horses ... rode out every morning ... widow of the late fergus keane ... died aged eighty ...'

eighty! so she was – let's see – thirty-five then at corbalton hall – and i was twenty-four.

so why am i crying as i type away, now? for a woman that i never loved, never dated, never even danced with?

because i did actually meet her again. the summer after that meath hunt ball i was taken out to lunch in a restaurant in a hotel above rathfarnham – not a place i would normally go – and patra keane walked past our table with a woman friend.

even from behind, i knew that it was her.

when i was on my way out, she was standing there at the garden entrance, at the top of a flight of steps, with one hand on a stone urn. she was looking at the city of dublin spread out below, in the sunshine.

she had waited for me.

'how is life treating you?' she said.

'very well,' i said.

when she turned to face me she was wearing a simple but elegant dress typical of her own design. a perfectly cut and perfectly pitched dress that neither boasted, nor attempted to conceal, that she was heavily pregnant.

she looked pre-raphaelite. regal. dynastic.

'i don't know what to say,' i stammered eventually.

'then don't say it,' she replied coolly, smiling like the cat that got the cream.

a flaming red haired galway woman, who had feared for twelve whole years that she was infertile, but never gave up.

they don't come more dangerous than that.

making 'katy daly'

the ambition of the bookie was to build a new house on lower ground for his family. his older daughters were in their teens and no longer content to sleep in a cramped room with a clatter of younger brothers. they were dark too, like their parents, and very good-looking.

in the present farmhouse they washed their hair for saturday night dances in a bowl on the kitchen table. the bowl was filled by way of a bucket at the spout and a constantly refilled kettle on the range. meanwhile the conversation went on all around them. in spite of the intimacy of the circumstances the girls kept themselves proudly apart, and any over-familiar remark could be sharply put down.

once the bookie was committed to building a new house, i offered him the chance of bringing his family to live with me until it was completed. he accepted at once.

laragh house had nineteen rooms. even if the duffys occupied three times the space that they were used to, it still left me ten rooms for myself. a constant fire maintained in the range, winter and summer, was the thing the house most needed. that they would supply.

living without a car makes a person many times more aware of all that goes on within a mile or two of their own house. i got to know laragh. above the village was the lake in which the millrace originated. at foot of the lake was a sluice gate, to control the flow of water in the race to the site of the mill above the village. water that did not get diverted into the race, overflowed into the river, which ran below at the back of the village.

the lake was broad but shallow, and slight variations in rainfall resulted in large variations in the acreage of land underwater. this resulted in wrangles between the farmers who had land along the lakeside, and those whose land was subject to being flooded by the river further down. the favourite tactic of the lakeshore farmers was to wedge a large rock underwater, so that the metal sluice gate could not be lowered.

although the country round about was completely rural, laragh had also had an industrial tradition. the country was pockmarked with six-foot-deep flax dams left over from the days of the flax industry; these were like tiger traps for stray cattle.

in buying the house, i also bought into the leftovers of the relationship between the mill workers and the mill owners. many big houses are like that. the incomer begins by inheriting the relationships of the earlier owners, whether popular or unpopular, and regardless of whether anyone has bothered to find out what he is like himself.

there was a ghost on the old mill site – supposedly of a girl who had jumped the race as a shortcut when late for her shift, become caught up in the wheel, and been dragged under the water. i never encountered her.

on the shore of the lake lived a poet, jemmy julia. he was also a farmer. his own name was james. his surname was duffy, but his identifying nickname was his mother's christian name (a system older than surnames). he came to the road by the shortest route, across the lake by means of a home-made boat.

i was curious about these few remaining old men who had lived almost all of their lives in a society that predated electricity, 'made up' roads, and when there were no cattle marts, but only fairs in the town street. with electricity had come the radio, and with the radio the popularity of homespun songs and stories had begun to wane. one night, with the bookie's help, we gathered up half a dozen of the men of the locality, who still had a song or a story. persuading them to meet us in mccabe's, we arranged a car to bring them around to the house at closing time. there we gave them a bottle of stout in the library (a library so designated for its tall shelves, rather than by any great quantity of books). bridie the bookie's wife had the kettle on to make punch – 'poteen', or home-made whiskey with added hot water and sugar. when this was handed around and the singing of songs had got under way, one of the storytellers went around the circle again, with a bottle of my gin, the only spirits in the house. this, he explained, was 'to cool it.'

after this occasion, i would not rest until i had seen 'poteen' made. what was the source? how was it obtained if no one seemed to know where it came from?

the source of poteen was closer than i suspected. the bookie himself had been a practitioner of the art. to the amusement of all the district, including the guards, he had decided to 'retire' and had presented the 'worm' or copper spiral tube, to the folk museum in town. this was a cool move. the 'retirement' was actually a cover for acquiring a new set of equipment, and this was again hidden where the old equipment had been hidden, by taking it apart and hanging it all separately here and there in the different trees of an orchard.

the process began with a 'wash' made in barrels, and concealed under a few hay bales in a loft. poteen can be made from barley or potatoes, but the superior monaghan product was made from demerara sugar. it also required yeast, which for some reason was hard to obtain outside of the north, and had to come over the border.

when the day came that the wash had matured and was ready, a fire was built in the middle of the yard. the distilling process proceeded out of doors. the fire needed to be very hot, and this was achieved by means of a drainpipe laid to the centre of the fire, connected to a fan bellows. a 'fan bellows' is a metal tube like a giant snail shell, with a wheel and a handle to turn the fan. these were thrown out of cottages when open fires first began to go out of date and solid fuel ranges came in.

my job was to turn the fan bellows to keep the fire reddened, and also to keep an eye out for anyone coming to the house. the greatest danger to a poteen maker was not the gardaí themselves, but betrayal by a jealous neighbour or rival producer, who had been tipped off by the tell-tale spiral of smoke from an outdoor fire. this was another reason for the fire to be really hot and not just smouldering.

the bookie was assisted by his uncle cuey (hugh), a little bent man who knew the business. cuey tested the product. he explained that the wash now had to be put through the system a second time, and there would be far less poteen after the second distilling.

'why is that?' i wanted to know.

'because he drinks so much of it the first time,' said the wee black bookie.

when the potato harvest came i went around with the bookie to harvest his neighbours' potatoes, which he had to do before anyone would help him with his own. there was a traditional crop rotation. after the potatoes came barley, for feeding and for straw. the barley was 'undersown' with grass and this was inspected by a department inspector, and if passed, saved for the thrashing and sale of certified grass seed the following year. then the field was kept for hay for the farm's own use, then for grazing – and back again, when ploughed, to potatoes.

when the tractor and spinner came for the harvesting of the potatoes, every man, woman, and child had to help. a child was nearly as quick as an adult, being closer to the ground. the potatoes were stored in the field in a straw and clay covered mound, what in monaghan is called a 'pit' but in england would be called a 'clamp'. this was also a use for a few mown rushes, used to cover the pit.

manual work was new to me. i enjoyed it, but i did not share the folk memory of hunger which made them work on into the dusk until it was almost impossible to make out the potatoes in the gloom.

i was an unemployed footman now, working not even for money but for a share of a harvest of spuds.

fools' paradise

at the beginning of the christmas school holiday claudia kenny came to stay. i was glad to have her back at last in my corner of ireland. the weather turned bright and frosty. we took a big brass bed to pieces and reassembled it in the smallest bedroom, the first room in the lower back wing. this room also had an open fire. by lighting this fire in the evening, and stoking it up last thing at night, and by staying under the blankets until well into the next morning we were able to make the warmth, and our fools' paradise, last a little longer.

christmas at corballis house

i had no intention, and little expectation, of resuming a life in domestic service, but in december there came an unexpected invitation to work over christmas at corballis house, near dublin.

the day of the big houses in ireland was coming to an end. the day of a large formal domestic staff, butlers and footmen, had more or less gone for good. the few 'butlers' were now usually glorified waiters hired out by catering companies. in the servants' halls of private houses i had seen the tail end of a system that would not return, even if the irish georgian society managed to preserve the beautiful shells of the houses for posterity. even so, i had never fully belonged to this world of domestic service 'below stairs'. come to that, i did not belong to the 'upstairs' world of anglo-irish society either. the no man's land, the borderland in-between upstairs and downstairs, seemed to be my precarious niche, and this niche, too, was closing.

the few surviving full-blown houses of 'the ascendency' were in rapid decline, but sometimes societies in decline – like great cheeses – save their most delicious flavours for just before they go off.

the job at corballis house was to act as butler to the family of an american friend of the talbots of malahide. the drawback was that only a couple of daily staff were kept, and there were some fairly strenuous aspects to my duties, including carrying brass coal buckets to fires in upstairs and attic bedrooms, from a basement far below.

corballis house dated from perhaps 1740, with the typical wings of the irish georgian house, and these faced to the rear and contained stable yards and other outoffices, but in more intimate proportions than at castletown. the presence of hens and horses in the yards made for a more authentic eighteenth-century irish feel, even though aunt laura knox, the american, had been reared in louisiana many thousands of miles away, and had no known irish connection. why i call her 'aunt' laura will become more apparent in due course.

aunt laura's husband, uncle jeremy, was an anglo-scot. he was also an old etonian, which had perhaps left more mark on him than his early upbringing in edinburgh. there were also two young sons and a teenage daughter, celia. the house was beautifully restored and decorated, heavily under the influence of the bold decorative style of mrs guinness and the irish georgian society revivalists. thus far so good. they kept wolfhounds, which being poorly house-trained were confined to the basement floor (i myself had seen the light and parted with my own intellectually challenged companion, 'murphy'). they also had a couple of kerry blue terriers, of doubtful temper, which were allowed upstairs.

aunt laura wanted to invite louisiana cousins for christmas, so she needed help. she and her husband were distinctly 'old south' american and lowland scots 'british', respectively. this made it difficult to fit in with their level of formality, since in this, as in so much else, they differed.

a trained butler actually prefers to be treated impersonally. this allows him to get on with the job. my life at corballis house was immediately thrown into a form of chaotic improvization. the family lived as though they were making life up as they went along, like a play with no script.

aunt laura addressed me by my christian name, uncle jeremy addressed me by my surname. she sent me for more coffee after dinner. he asked me to sit down at the table and have a cup. all of this was hard to deal with.

the other staff, both women, were dailies and there was no servants' hall to speak of, just the cook's television room in the basement, where the boys sneaked in to watch things they had been forbidden to watch upstairs.

gradually i fell into some kind of routine, but though very busy at certain times of the day, the real problem for them was where to put me and what to do with me, when i was not busy. i spent quite a lot of time reading in the afternoons, in my yellow bedroom high on the top floor.

this was the winter of a foot-and-mouth scare. first, all hunting was banned, then even riding or unnecessary walking in the fields was banned. the land at corballis house was let to local agricultural contractors, and as a result, for us, there was no access to the fields at all. the horses had to be exercised by riding up and down the avenue, but at least it was a long avenue.

uncle jeremy asked me if i could ride. i could, although it was many years ago that i had learned while on holiday as a child, so i took over the job of exercising 'plato', the smaller of two hunters. in a borrowed hat, and wellingtons for riding boots, i rode down the straight tree-lined avenue, and back again. half a mile down, half a mile back. half a mile down, half a mile back. the half mile back, facing the house, was the one which gave pleasure.

one afternoon i strayed too far into the grass beside the avenue, and plato put his front hoof into a hidden drain, stumbled, and pitched me slowly, but inevitably, over his head. making a last grab for his neck, i swung beneath it and into the grass, where he managed to step neatly over me and continue on. i walked back to the house, my pride more bruised than my backside, to find plato home before me. he had put himself back into his stable.

i limped into the house, where i met uncle jeremy on the stairs.

'how did you get on?' he enquired, perhaps sensing my discomfort.

i confessed my mishap. i began to reassure him that i had come to no harm, but he cut me short in mid-sentence.

'is the horse all right?' he asked, sharply.

humbled, i went back to the stable yard, to check.

the best times at corballis house were parties. extra staff were brought in, and because aunt laura and uncle jeremy were enthusiastic members of the georgian society, i often held open the door to people that i had waited on before. one of these was mrs guinness's great friend major synnott, who remembered the pre-war days of anglo-irish society, and was delighted to have his coat taken at the door by a butler, as if it all were still in full swing. his own house, furness, was one of the prettiest, most mouth-watering, of the irish georgian houses around dublin.

there comes a time in the life of a great house, when it is almost gone. the staff are paid off, the gardens are shrunk to the little bits at the approach to the front door, and bullocks graze close under the windows. the owners retreat to the warmest wing or a small back sitting room. then the house only comes alive for parties, when the shutters are opened and fires are lit in grand rooms where an ethereal frosty calm prevails for most of the rest of the year.

corballis house, on the other hand, was warm through and through, not least because of my trojan labours with the coal scuttle. here, as at leixlip, the house was heated and the furniture all appropriate to the georgian period. other houses, which had not been renovated, and which had remained in the same families for generations, tended to be half filled with nineteenth- and twentieth-century tasteless clutter. leixlip and corballis were not. paradoxically, you could say that only a newly restored house could be entirely and consistently old.

the major thoroughly enjoyed the party he came to. before he left he invited the entire knox family to pay him a return visit.

CHAPTER FOUR 1968–9

new year

it had become difficult to get staff to work in big houses. this was to do more with the hours than the wages – the awkwardness of being free and idle in the middle of the day, but then still busy working at ten o'clock at night. as once before i dropped the hint to aunt laura that i knew someone who might be willing to cook, temporarily.

'we would have nowhere to put her,' was her reply.

'she could sleep on the top floor,' i suggested, but aunt laura unfortunately took me up wrongly on this suggestion and was offended –

'this is not leixlip castle!' she said, primly.

the foot-and-mouth scare was still on when uncle jeremy's niece, octavia knox, came to stay. she was apparently recuperating, but from what, no one explained. connie the daily help thought it was a broken engagement.

she was a tall girl, dark, about my own age. she was witty, but inclined to melancholy, and aunt laura would do anything, including breaking out champagne in the middle of the afternoon, to cheer her up. in the long winter afternoons i would see her from my room, walking the same path as plato down the tree-lined avenue – half a mile to the middle gate, half a mile back.

it was celia knox, the fourteen-year-old daughter of the house, who first noticed me taking notice of her cousin octavia. in the matter of ponies, dogs, and servants, celia took her father's view more than her mother's. all of the above should know their place.

it was after dinner. i had retired to the basement, before going up to bed. celia appeared in the doorway and announced that she would like two buckets of coal for the fire in her bedroom. aunt laura was coming down the back stairs behind her, and must have been aware that her daughter was addressing me in the same high-handed tone used for erring kerry blue terriers.

aunt laura dismissed the idea of coal at this hour of the night, and to make amends (i felt) asked me to come upstairs to open champagne. there were no visitors, they were just playing music on a gramophone for the cousins and themselves.

i had the knack of being able to open champagne without causing a 'pop'. this is a kind of snobbery, and the trick is to keep a very tight hold on the loosened cork, while twisting. a moment comes when the cork wants to 'pop' but if a firm grip is maintained, it can be removed, and the champagne can be poured into a glass noiselessly, and without spilling a drop. some people appreciate this, despising foaming champagne as being 'too formula one.' others, equally, don't see the point and think that the 'pop' is half the fun, if not three-quarters of it.

aunt laura must have being talking about this, because she said –

'now shut up for a moment, everybody, and watch how gillies does it.'

the louisiana cousins shut up. like any knack, noiseless champagne is extremely difficult to do when people are watching. this time as i loosened the cork, which was at first very stiff, it flew out with a sharp report into a chandelier. bubbly froth everywhere.

failure.

in spite of this, when the glasses were filled, i was offered one for myself. the side table needed a wipe of a cloth, but aunt laura was a true american. defeat was not an option. we would open another bottle.

which we did.

this one worked.

then one of the louisiana cousins was bet that they couldn't open a bottle without noise or spillage ... it was not very long into this impromptu party before i was asked if i could do a 'charleston'. now i was not a good ballroom dancer, i was one of those who tend to mutter 'one, two, three' under their breath when waltzing. However, in my teens i had been at first captivated, but then baffled, by the rhythm of the charleston. i had persisted in making a cousin of mine demonstrate it to me till i had mastered it.

so yes, i could do a charleston. In fact the charleston was the only dance that i could really shine at.

the record was put on again, more than once.

even celia knox got caught up in trying to learn it.

this was a typical aunt laura evening. by sheer force of personality she had transformed a wet january night into a bright party, even without guests. she had rescued a solitary butler, a sulky daughter, a melancholy niece, and the louisiana cousins. she had turned up the music and turned down the lights and had everybody hopping. uncle jeremy went along with it but i am not sure what he thought of it.

before the night was over i was dancing with his niece, octavia knox.

old soldiers

for quite a time after the second world war, people were afraid that war could break out again at any moment. in england, people of my age, born during the war, lived through a whole childhood decade of post-war food rationing. with this constant reminder, it was difficult for a time to escape the shadow of conflict. but then in the middle 1950s there was a hit musical, *salad days*. one of the ditties in this show went —

'... don't ever ask who won the war,
don't ever ask what the war was for ...'

this was perhaps the first time anyone had dared to take the subject of the war lightly.

then later, in the early sixties, there was the cuban missile crisis. after that scare, the idea of gallant foot soldiers with bayonets led by red-faced and shouting officers did not seem to carry the same clout any more. and now, a further five years later, the long-haired youth of the 'beatles' and 'rolling stones' generation took to wearing uniforms as a kind of mockery of their elders' military ideals.

the older people of the sort who still wore their hair short, stood ramrod straight, and shone their shoes every morning, gritted their teeth and secretly longed to cut these peoples' hair and 'smarten them up.' it was a time of social watershed.

when the day came for the return visit to furness, i expected a quiet evening at corballis minding the house. however, aunt laura, who was a dominating but genuinely kind creature, suggested that i go along with the party. she knew of my interest in eighteenth-century houses, and in her mind i was a member of the irish georgian society, even though i had in fact never joined it, and had only been an employee of the society's founders.

i demurred. i felt that i had not been invited. but aunt laura was not to be gainsaid. major synnott had issued his invitation to *everyone* at corballis house, she said, and i was one of those at corballis house. anyway, one extra would make no difference.

before we left, she also suggested that we wear the uniforms. these were three or four early nineteenth-century military uniforms from the attic. they came from some house whose contents had been dispersed at an auction which uncle jeremy had attended. the family were rather reluctant to fall in with this plan, but she was insistent.

one particular red coat with trousers was not going to fit any of the shorter members of the party, and these were thrust at me. i hastened upstairs with them, trying hard to get into the spirit of the thing, as it was nearly time to go. fortunately the long mirror in my room showed that this uniform fitted me perfectly, and was extremely impressive, being scarlet, with gold embroidered shamrocks and other remarkable elaboration, and a golden and black stripe down the side of the trousers.

i was the last out of the front door, and as i closed it behind me, found to my dismay that the rest of aunt laura's family had rebelled against her plan, and were already aboard the two cars, but in their ordinary clothes. by this time it was too late, and for me it now became an uneasy journey to furness house, twenty-five miles away in the neighbouring county of kildare.

it was almost dark when we came to furness, but the major had put on enough lights to show the house off well. as we stepped out of the car at the front door, the door opened wide ahead of us, and there he was. he held the door back to let in the louisiana cousins, standing at exaggerated attention with his arm held out to receive their coats.

as aunt laura, uncle jeremy, and celia followed in their turn, he announced –

'i am mr gillies tonight!'

he was acting the butler for their amusement …

there was no turning back, and so i stepped on past him into his hall, dressed in scarlet, in the one-time full dress uniform of the deputy lord lieutenant of the county tipperary.

the major managed to carry this off very well. he was one of those very clever people who hide their intellect behind an appearance of bumbling stupidity, and thus steal a march on the unsuspecting.

he entertained us with wine and some of his poetry. the poetry was very bad. i suspected he had composed it that very day and was having a practical joke at his guests' expense.

there is a peculiar form of modesty among the anglo-irish – if it is modesty – in that their most important photograph, memento, or trophy is often displayed in the *downstairs lavatory*. this serves a number of purposes; it suggests that the owner of the house is suitably humble about their achievements, and is not particularly drawing attention to them. but at the same time it puts the item in question in a place where the visitor is bound to go, bound to have a moment to themselves, bound to see it, and free to look closely to see if that really is the queen mother, or lord mountbatten, who has been caught by the camera in intimate conversation with their host.

the downstairs lavatory is an essential part of a distinguished house, as essential as the nursery, the library, the wine cellar, the walled garden, or the stable yard.

what your house must also have, to qualify as a really great house, is a retinue of enthusiastic young aesthetes, of doubtful heterosexuality, who know more about your house and pictures than you do.

the laboratory assistant

i myself had now joined, at the age of twenty-five, that class of people who have a house too large for their needs, and who have to cast about for a way to support it. i braced myself to look for a job in the immediate locality of laragh – however unsuitable the job might be, it would make more sense than owning a house and not living in it.

how can i explain the strange course of my life and the choices that i took?

i think that i lived a sheltered and isolated childhood, with the result that most of what i knew about the world came out of books. i was always going to write a book of my own. i always saw myself in the role of narrator of a tale, rather than living a life or pursuing a career. people write autobiographical books about their lives – i lived my life around a projected autobiography.

this is not a very good way to approach things. laragh house was romantic, yes, but utterly impractical from the start. as a purchase it was little better than high island off the coast of connemara would have been.

but if all had proceeded in a normal and orderly fashion, there would have been no book – no life.

the milk from local farms in county monaghan went to a creamery at a crossroads at the head of lough egish, the lake from which the millrace and the laragh river flowed. here beside the creamery was now being built an ultra-modern dried milk production plant for 'glaxo'. i went for an interview and immediately obtained a job as a laboratory assistant with the giant company.

the job included training, as the local applicants were mostly farmers' sons, and with the exception of the nineteenth-century flax mills there had been no local tradition of industry. here i spent the day, or rather, the shift, sampling milk from pipes in the factory, diluting it on to plates of jelly, mildly heating it in electric ovens, and then counting bacteria to assess the purity of the milk.

we did the same with samples taken from the bags of dried milk replacer, which was what the factory produced. in the breaks, which were as regular and predetermined as the work itself, we drank tea, everyone (other than me) talked about football, and we played poker.

i don't know what kind of poker we played, it was 'factory' poker. we played for money, but nothing that would break the bank. we earned eleven pounds a week.

with savings from my wages i bought a pedigree boar pig. he was a 'large white', and extremely long in the body. he cost me a further pound per week to feed, and local sows came on foot, driven along the road by boys with sticks, to visit him.

i called the pig 'gilbert'. when gilbert tode-kerr got to hear of this, he was less than amused. i hurriedly explained that 'gilbert' was very well-bred, of long and distinguished pedigree, and had his pick of the local women. this seemed to mollify tode-kerr. pigs are dangerously intelligent and resourceful animals. gilbert learned to excavate the crumbling stone walls of his pigsty, eventually gaining his freedom. he could not be driven or intimidated. the only way to get him back was to rattle his feeding trough and call him. after a while the call alone was sufficient. even if he had rambled so far that he was no more than a pink dot at the crossroads half a mile away, i could go out and call him home from the field at the back of the house.

even though i had come home to laragh, i still lived between two worlds – the depressed world of mid-century rural ireland, where land was still sold at under one hundred pounds per acre, and the high technology world of glaxo's factory. each day at the glaxo factory was the same. that was the point. there was no creative element in the place. the whole idea was to keep things turning over, and the milk powder bags going out of the door, while eliminating every possible upset or variation.

my moment of true usefulness was brief. one day i was taking a sample from the top of the milk tank that fed the factory. it was half past seven in the morning. this tank was the height of a four-storey house and gave a great view of the drumlin country round about. the sample that i collected eventually returned a very high bacteria count. i reported this. more samples were taken and more tests were performed, and each of these confirmed the accuracy of the first result. there were consultations at management level. a decision was taken. under their quality-control rules, all ten thousand gallons of milk were to be discarded. i had served my purpose and performed my role. the valves were opened and the contents of the tank, collected from hundreds of dairy farms from here to far down in county meath, were discharged. no wonder a bloom of green algae sometimes grew, in warm weather, on the shallow waters of the lake.

in between the shifts at the factory i began to take more part in the farming life of the locality. children usually stayed home from school on the big days like their own potato harvest.

one bright autumn day when it was the bookie's family's turn to gather spuds, claudia came to see me. no one stopped working but everyone in the steep field turned to look. she had left school. she seemed taller and leaner than the last time that i had seen her, and was dressed in a cream linen suit. she was with her sister, also tall and red haired.

the contrast with us, the potato pickers, was extreme. the sort of contrast they seek when they fly the fashion models to africa, to pose among the desert nomads' children. i could not even leave the field to bring her up to laragh, the small farm work ethic was strong and binding. so she and her oldest sister had to sit in their borrowed car, until darkness fell and the work was done.

loving a girl like claudia could only end in disaster – and to disaster, in due course, my long tale would come.

snaffles restaurant, 1969

i have now forgotten why i left the milk powder factory. whatever the excuse was, it must have been a thin one. basically, the strict routine of manufacturing industry was starving my soul of meaning, or excitement. the tinnés, friends of gilbert tode-kerr, had decided to open up a small restaurant in dublin. they invited me to be the waiter.

at the time there was only one discotheque in dublin, a small basement room called 'le disque' in molesworth street, and there were very few restaurants. most of the world ate at home, while the prosperous and the tourists ate in the bigger hotels. 'the bailey' had a fish bar, and there were also the famous 'jammet's', and the 'red bank' oyster bar. pubs served very little in the way of food, and bars were mostly full of men, drinking, while their wives remained at home to get their supper on their return. so opening a boutique restaurant in a basement on leeson street, was a novel enterprise. nick tinné was an old etonian, a connemara resident who had tried his hand at stockbroking. he was not very much older than i was.

his inexperience, and mine, made us think that being a butler was the perfect training for the dining room of a smart little restaurant. i was to wear a green apron over my white shirt and black trousers, as i had done in my previous employment when polishing silver. this was an effective gimmick.

butlers and waiters are, however, different. the butler is the conductor of a symphony. when things are going well, there is a rhythm to a formal meal that is largely under his control. in a restaurant a waiter is constantly interrupted, 'i want this, i want that, i have no mustard, my wine is cold, my steak is rare and i said medium rare …' there is no set menu and no set time to begin the meal. there is definitely no set time to leave.

'snaffles' restaurant was designed to look like the dining room of a country house, not that that was fooling anyone, that was just its theme. there was a large console table and mirror, and the tables and chairs were, if not antique – wooden and old. nick tinné began with a couple of advantages. he had a wife who could cook. he also had a large circle of acquaintances from the west of ireland and from long attendance at hunt balls up and down the country. these would start the thing rolling. the menu was good, but the names on the menu were almost pretentiously unpretentious. there was 'game soup', 'fish pie', and 'pigeon breast in red wine sauce'. the big hotel menus at the time tended to be in french, or partly so. down the country the food, even in hotels, was still meat plus two veg in massive dollops – the kind of plateful demanded by cattle dealers who have risen early and travelled far.

to live in dublin i had to have a flat to stay in for five nights a week, and i found a room in upper mount street, off merrion square. my wages were now fifteen pounds a week. these had to cover the rent, my travel up and down, and keep me alive. the irish pound was still tied to the pound sterling, and divided into shillings and pence. the coinage still bore the beautiful, almost heraldic, farm animal designs selected by william butler yeats's committee.

the opening night was one of those successes that should by right have been a disaster. there was no 'dress rehearsal' for the night. the cooking had been well-planned but many of the smaller points had been overlooked. not least of these was the counting of the cutlery. my memory of that night is vague, but molly o'rorke – lady cusack-smith of the bermingham hunt – had to eat her pheasant with a teaspoon.

i doubt if i made a very good waiter. i did make a good doorman, and i soon became one of those dublin faces that everyone knows, but few can remember where they have seen it. it was not long before the restaurant took off and was making a hundred pounds or more a night.

the wine waiter, cobby, was like myself an enthusiastic amateur. he was also another friend of ursula, who had by this time abandoned her rented glebe house and bought another county meath property not far distant. she became an occasional customer of the restaurant. thus the story of my life resumed, in the no man's land between the insiders and the outsiders, the tippers and the tipped. the wine list was catered for by a dublin wine merchant, the young inheritor of a long-established family business.

myself, i was quite a connoisseur of wine, and this was the result of some years of finishing off the dregs, usually from red wine bottles. (white wine or champagne is more likely to be drained to the last drop.) my taste was in fact for the leftover sludge in the older clarets. butlers have little motive to steal from their employers, there is just too much opportunity to scavenge legitimately. as for the names of the wines i was drinking, i did not buy the wine, nor select it, so i had no real need to memorize them. even if a wine was exceptionally good, i was unlikely to encounter the same one the next time. i had to take what came my way.

there are many wine experts, but i would guess from my restaurant experience that nine out of ten of them are wine *label* experts. soak off the labels, or decant the wine, and most will at once become lost. that is why there is so much emphasis on different shaped bottles and different shaped glasses for different drinks. it helps people distinguish between them.

since at least as long ago as the wedding at cana, it has been known that you serve the good wine first, because at a later stage people neither know nor care what they are drinking. by then some of them, of course, may not know the way home, or their own names.

one quiet night we sat down, cobby and the tinnés and i, and tested various wines in identical measure in identical glasses. the three of them had become quite good at distinguishing the wines that we ordered regularly. my selection was more eccentric. they soon spotted that i always picked as my favourite the glass that had been poured from the dregs of a bottle. my scavenging habits had caught up with me.

as with the wines, so with the food. especially late on the saturday night, before the restaurant was cleared (and time moves slowly for customers who have had a bottle or two), there was often food to finish up that would not last over until the following week. i developed a taste for raw scallops, eating them like oysters.

i think that my brain must be wired differently from those of the general run of peoples' brains. to savour a dish i would really have to eat it in silence, just as most people need silence, first, to enjoy classical concert music.

for a brief time during my employment at snaffles, i again shared the mount street room with sketchley. this did not end well. sketchley had taken to the drink to the extent that he was no longer capable of saving up his share of the rent. nor could i afford to support him. i foolishly thought that i could train him to pay up by opening the front door to him on the chain. when he passed in his three pounds on tuesday evenings, i took off the chain and let him in. but the day came when he came empty-handed. i held to my threat and would not open up.

sketchley stumbled off into the night, muttering pompously. he had introduced me to dublin society, he declaimed, and now he would make sure to ruin me. if he had spent a cold night on the canal bank, i might have had some luck with my methods, but i learned later that he had gone and woken up his sister in ballsbridge and was allowed to sleep on the floor of her flat.

cobby the wine waiter was a confirmed bachelor. cobby also drank, as i suppose we all did when we could afford to, but not in any self-destructive way. being another friend of ursula's, he drove me out to see her one weekend. her new house was only a couple of miles over the fields from the glebe, and i knew that part of county meath well.

we did not talk much to her about sketchley, but i sensed that the affair was not likely to survive for much longer. i am of course telling my side of this tale, and from a mere bachelor's perspective, whereas ursula, even though now divorced and independent, had at all times her family and the upbringing of her children to take into consideration.

like a high wire juggling act: it looked easy – but it wasn't.

cobby was a bit of an interior decorator, having worked in the business. he was horrified at ursula's decorating method, which was to get the painters in first and in a few days paint the entire house pale cream, including doors and windows – from top to bottom.

on the way home cobby confessed to me that he would like to tackle the restoration of a house himself. he had even looked at one or two around dublin. i had often walked and driven these back lanes in meath, and i made him turn the car up the hill and took him to look at a yellow ochre house standing in a field. it was three storeys over a basement, a house of about 1790, with a flight of stone steps to the front door. we pushed the door and found it open. inside all was intact until we came to the upper bedrooms, where one chimney had collapsed through the roof and in to a room. this room was also full of sticks accumulated by the jackdaws. the windows commanded a wide view over the plains of meath, looking due south in the direction of the far-off wicklow mountains.

this was to be cobby's house, and eventually, the one in which i would spend my honeymoon.

cobby came back on his own, on another day, and sought out the owners. he then made an offer for the house and was about to buy it for eleven hundred pounds sterling when an emigrant sister of the family, home from england, intervened and told her family they were mad to sell it for that as property prices were rising. this was unfortunate, and cobby ended up having to pay fifteen hundred pounds.

when the romans and their legions pulled out of britain, the roman villas often stood empty, while the saxons built their own-style dwellings alongside. similarly, when landlords' estates were divided in ireland, or fell into decline and were sold off, the local farmers were quite often reluctant to move in. houses stood empty, while the new owners of the land built new bungalows alongside them for themselves and their families. perhaps it was not really until the third generation that the big houses were seen as desirable again, or perhaps not until after a somewhat later irish government had decided to remove the rates from private houses.

before farmers were required to pay income tax, the rates – a property tax – were their only direct contribution to the state. unlike income tax, these rates had to be paid year in, year out – even in a bad year when the farmers had made no money at all.

it would be nice to go back to those days, and buy up a good slice of the county meath for peanuts, but at the time the recollection of hardship was too fresh in many peoples' minds. large properties were considered a liability, and the recent memory in many places was of the last of the 'ascendency' hanging on to faded glories, with basins and buckets here and there in their crumbling houses, to catch the drips from the ceiling.

if a property was sold, it was for the value of the land. houses, like hedges and gates, were expected to be thrown in for free.

meeting his family

small as snaffles restaurant was, sooner or later everybody dined there. inviting my aunt mary and a cousin of mine over from england, i was allowed to have supper with them myself, and i invited claudia kenny to join us. it was a quiet night, and cobby stood in for me in the waiter's role. with claudia i affected a nonchalance that i did not feel. she tended to be more interested in people who did not show obvious interest in her. she needed a challenge, if you like.

my cousin began to marvel at her stunning appearance only minutes after we had sent her home in a taxi after the dinner. there are obviously genes for red hair – whether expressed or recessive – (my cousin had red hair himself), but perhaps there are corresponding genetic compulsions to '*fancy*' red hair? i know there are.

but i was not entirely in a good humour with claudia.

something had finally opened my eyes and i had formed this cynical view: that all women who are given by nature more than their fair share of that mysterious power that turns all men into their slaves – *are going to make use of it* (even if it is only to get a dented mercedes benz pushed to the side of the road). a few martyred virgins in the early christian years voluntarily gave up their power to attract, in order to live holy lives – but these were surely rare and exceptional?

in connemara when i first met her, an age difference of eight years was enough to make claudia and myself equals in spite of my immaturity. now already, a mere three years later, she was growing in poise and confidence. i was still a waiter – (even if this was my night off!) i was ready to settle down. claudia kenny was only now trying her wings, and ready to fly.

nelly, you think me a selfish wretch, but, did it never strike you that, if heathcliff and i married, we should be beggars?

cathy earnshaw in *wuthering heights*. chapter ix.

and another thing. if claudia grew up to be another patra keane, that would be fine for her – *but was i prepared to become another mr keane?* it did not matter if i did – it was by this time very unlikely to happen.

political divisions

another person who came to the restaurant was the unionist politician, john taylor. the occasion was an invitation to him to dine with, and afterwards address, the trinity college conservative club ('conservative', here, as in 'tory party').

the address came after the dinner was over, at the coffee stage, so there was no choice for me but to wait and hear out what he had to say – but i was fascinated, anyway. he gave a good rundown on the current troubles up in the north. the troubles were then in the early 'civil rights' stages, but the situation was rapidly deteriorating into out and out violence. he could see what was coming.

the student speaker who had introduced john taylor had gone on for a long time about 'the independent deterrent.' this referred to the british having nuclear weapons of their own make, with their own delivery system, under their own control. it was the major topic of debate of the day – at least it was, over across the water. i think it was to do with the british desperately clinging to the last of their imperial importance. there was no point at which the two speeches intersected. it was as if the unionist politician, and the english students, lived in separate universes.

this was all a poor omen for the future.

the events in northern ireland and their side effects on the politics of the republic never intruded upon the world of snaffles restaurant, but for us, as for everyone else living in this part of ireland, they were like wallpaper, an ever-present pattern in the background.

aunt laura and uncle jeremy came to snaffles, and came more than once. aunt laura was most encouraging, while uncle jeremy tipped ten pounds on top of the bill. this was an enormous amount for a tip, but i was left with the strange uneasy feeling that his generosity had an edge to it. he doubled my spending money for the week, and at the same time he put me back firmly in my place.

while the rest of their world were fretting about whether it would still be safe to visit their friends in northern ireland, the knoxes had actually decided to move there. a house in derry city had come up for sale, being both unrestored early georgian and with a distant but definite knox family connection. this was more than aunt laura's pioneering spirit could resist, and the project was to buy it and restore it.

the beautiful corballis house was to be sold, and being near the airport its extensive acres would make lots of money. this alone had reconciled uncle jeremy to the move.

another visitor to snaffles was octavia knox herself. the selling of corballis house would not mean an end to her visits to dublin. she, too, had done a three-year course at trinity college, and, i think, repeated a year – making four. thus she had many friends still in dublin. she was now living in her late grandmother's old house in london, but greeted me as an old friend from a familiar past.

she was out on the town for an evening with former trinity contemporaries, several of whom had been around during the summer of the georgian society volunteers, at castletown house.

they were the very last to leave that night, and she said –

'why don't you take that apron off and come with us?'

which i did.

the film set

my friends said that i would go mad, living the way i did. perhaps they were proven right in the end.

after snaffles restaurant closed on a saturday night, or rather in the small hours of the sunday morning, i would go back to my room in mount street. later that morning – and often in summer i might not have got to bed much before the first light of dawn – i rose early, and walked across the liffey to the railway station. there i got the train to dundalk. some sundays if i was lucky there might be coffee in a restaurant car on the train. at the station in dundalk i then got a bus for castleblayney, and five miles beyond carrickmacross i got out at an isolated crossroads and walked the final four miles to laragh. it was now still mid-morning and my head had barely cleared of the music, voices, smoke and rich flavours of the night before. the contrast was unsettling. there was little out here except a few cattle, the whins (gorse) and rushes, and the birds. unless you are on a road to mass, or to a football match, the back roads of monaghan are silent as the grave on a sunday morning. however, any car that came along was likely to give you a lift – even if only to find out who you were – but few cars came.

on one of these weekends off i was invited to work at castle leslie. this house right on the border in north county monaghan is now a guest house, famous for the wedding of paul mccartney. in those days, before attaining this distinction, it had only been remarkable for the leslies themselves and their connection by marriage to someone called winston churchill.

desmond leslie was an intimidating man of about six feet six inches tall, married to an austrian jewish actress and cabaret entertainer (i hope i recall this last bit correctly, but it is sufficient for my story that she was by this time middle-aged, dark, still exotic, and definitely not from monaghan).

desmond leslie himself was a determinedly eccentric man. in my not so distant schooldays, i had read his book – *flying saucers have landed*. he had once taken exception to being described in a local newspaper article as 'fairly eccentric.' he rang the startled editor to point out that the leslies were not to be described as 'fairly' eccentric, they were, and had been for several generations, *very* eccentric.

the leslies, to make ends meet, were proposing to take in american visitors, and to justify the prices these people would be charged, it was necessary to hire temporary staff in order to recreate some of the formal and pampered feel of a previous generation. my interview with desmond leslie, in preparation for the first arrival of visitors, was more like a rehearsal for a play, than a plan for a dinner. naturally, if visitors encounter a butler on arriving at a house, they assume that he is part of the general family set up. it does not occur to them that he has only managed to get to the house a few hours ahead of their arrival. but anyway – what does it matter? this particular kind of entertaining is based on suspension of disbelief. the visitors are paying to be entertained as though they were 'friends of the family', which they clearly are not.

i, on the other hand, was being paid to pretend that i was *not* a friend of the family, when in fact i was (or at least, a local acquaintance).

for the purpose of this charade it was a great help that my christian name, 'gillies', sounds equally like a surname, and so could be used without attracting undue attention.

that there had been a full-time butler at castle leslie within living memory, i knew for a fact – because this individual had become very old and had developed a shake in the head. this had had the result of some of the more observant guests of the leslies refusing pudding or other dishes, assuming that the head shaking was a quiet tip-off to avoid certain of the cook's concoctions.

dinner for the americans started well with drinks beforehand. desmond leslie accompanied this with tunes on a small pedal organ at the back of the room – a common piece of furniture in ulster protestant homes, but not at all typical of a house like castle leslie. he was able to indicate to me with a nod of the head, without pausing in his playing, to place his own drink down on the top of the instrument. he then treated me to an enormous conspiratorial wink.

the dinner proper began and continued fairly smoothly. mindful of the story i had been told about the old retainer, i kept my head motionless.

with the main course served, and the wine served, i realized that after several welcoming cups of tea i badly needed to locate a lavatory. i knew there was one near the hall, but i assumed that there would also be one for the staff in the kitchen corridor. there was not. undeterred, i guessed it must be up the backstairs and ran lightly up to the corridor above. still no luck. try once more. i ran up the second flight of stairs to an identical corridor, except that this time one of the doors that i tried turned out to be what i was looking for. the whole wing appeared to be the disused staff quarters. on coming out of this loo, i took a wrong turn and came to an upper staircase hall with an enormous skylight, at the far end of which was a door. daubed on the door in red paint was the legend – *go away!*

i went away, and unperturbed by the message i retraced my steps, found the stairs, ran down again to the darkening corridor, and along it to the end where i had begun. i then opened the door to the dining room to find a completely empty room.

nothing.

things covered in dust sheets, in the pale moonlight …

what had happened, as you probably guess, was quite simple. i was still exactly one floor above where i thought i was. but for a moment i was baffled. i had left a busy kitchen, and a lighted dining room smelling of candles and claret and irish stew, womens' perfume and cut flowers, and a blazing log and turf fire. for a moment only, i was stranded in musty emptiness in an identical room as though the whole dinner were some ghostly figment of the imagination.

perhaps it was?

no, it was real enough. i found the stairs and was back just in time to clear for the next course, before anyone noticed that i was missing.

the film producer

Sometime later that year, castle leslie was again rented out, this time to make a film. the house was to be the film set, and also the lodgings for the director and a few of his favoured friends. the film crew would be based in the gate lodge, but this had in the past been the agent's house for the estate, being a large three-storey house and a substantial building in its own right. the thousand-acre estate, which included wooded areas and rhododendron walks, and a spectacular lake below the house, would also provide most of the locations for filming.

my first encounter with the film people was in the restaurant in dublin. i had never set eyes upon a film producer before, and so i accepted the flamboyant jerome tate's manner simply as being typical of film producers. he was a fat man, young, perhaps in his early thirties, and very noisy. when the table became too small for the party, the film people dragged another one beside it and joined the two together. when the second bottle of wine was quickly drained, tate said –

'waiter, another dozen of these.'

i was not sure if we had a dozen of anything, let alone that particular wine, but began hunting out and opening bottles of claret as fast as i could.

tate then wanted to know when the wine was coming. so i hurried along with the bottle.

he tasted this in an elaborate pantomime, held up the glass to the light, and pronounced it too cold (of course it was cold, it had not been given time to be anything else!)

i retreated to the kitchen and did the old butler's trick with the hot water. now the wine was magically and suddenly at room temperature, but this time tate pronounced the bottle corked. he insisted that i try it myself.

i never liked to pick an argument with a wine connoisseur, not trusting my own judgment, but at the same time i suspected that tate was only showing off to the film crew, so i simply said diplomatically that i would bring another bottle …

i hastened back to the kitchen and returned again bearing the same bottle. this is worth the risk as it almost invariably works. he tasted again and pronounced this one acceptable.

collins the dublin art dealer, whom i knew, and who had somehow managed to insinuate himself into the party, was obviously finding all this fuss tedious. he said –

'why don't you just sit down, gillies, and have a glass yourself?'

this he said out of mischief, to show up tate and to embarrass me, all in the one go.

the irish and the english have certain ways of making each other look ridiculous, a contest which goes back a long way.

tate looked as though he were about to explode, but then looking around the table at the surprised faces, and deciding to milk the situation for more drama, burst into roars of exaggerated laughter that silenced the entire restaurant.

thus i found myself sitting at the table. i sat, not beside tate but opposite, talking to james, the director of the film, and next found myself having to explain the origin of my green baize butler's apron.

as i write this account, i realize that all of my stories are essentially the one story – a story of gatecrashing across the frontier between the servants and the served.

tate was rich, and noisy, and selfish. everyone referred to him as 'tate' except his director, who had been at english prep school with him years before. these two called each other by the nicknames 'rombo' and 'jimbo' that they had been known by when they were eight years old.

as soon as tate knew that i had been trained as a butler, he wanted a butler. no matter that there is not a lot for a butler to do on a film set, there was no stopping him. like *toad of toad hall*, he had conceived a new enthusiasm. he had to have a butler. at this point i had to leave the party and serve them their food, before it went cold.

it was well into the small hours of the morning before they all left, but before they did, james, the director, had a proposition for me – would i like to return to work in county monaghan in castle leslie for the film? i would have to drive a land rover, and take out the sandwiches to the film crew, to whatever outdoor location – lake, field, or wood, – was scheduled for that day's shooting.

james had seen a way to indulge tate's latest whim, while getting on with the serious business of making a film. i could see that while tate used his money to dominate 'jimbo', jimbo in return used his wits to manipulate 'rombo' and flatter him, while making sure that he himself got what he needed to achieve his ambitions.

i said that i would think it over.

my irish family

the bookie and his wife bridie, who by then had a family of eight children, eventually growing to eleven, became my own family. i say this because i was not brought up in a family, or even in a private house. the duffys were in many ways the first family i had ever been part of. they were all small and dark and lively, like peas in a pod, the children's ages like steps of stairs. the bookie, for all his small size and lively manner, was a patriarch, and his role and that of his wife were governed by long custom. if he came home from a cattle market to find her gone to visit her mother or married sisters, he would wait for an hour if necessary for her to return and make him a cup of tea. he would not lift a kettle himself.

no physical sign of affection passed between them, in spite of the close cooperative effort that their farm life and large family must have entailed. at sunday mass they sat separately too. the women sat on the left-hand side of the chapel (as you face the altar), the men on the right. the women went straight in to mass, while the men stood talking under the graveyard wall until the last possible minute.

although the intention had been for the duffys to live in their own separate quarters, it was only natural that in time i was asked into the big back kitchen of laragh, to share cups of tea, or occasionally, punch made with poteen, or invited to throw a few more clothes into the large family wash. on a farm there were other things which needed help – herding cattle, bringing a sow to a boar, castrating young pigs, tying and stooking oats, throwing up hay into a shed. the bookie found my abundance of unused stables and lofts very convenient and desirable, and bit by bit our lives became more intertwined.

rural areas run on credit. there was the monthly or annual credit extended to the farmers by the shop and the creamery, but there was also the social form of credit, whereby nothing is demanded in return for a loan, a gift, or a favour – but at the same time everyone remembers exactly who helped whom and when. this also ran in reverse. the bad turns were remembered, cherished almost, in the knowledge and hope that a day would come when, one way or another, just return could be made.

monaghan revenge took some strange traditional forms. sawing a man's wooden gates in half in the middle of the night being one of the more extreme ways of indicating displeasure.

after generations of local intermarriage, family relationships were many and complex, and to make an enemy of one person was often to make an enemy of several. jokes were equally savage. one halloween trick was to quietly tie all the doors of a cottage with twine from the outside, then to put a ladder to the roof and place a slate over the chimney pot to smoke out the inhabitants.

these fierce hostilities were matched by equally intense hospitality. to enter anyone's house was to be offered a cup of tea. to decline this without good excuse was to give offence. it took me a long time to learn not to enter the door of a house unless i had time for tea. you had to stay outside, even if you had to conclude your business in the rain, unless you intended to sit down at the table and be waited on. to enter anyone's house was to see the kettle quietly pushed from the edge of the range on to the hotplate.

perhaps considered the greatest form of rudeness was asking too many questions. all conversations were conducted warily, like a card game with your cards held close to your chest. the one thing that you were not to do was to ask straight out what was in the other person's hand. to ask direct or pointed questions was the function of guards, customs men, and farm grant inspectors, and considered an indication of hostile intent. even for a simple question to be answered, it was necessary for the person asked to establish first, before answering, your reason for wanting to know. anyone asked for directions to a nearby house would remain mysteriously confused and ignorant of the layout of the neighbourhood until you agreed to let slip the reason for wanting to go. ask a true monaghan child 'is your father at home?', and there are a dozen possible replies – which do not however include the answer 'yes.'

in conversation, to ask unwanted questions was to invite the answer, or non-answer –

'aagh now ...'

this can only be translated as 'i can guess why you are asking that – and are you expecting me to be innocent enough answer it?'

the skilful conversationalist nevertheless left you having discovered everything about your day's business, without your realizing that they had been probing, and with you still not knowing the first thing about theirs.

down on a rock between the road and the river was a tiny church built of cream and maroon corrugated iron. the mill owners being protestants in a valley where everyone else was catholic, had built their own place of worship. this was called 'saint peter's' – a clever reference to the rock on which the church was built.

one day i came around the corner of the road to find a raggedy man removing a ladder from the building, which always stood open, in spite of having lost its congregation. the church was not mine, having been excluded from the sale of the house and given to the representative church body of the church of ireland, but i still did not like to see it robbed.

i confronted this man, and asked him what he was doing. he replied that he had been told to take out the ladder and paint it. this was a most unlikely story.

'who told you?' i asked him, 'was it the man up at the big house?'

thinking he saw a way out he replied that it was.

'well that is not true,' i said, very pleased with my cunning question, 'because i am the man at the big house and i never saw you before. so you had better put it back before the guards see you.'

i then expected him to put back the ladder and be grateful to get away without further trouble. but there i was wrong. i had challenged him too directly, and honour was at stake. muttering under his breath he shouldered the ladder, turned his back on me and went off purposefully up the road.

now it was my turn to feel humiliated. it was not my church, or ladder, but i was damned if i was going to see it plundered in broad daylight. what would disappear next?

so i walked smartly down to the post office and rang the sergeant in shantonagh barracks.

i told my tale, was thanked, and within less than half an hour the ladder was back in its place under the little iron belfry, and the squad car was on its way back to town. how did the guards know immediately where to look for it?

when the bookie returned from milking i told him the tale of my little triumph. when i told him how the thief had continued taking the ladder even when caught out red-handed, his face darkened.

'aye, and i would have done the same,' he said, 'surely.'

this pulled me up short.

for the first, but not for the last time, i had offended against some clause in the small print of the unwritten laws of the border. a petty thief was a nuisance – but no one would actually have missed the ladder for months, if indeed ever …

acting as a police informer, on the other hand, was to risk becoming one of the lowest of the low.

this might be the place to say something about the history of the IRA. firstly, there was at this time no 'provisional' IRA. people tend to forget that the first 'round' of the long period of northern troubles which began at the end of the sixties, was fought between the civil rights movement and the RUC, the royal ulster constabulary.

so the IRA was not there at the start and did not exist, or definitely not as an effective organization, until later on.

nevertheless the political and sectarian tensions out of which the IRA grew, did exist, and had done for many generations. partition did exist, and the border did exist – even though unnatural, convoluted, and porous. the border would also have been almost invisible, had it not been for the giveaway of our cream and green telephone boxes, versus the red of the telephone boxes and royal mail letterboxes on the far side. but, even at that time, whereas in a dublin bar you might meet a man mouthing off about partition and the (old) IRA, you would never hear that on the border. the topic was avoided, and you had no clue as to who was who, with this one exception – if you did meet a stranger in a bar ranting on about the IRA you could be absolutely sure he had nothing to do with it and knew nothing about it.

usually such a man would turn out to be a returned emigrant, one who might have paid his taxes and PAYE to the queen, for decades. you were suffering the small talk (or big talk) of kilburn or coventry – not that of carrickmacross.

one day a young man, twenty or twenty-five perhaps, came and shot crows out of my trees very expertly with a .22 rifle. i did wonder about him. i felt that the crows in my tall trees at the bottom of the avenue were '*my*' crows. even though they did me no good, they did little harm, except the mess of small sticks at nesting time, and the droppings on the road beneath the trees. when i came down the avenue this youth gave me a very direct look and a smile, as if to say, 'want to make anything of it?' and i went on past him about my business. he had an unsettling self-confidence in the way he handled the gun.

i have never encountered a professional hitman, but i am sure that after a shooting there is this same moment of evasion, a silence, a brief window of uncertainty, through which he can calmly walk away unchallenged. he does not have to run.

dublin friends

i now had given up my flat in dublin, and when going up to work in the restaurant i stayed with various friends. one of these was collins the art dealer. he lived in the inner suburb of rathgar, in a run-down rented house that by now has probably been gentrified and worth a million euro. it was certainly convenient. collins later prospered and ran a string of polo ponies, but there were also lean times in the picture trade. sometimes when you rang the doorbell it was answered by a voice through the letter box, checking first that you were not another debt collector.

collins had a younger brother, fintan, who was an artist, and his girlfriend of the time, antoinette, who rode around with him in his big old daimler car, worked occasionally as a waitress in the restaurant. she sometimes posed for fintan collins as his artist's model. a huge pink nude oil painting of her dominated the back kitchen, and never failed to stop visitors dead in their tracks as they came through the door.

in return for collins's hospitality, i in my turn invited fintan, the artist, to stay with me. this suited all parties. i was glad of company at laragh. i knew the ways of artists and enjoyed the smell of oil paint and turpentine. fintan was glad to escape the stressful existence of 'ducking and diving' and being required by his elder brother to give endless evasive replies to creditors at the door.

while at laragh fintan continued to paint versions of his successful portrait of antoinette. friends noticed that these became ever more and more abstract, until finally, after a visit to the house in dublin, they would revert to intense realism once again. i tried not to comment.

antoinette was a good-looking irish girl. she was not beautiful to me, but she was to more than a few. beauty is an elusive thing.

i realize that i have called her 'irish' which may seem pointless, because all dublin-born girls are irish. now that i write it i realize that, to me, certain dolichocephalic (long-headed) dark, dense-haired girls are 'classically' irish, the ones who tend towards being almost spanish in racial appearance.

there are also bubbly snub-nosed blonde dublin girls, who have equal claim to be irish, but these are part of other people's sagas.

we will ignore them.

fintan fitted in well with the pace of life in the country. he spent a little of each morning sawing damp laurel logs for the fire in the room he used as a studio. then he settled down to painting for the rest of the daylight hours.

i always got on well with artists. we lived austerely when at laragh, except for the ten shillings each that we blew every weekend on drink.

the film

summer came and the actors and crew assembled in castle leslie.

having no car, i often got friends to drive me to places, on the promise of a little social life or adventure. that was how i got up to castle leslie. home was only thirty miles away, so there was no need to take much luggage along.

the former agent's house at the gate was to be the base for the film crew. the actors were lodged in the village of glaslough in a guest house, and jimbo and rombo stayed in the castle itself. the castle was in fact a very large plain victorian house, the successor of a couple of earlier houses on the same site.

desmond leslie and his wife aggie were in the course of a difficult separation, in a country which then had no legal form of divorce. aggie was still at castle leslie. she had to remain in residence, i presumed, to keep a claim on her part of his property. this made for a tense and upsetting situation, even in a very large house, where they both continued to live alongside the film-making. she occasionally went away to a clinic 'for repairs' as desmond rather unkindly described it.

desmond leslie also had a tall blonde girlfriend, physically very different from his wife, and who in the course of time duly became his second wife. aggie leslie was aware of this but could hardly up sticks and go home. where had home been anyway? i had no clue. an austrian cabaret artist's wartime flat in east berlin? i did not know and i made no attempt to work it out. i tried to stay on good terms with them both. for the moment i was at castle leslie as film crew, not in domestic service.

stepping in to the agent's house, although i did not immediately realize it, i stepped once more into the period of anglo-american history which is labelled as 'the sixties'. there was a languidness about the early arrivals that i gradually realized had something to do with what came out of a little carved indian box, belonging to one of the crew, and became incorporated into hand-rolled cigarettes. not being a smoker, i was in no danger of becoming part of this ritual, but the prevailing mood was easy to fall into.

the record of the musical show 'hair' was being played (records were then still like grooved black plastic plates), and when it finished the needle was simply put back to the start and it was played over again.

there was lots of talk, lots of meditative silences, a little eating and a modest amount of drinking – but not much sign of making a film. leo, the rather restless cameraman, had already shot a lot of background footage of dawn over the lake, sunset over the lake, the lake in the rain, and similar stuff. for a day or two we seemed to be waiting for the leading man to arrive, then when he had purred up on his powerful motorbike, for the leading lady to arrive. in the yard behind the house there was a small hairy cob in a stable. this quiet animal was destined to play the part of the heroine's highly-bred hunter in some atmospheric shots along the lake shore. no doubt a highly skilled cameraman would have no trouble in creating the right illusion.

on the third day we were at a loose end. we were like schoolboys after term has ended, but before the holidays have begun. things were happening, but elsewhere. there were rumoured to be rows about money.

it had crossed all of our minds that rombo the film producer might be a con man. there was something insubstantial about his knowledge of the film industry, and yet, who could he be conning? he made his telephone calls to the bank in monaghan town from a coinbox phone in the hallway of the guesthouse in the village. this in itself seemed odd, except that he was perhaps the world's greatest extrovert. he talked loudly in terms of tens of thousands of pounds, and yet, when we had just begun to suspect that the bank manager in the town square was right to play it cautiously, another five thousand pounds would unexpectedly arrive to cover the bills for the next few days.

on the fourth day, after a spectacular bust-up, on the guesthouse telephone, with the bank, rombo once again prevailed over the deputy manager of 'the provincial bank'. to celebrate this he offered to treat the restive film crew to champagne, and as border village guesthouses are not noted for their wine cellars, a crate had to be sent out by taxi from the town. the problems of film-making were then once again forgotten. the inhalers of the fragrant homemade cigarettes seemed comparatively uninterested in alcohol, so there was plenty for the rest of us.

jimbo the director steered clear of this scene. he looked increasingly anxious, and spent his evening up in the castle supervising the laying out of a little metal railway through the hall and the drawing room that overlooked the lake. this was the track for the camera to run along. later the crew assembled in the agent's lodge. more cigarettes were rolled, and the talk came around to what would happen if the film fell through. the leading lady, who alone seemed both a nonsmoker and sober, was more concerned about her career than her salary. could she afford to be associated with a film that might possibly flop?

the men who worked behind the camera were only concerned about financial arrangements. they each in turn confessed to the terms of whatever contract they had negotiated and signed. then leo the cameraman asked me –

'what are you on, gillies?'

i said –

'twenty pounds a week cash, every friday.'

this was apparently not how film contracts were drawn up. the entire company, actors and crew, burst into loud laughter at my expense.

the following day it was revealed that radical alterations were to be made to the filming schedule, the plot, and the script. there was to be no change in the title of the film, as at this stage they did not have one.

in the morning they filmed the hero rowing the heroine across the weedy lake in a small rowing boat. the weather was good, the breeze gentle, and it was a day and a scene out of which any fool with a kodak brownie could have made a good photograph. there were large lazy carp in the lake, visible in a certain light just beneath the surface of the water.

i hung around the filming with little to do, meditating upon what made a successful film star. to meet the star (or aspiring starlet), in her jeans and sweater, was to meet an unexceptional and fresh-complexioned girl, about twenty years old. she was mousey-haired, and about five feet six inches or seven. she was not stalked by paparazzi, nor in any way striking, and yet seen in a close-up she had some special quality that survived the inspection, whatever angle the camera came from. she was some kind of cameraman's ideal – there was certainly not much about her that a fintan collins could celebrate on a large canvas in hot swirling red and pink oil paints.

in the afternoon they decided that the next scene, which was a feast in an orchard, would be improvised. tables and benches were laid out. the cameras were set up, and a token amount of food and drink was left out on the tables. rombo was away negotiating the transfer of funds from england. jimbo the director also seemed somewhat surplus to requirements, as a result of his decision to improvise, and he hovered uncertainly. i hung around too, my job was to bring the sandwich lunches out to the locations, but today this location was right beside the house, near the garden. the actors, so laid-back in their late-night conversation the evening before, now became oddly stiff and stilted. when pushed in front of the cameras without either cigarettes or a script, they barely knew what to do. improvisation, like blank verse, looks easy, but is the hardest act of all to carry off successfully.

the day's work ended just as rombo came back from the town in a taxi. he was in expansive mood, so he must have triumphed over the deputy bank manager again. he had taken to wearing a kilt, on the strength of some tenuous connection with scotland on his mother's mother's side. his legs were fat, and he wore nothing under the kilt, as we discovered later.

the camera was carefully put away and the little rail track dismantled for the night. but rombo had been in negotiation with the wine merchant, as well as the bank, and the taxi driver carried over a couple of crates of champagne, and two dozen bottles were placed among the remains of the cinematic props on the tables.

newly confident that he knew how things were done socially in ireland (i.e. very democratically), rombo now invited the taxi man to take the head of the table, and cracked open the first bottle, foaming racing-driver style.

it was a pity that the camera had been put away. a real 'feast in the orchard' now ensued, that would have been the making of any film. now they were really laughing and shouting. art had once again come a poor second to reality.

in the morning it transpired that the leading man, whom nobody had seen leave the party, was now already back in dublin, en route for the airport, and unlikely to return. nor was he the first to leave. early on, an anxious little person – whose job seemed to be to go around with a clipboard and coordinate the schedule of the many different things that have to come together each day to create a film – had blown a fuse. so already, those of us who suspected that the leading lady would be the first to crack had been twice caught by surprise and proven wrong.

the day had dawned wet and the morning's filming was put on hold. the film crew retreated back to the lodge, where they played 'hair' on the record player, and smoked. they also opened a 'book' – laying bets on who would quit next. no bets were accepted on the leading lady, who had been overheard arranging for her mother to fly over to meet her the next day. my odds were the longest – they figured that i was unlikely to quit, and certainly not before being paid on a friday.

they then decided to hold a 'seance' in the lodge that evening, to help pass the time.

dave, the sound boom holder, seemed personally affected by the uncertainty and inactivity, also by the scented smoke and the constant champagne. he was, furthermore, disapproving of attempts to contact the dead, and of the whole bizarre scene, and went off in disgust to drink newcastle brown ale, or its nearest obtainable substitute, in the bar in the village.

later that evening we decided to play a practical joke on dave. when most had retreated to bed, we carefully led 'jacko' the hairy cob from his stable, and up the front step into the lodge. we led him through the hall and up the wide wooden stairs to the first floor, then again to the second floor, where dave's quarters were. here, knowing dave would need to relieve himself of the contents of several pint bottles of ale, we backed the cob in to the bathroom, and thoughtfully filled the bath with hay to keep him quiet and entertained. we then removed the light bulb from the top landing, and went to our respective beds to await dave's return, expecting to hear a startled roar when he opened the bathroom door and met a hairy face in the dim light.

it must have been late when we went to bed, and even later when the pub closed in the village, because it was broad daylight when i awoke. i had slept undisturbed. dave was already down in the dining room making coffee. the joke had failed miserably. dave had apparently come home very drunk, gone to the bathroom exactly as predicted, failed to find any of the light switches, and pushed his way past the patient cob to the toilet bowl, and back again, without noticing the hairiness or bulginess of the wall he was supporting himself by.

the joke was now on us. 'jacko', who had patiently picked his way up the stairs the night before, now looked upon the downward path as leading over a dangerous cliff, and sensibly declined to go an inch beyond the top step. in his days as a riding school trekking pony, this might have been a useful virtue. now we did not know what to do. the more we dithered the more the sensible 'jacko' sensed that he had fallen among ditherers, and must give us a lead in the face of common danger. so up on the landing he stayed, outside the open bathroom door and the hay-filled bath.

i went back down to dave for more coffee and to think out what to do now.

leo, the cameraman, who had been out early, came in to the kitchen.

'there's a bloody horse blocking the bathroom, i am going over for a shit in the guesthouse, and you are wanted, now, this minute, up at the castle.'

the odds had shortened.

i assumed that these remarks were connected, and feared the worst. and it was still thursday.

in the drawing room of castle leslie, apart from the little metal railway sneaking through the double doors, peace and normality reigned. jimbo was pacing the room, alone in the morning sunlight. i stepped over the railway tracks and waited in the doorway, butler-like, for instructions. whatever jimbo wanted to say, he was having difficulty coming out with it. he went off on a preamble about the film – we now had no leading man, no leading lady, very little in the can, and – without either of the principal actors – no immediate prospect of keeping the film going until new actors were found. the crew would become restless with nothing to do. even the producer might lose interest.

gradually it dawned on me that it was jimbo who passionately wanted, against all the odds, to become a film director. rombo was not a con man. he was simply being manipulated by jimbo in some subtle way. rombo did not care about film. as long as he could go around opening champagne, and being rombo, he did not mind whether he was fantasizing being a film producer, a circus act, a victorious general, or a great scottish landowner.

jimbo came to the point. would i, for the moment at least, like to step in to the departed leading man's shoes, so that the filming could continue? there were no lines to learn. there was not even sound – sound would be dubbed on later. the film was very free-form and could evolve in any direction, but even to create the shots leo and he needed a character around whom to work and build up what they wanted to create ... would i help out?

the japanese say that the warrior is a man who, given the choice between life and death, goes for death – every time ...

i went for it. unlike the sensible 'jacko' i stepped forward.

'yes, of course i'll do it.' i said.

back at the lodge the couple of remaining actors and several of the crew were nursing hangovers. by now they were interested in little but coffee, peace, and not being asked to work before lunch. i changed into my footman's suit and a black tie and prepared to return to the house. then i had to explain what had happened. this was met with incredulity and a stunned silence that i feared, for a moment, indicated professional outrage. should i really have obtained an 'equity card' to embark on this? peadar lamb, a 'character' actor, was after all a real actor who could be seen on the television or the abbey theatre stage – would he call up the actors' union, and make objections?

then leo said –

'so what is your deal, gillies?'

in the general excitement of the morning so far, and the relief of finding out that i was not going to be fired, it had not crossed my mind to open the subject of remuneration with the director.

'i suppose,' i said, 'it will still be the same. twenty pounds cash.'

a roar of derisive laughter at these terms for acting the leading role in a full-length feature film, convulsed the whole company.

what looked for a moment like an awkward situation, was defused. no one made further comment, even when i was invited to move out of the crew's quarters, and – the guest house being full – into the castle.

so i began my days of filming. the sandwiches were forgotten and everyone got their own lunches, which they already had been doing for much of the time. the weather turned wet again, so filming indoors made sense, and avoided the hassle of setting up outdoor locations.

the house was a film set as it stood, not needing any rearrangement of the pictures or furniture. whichever direction the camera pointed, or wherever the director chose to place me (for the moment the sole actor), the family trophies of the leslies formed a glittering background. if the action took place before the windows, there was then the grassy slope to the grey-green lake, and the scudding clouds and sudden showers of an irish summer day beyond.

i was asked, at first, to play the grand piano. i cannot play, but without sound, this did not matter. to begin with i hit the keys, and the crew had to endure meaningless discords as they lined up the camera on the railway tracks. then i got into the whole thing. they did not need to focus on my hands, indeed it was silly to do so, so why hit the keys? they were filming from the front, so that my hands were not in shot.

although i do not play, i can remember some of the more famous bits of beethoven. humming ever so slightly i let myself be carried away by the rhythms and melody in my head, which was in fact not the music of a piano piece at all, but the whole berlin philharmonic doing all-out beethoven from one of fintan's favourite records. i was aware of jimbo muttering behind the cameraman –

'good … good … good.'

it was going well. we were in business again.

friday came and i got paid. in the early evenings the whole crew piled into the land rover (the sandwich transporter) and aggie leslie's borrowed car. we drove the few miles into monaghan town where jimbo had hired out the local cinema, and we played the previous day's 'rushes'. these are a first hasty printing of film, shown so that the film-makers know whether to go back and reshoot any bits that are, for any reason, unsatisfactory.

this was a shock. i had never been to the cinema house in monaghan town, but i had been in other similar places.

like a savage confronted with his own picture for the first time, i was faced with the rushes of myself playing the piano in the castle leslie drawing room. to my surprise it was utterly convincing. there on a screen twenty feet high, in an almost deserted cinema house, was my own face, complete with all its moles and spots, in colour, in close-up, and i was playing the piano. if it had been anyone else in the scene, i would have been utterly convinced that they were playing the piano, i would have had no reason to doubt it. the illusion worked. the scene was as if from a mysterious grand house in a far far away country.

desmond leslie came to this showing. he looked pleased, and as we came out of the cinema he said to me, conspiratorially –

'you … are going to be the star of this film.'

with desmond you never knew if he was serious, or not. he was no doubt watching the way things were going, just like everyone else. he was as anxious for his next month's rent as the crew were for their next month's salaries. for the moment we were all on the same side. we wanted jimbo's career as a director to flourish for a little longer.

that night fintan's older brother, collins, my art-dealer friend, rang up.

'how's the filming going?'

i knew that he would not just ring up to enquire after my health. some rumour about the film must by now be circulating in dublin.

'fine.'

'what are you doing, yourself?'

'i am the star.'

sensing drama from afar, he said that he would come up, bring up antoinette, and visit fintan (in exile at laragh) on the way. i told him to come as soon as he could, if he wanted to see the filming, as it could all run out of money, and fold, at any time.

that he already knew. he was able to fill me in that rombo was the heir to a fortune made in the west indies before the turn of the century, and the beneficiary of an enormous trust fund. he had been spending wildly for some time, and his trustees wanted to have him declared insane as the only way to protect him from himself, and others.

this sounded unlikely, to me. rombo was eccentric, over the top even, but hardly insane.

then collins repeated to me a story going around dublin – that rombo had recently been on a flight to paris which had encountered severe turbulence, alarming many of the passengers. tate had unstrapped himself from his seat and stood up at the front of the bucking plane – to announce that he was jesus christ, and would save them all. the flight had eventually landed safely, but been met at paris by the french police. i could picture this happening. immersed as i now was in the filming, i could only respond by wishing that jimbo and leo had been there to record the scene on the plane for the next evening's rushes.

collins, who had good intuitions about people, and about money, suspected that rombo had been lured out of the british jurisdiction by his friends and hangers-on, deliberately, because that way his family and trustees were rendered virtually powerless to make any legal move against him.

collins travelled the country in a large daimler car. it was about twenty years old. if it had not been his it would probably have been painted white and been some rural hackney driver's wedding car. this car looked very appropriate sweeping up the drive to castle leslie. rombo was in the conservatory. above all rombo required an audience, and as collins and antoinette and a couple of their dublin friends came into view, he waved a hand to bring the day's filming to an end, welcomed them, and offered them a tour of 'his' castle. he was wearing his kilt, and, rather unnecessarily, he ascended the conservatory stepladder by which the gardener tended the vines growing up under the glass of the roof.

rombo addressed the half-dozen listeners as if we were a crowd of a couple of hundred people, with a largely inaccurate account of the house and its history, as if it were his own. the listeners stood as if spellbound by this dubious tale, and only then did it dawn on me that by ascending the ladder, rombo had revealed (to those strong enough not to avert their gaze), that he was wearing nothing under his kilt.

he then descended and began to play the part of the great director, even though he was meant to be the producer. we went in to the drawing room. he seated antoinette at the grand piano. without explaining what he was doing, he then looked at her through his fingers, making significant 'hmmmms' all the while.

i do not want to exaggerate antoinette's beauty, but she was striking enough to have served as artist's model for more than one dublin painter. she began to pose, and show tate her best side. i did not like the way this was going. some tiny tinge of jealousy came out of nowhere to infect my thinking. rombo spoke to her in flattering terms.

rombo was lining up his next star ...

the evening ended up as had several others, with champagne on the guest house dining room table, and rombo playing his part as millionaire film director to antoinette, as if there were no one else in the room. great wealth is known to be an aphrodisiac, and i was surprised how coolly collins let this go on, in front of everyone. i was even more surprised when rombo popped the question.

'jimbo and i think that you would be perfect, my dear, for a little part in the story.'

antoinette looked at collins, who did not bat an eyelid, but grinned, wickedly.

'but i have nothing to wear,' she said.

'then we will have to get you something, won't we?'

rombo burst into his trademark roars of loud laughter, at which anyone within earshot could not help but join in. i had visions of rombo and jimbo conducting antoinette around the dublin dress shops with an open cheque book.

so had she.

so had collins perhaps, for he excused himself and his fellow guests, and thanking his host, ushered them out to the car for the drive back to the city, leaving antoinette to her fate.

when everyone had gone back to dublin, or up to bed, it was left to me to drive rombo and his new star up the winding avenue to the main house in aggie's old car. rombo had ushered antoinette into the back of the vehicle, as if i were a taxi, and driving very slowly in the unfamiliar car, i became aware of some kind of kerfuffle going on between the two of them.

the castle door was open, and lights were on in the main hall. i followed them in, painfully aware that antoinette was slightly less happy than her producer at the scene that was now beginning to unfold itself. at the foot of the stairs, rombo turned and said –

'you can go and put away the car in the garage.'

i began to say that it was late, and the car would come to no harm left out on the gravel for the night …

rombo said sharply –

'when i hire a butler, i expect him to follow orders.'

i went back out of the front door, feeling that he did not care a damn about the car, but just wanted to get me out of the way. i felt humiliated. one moment i was a leading actor drinking champagne, and the next a badly treated domestic pulled up for questioning instructions. i had had enough.

a fuse blew in my head and i turned back into the house, leaving the car where it was. he could put it away himself.

as i came past the bedroom on the first-floor landing, there were alarming noises. it was the booming sound of rombo, ranting. the lights were on, the door was partly open, and face down across the four-poster bed was antoinette, and she was sobbing hysterically.

this had gone too far. this had to be stopped. but rombo was a big man, drunk, and possibly violent. what on earth could i do?

i am a coward, in certain respects, and i ran down the stairs again to the hall. there from the mantlepiece i took a mediaeval iron mace – about eighteen inches long, a weapon that had served no more than a decorative function for the last several hundred years. taking a firm grip on this, i raced up the stairs again, two at a time, threw the bedroom door wide open, and advanced on rombo. he stopped shouting. he stood there in his shirtsleeves, transfixed. antoinette lifted her head from the pillow. for a second the three of us formed a tableau.

i said to her –

'go to the car, we're getting out of here.'

there must have been an unaccustomed decisiveness in my voice, or it was the iron mace i was holding at shoulder level ready to strike – but antoinette scrambled up, and out of the room. i backed out after her, slowly. rombo stood shocked and motionless. i moved off along the landing, alert to any sound of pursuit. there was none. i shouted down to antoinette in the hall below –

'go and get in the car, *now.*'

she ran outside.

in the room beside the top of the long flight of stairs, the light was on. the door ajar. there in another large four-poster was aggie leslie, a book in front of her on the eiderdown, unread. she was sitting bolt upright in bed. she had overheard the drama along the landing.

i went straight in, i said –

'aggie, i need to borrow your car, now.'

i held up my other hand in which i still held the car keys. i got what i took to be a wordless assent. the last thing i said on the way out was –

'we'll bring it back in the morning.'

i then went down the stairs, through the hall, carefully putting back the mace in its accustomed place as i went, and out to the car. we took off, scattering gravel.

there was not a camera in sight as i drove the heroine through the gates of castle leslie, and out on to the dark roads of county monaghan, on our way home back to laragh.

the end

in the morning i found the bread knife on the bedside table, a sign that i had gone to bed feeling insecure and half expecting us to be pursued.

i left fintan to make pots of coffee for antoinette, and soothe her with his sergeant pepper records and a little beethoven, while i went off to return the car back to glaslough.

there was no one about when i parked the car at the front door, and went in to collect my belongings from castle leslie. desmond's old uncle, the one that always talked about monsters, appeared and followed me about the house suspiciously, but it only took me a few minutes to gather up my bits and pieces. i simply left the car at the door with the keys in it and walked down the avenue and back out of the gate. i now had to try and hitch-hike the thirty miles home.

so ended the story of the film – and it was some weeks later that i heard the rest. rombo had reverted to english ways and called the police out in the middle of the night. between the effects of champagne and his usual extravagant mannerisms, his tale of being attacked by a mad butler had fallen rather flat. there were no injuries, no blood, no body, no aspiring film actress – and the mace, though real enough, was over the hall mantlepiece where it had always been. the squad car were fairly unimpressed to be called out so late about so little, and had wondered aloud to aggie if it were not in fact rombo who was off his head?

so the glaslough filming ended and the crew quickly dispersed to work on other projects and in other countries.

apparently the rombo trustees got their act together, and managed to staunch the haemorrhaging of funds out of the country. when the actors and crew got their pay-off in london, in accordance with the terms of their contracts, all their cheques bounced.

no doubt they wished they had agreed to my own deal of twenty pounds, cash, at the end of each working week.

CHAPTER FIVE 1970–1

unemployed

i was now out of work, as a direct result of seeking interesting adventures, rather than settling for steady employment.

i qualified for unemployment benefit. the single man's dole was at this time still three pounds ten shillings per week. with this i attempted to feed fintan, myself, and gilbert the large white boar – all of which cost three pounds – and we drank the last ten shillings. fintan, as a struggling artist who did not stamp a card, did not qualify for dole.

i resolved to hold out for work locally. to have a house like laragh and not live in it made no sense. i would have to adopt the local tactic of being prepared to take anything that came up. full-time jobs were not to be had too easily, so you had to be satisfied with scraps of work here and there. the traditional alternative was emigration.

the first job i got was helping to rebuild the graveyard wall. the builder, who was a neighbour of mine, did the actual building. i shovelled the gravel, sand, and cement, for him. the work was at the chapel in lisdoonan village. this job was rather public, as sooner or later everyone in the locality passed up the road. what is more, they all made the same joke:

'that'll keep them in a bit longer!'

in a community where much work was still manual, a lot of graves in the graveyard were dug by the families themselves, or their neighbours.

the community even seemed to think communally, and were able to work out, together, things that no individual mind would have managed to disentangle. conversation was peppered with certain well-worn stock phrases, like the recurring epithets found in homer. once a communal judgment was reached on a person or a deed, people rarely went against it. thinking independently was typically the mark of a blow-in, an intellectual (known as a 'head case'), or a returned emigrant. any returned emigrant who had changed their accent or ways of thinking was automatically demoted to 'blow-in' status at the back of the queue.

a funeral

while we were working on the graveyard wall, word came that a brother of the bookie's uncle cuey had died. cuey and his brother and sister, all unmarried, had lived together on a farm of about thirty acres, not all of it good land, and some of it rushy and north-facing. the farm was not large enough to support a family, but could support the three siblings as long as they remained single. i knew that i would be expected to go to the funeral, not because i knew the dead man well, but to show sympathy with his relations.

uncle cuey's house was one of those which had not yet entered the twentieth century. although it was now over twenty years since the first scheme for rural electrification had been launched, it was not connected, and the house was lit with oil lamps. when i got there the half door was open at the top, and the first room, the kitchen, was full of women and girls making tea and sandwiches, pouring stout from bottles into cups, and washing whiskey glasses. i was given a small glass of whiskey, but this was to be filled and refilled as the evening went on.

i now took a bit of a deep breath, for although i was in my late twenties, i had never seen a dead person. the house was small, and i had to push my way between the women in the kitchen to get to where the men were gathered in the bedroom beside it.

cuey's brother lay propped up in bed. the sheets were clean. he wore a clean shirt, open at the neck, and his best and only suit. his eyes were closed, his face composed and waxen. i paused at the foot of the bed, i am not even sure that i blessed myself in the uncertainty of the moment. somebody gestured me to sit down by pushing forward a chair.

the bookie had helped with the washing of the body. things like professional embalming, and funeral homes, still lay in the future. funerals were usually held on the third day after a death, which just gave time for emigrant relations to make it back from england.

conversation was at first intermittent, but as more people came in and glasses were refilled, flowed more freely. the first talk was of the dead man, his fine character, and his long life in the parish. we were all so close together in the confined room, that some had to stand in the doorway, while others had to share chairs and rest an elbow on the deceased's bed to keep their balance.

more people came. a couple of men went out to milk cows, or some other task that could not be put off, but came back again after a while. talk turned to the possibility of the country's entry into the european common market. as one who got my information from the newspapers, rather than by being part of the communal mind, i could hold forth on this subject.

there is great wisdom in the wake tradition. cuey's quiet house had not been so busy for a generation. warmth, friends, food, drink, reminiscence, and conversation, are all remedies for grief. instead of a solemn atmosphere of mourning, the dead man was honoured by the number of his friends, relations, and neighbours who had turned out on a wet night to be present in his house. as the evening wore on, the women put down their tea towels and butter knives in the kitchen, and, in relays, had their own tea. in such houses the old turf fire with its crane and kettle and pots still survived, alongside a more modern solid fuel range fitted into one corner of a wide arched fireplace.

i don't know if cuey's sister catherine was very old, or whether she looked older than she was as the result of a hard life. i remarked upon her blackened kettle, with its iron scalloped lid. pouring more water into the teapot, she said that she could still remember the day she brought the kettle home from crossmaglen fair on the handlebars of her bicycle:

'it was a divil of a long ride home and benny quinn was cutting oats with a scythe in the high field.'

again i was struck by the difference between the cut of the local mind and my own. here were a people and a generation who did not travel, read much, or (so far) watch television. their minds made little use of generalization, but instead relied upon a precise recollection of the details of everything local and particular.

their lives, farming, education, entertainment, feuds, and courting (if any), all took place within walking distance of here. hence they knew every rock, bush, pothole, fence post, and piece of thorny wire in the townland. cuey himself did not even get to the town until he was fifteen. then he was allowed to help bring cattle to the market with his father. you had to be big enough to get up before dawn, walk the cattle the eight miles into town, spend a long day at the fair, stand behind your father in a bar for an hour or two, and then walk the eight miles back.

people came and went to a house where there was a wake. no doubt some men's wives resigned themselves to being left with doing the milking and feeding calves, until after the funeral was over. things changed when more people had cars and were commuting to regular paid employment. the country could then no longer afford to drop everything for three whole days.

it was very late when we left the wake. the pros and cons of common market entry had had a good airing by then. absorbed in the discussion, i became accustomed to the dead man lying in the bed beside me, once even, absent mindedly, turning to him to seek support for the point i was making. but cuey's brother had chewed his last plug of tobacco, and his long life of hardship and troubles was over.

the bedcover

i made one more attempt to get work in dublin. in spite of the glaslough film and its disastrous ending, aggie leslie must still have trusted me, as she kindly lent me their flat in dublin to stay in, one weekend. she was not using it herself, and simply told me how and where to ask for the key.

it was a downstairs flat in the south of the city, not far from the canal. the attempt to find employment quickly came to nothing, so i decided to only stay one night. the flat was very nicely furnished, and i did not find this particularly surprising, as a house like castle leslie can often provide enough furnishings from its back rooms and attics to fill a dozen flats. it did not occur to me that the flat might also be part of the battleground of the disintegrating marriage.

the bed was made up in a front room. the bedcover was an unusual and heavy embroidered thing, but the night was cold, and i was glad of the weight and the warmth.

the next morning i slept late, and was just up and dressed when the doorbell rang. it was the towering figure of desmond leslie, and when i opened the door he strode past me into the back bedroom, then in to the front room.

he hauled the heavy bedcover off the bed, folded it once, folded it twice, and bodily lifted it off the bed.

'that,' he said emphatically as he strode out, 'was william iv's funeral pall!'

– and he slammed the front door.

the suit

i had now allowed myself to get poor. there was enough to eat, sure, and firewood if you took the trouble to get it in in time, and did not let yourself get caught without fuel in wet weather. there was little money left over for clothes.

i had now reached a point where, if a suitable job came up, i did not even own a suit to wear to an interview. nor had i the bus fare to get out of laragh or down to dublin.

it was round about this time that the trouble had started up in the north.

gilbert tode-kerr sent a message one night to ask if i would play host to his cousin peregrine. the telephone, which had the beautiful number 'tullynahinera 12' had been cut off as an economy measure – by the phone people. the postmistress's husband, who drove a milk lorry for the creamery, used to bring up messages for us. he came up the avenue from the village in his very long silver articulated tanker, rather than walk the couple of hundred yards.

tode-kerr had a way of making every request seem urgent and special. when i rang back, he gave little explanation, but said that peregrine could make his own way to carrickmacross, where i could meet him off the dublin bus.

two days later i made this rendezvous. peregrine arrived looking rather thin, pale, and distant. the customs officers at holyhead had confiscated his vitamin pills. they had probably looked at the colour of his eyes, which were a tired pink, and decided to take from him anything that could conceivably be eaten or injected. it occurred to me that tode-kerr had guessed this – that whatever substance peregrine might be purchasing in london, would not make it through the customs, or be easily obtainable at laragh. laragh was to be cold turkey farm for the moment.

there is not a lot to do at laragh to entertain the son of an english duke. peregrine had little money with him, and perhaps this was another sensible ploy on the part of his family. drinking was not much good to him, and did not seem to alter his mood. dancing was out of the question. even if we had the price of tickets in to the castleblayney dance hall, three step waltzing to the local band 'big tom and the mainliners', whether drunk or sober, was not a ritual for the uninitiated. i knew that the girls lined up inside by the mineral bar would possibly decline to dance with us, in any case.

the bookie came to the rescue with a suggestion of an outing across the border to 'cross' (crossmaglen) fair.

although the bookie had no transport, beyond a small working pony and cart, he had a network of contacts. he had begged the three of us a lift in a tractor and trailer. the journey of about twelve miles took most of two hours. this was not unpleasant, as we travelled at a speed which allowed us to see the country in detail, and even exchange shouted remarks with people we met on the way. the farms were small and the drumlin fields sometimes good, but more often rush-infested. if you saw a newly built house standing on poor land, it almost had to be the home of a smuggler. some of these places had farms with fields on each side of the border, and such holdings, though rarely sold, commanded a premium.

contrary to everything written in the newspapers, or shown on the television, the parishes on both sides of the border were quiet, deserted almost. if you had actually needed a soldier, customs man, or a policeman, there would have been very little chance of finding one. later, of course, the situation in south armagh became close to impossible for the forces of occupation, and the troops abandoned the roads altogether and only moved on foot across the open fields, or by helicopter.

we crossed the border illegally, on an 'unapproved road'. this was not because we were engaged upon anything shady – but just because the proper way round, by the army's manned checkpoint, was too far to travel in the tractor. there was no mark or sign at this point of the border. when you met the first red telephone box at cullaville, you knew you were on the far side and in county armagh. sometimes there was a slight bump in the road, because up in the north the roads were resurfaced more often. occupied regions often have better road systems, for logistical reasons.

in the fair in the square at crossmaglen goods were noticeably cheaper than on our side. many of the traders must have been getting their stock in england, where there was a much wider selection of second hand stuff. i bought wellington boots, and a greatcoat that showed by its navy colour that it had once been issued to a customs officer. the quality of these was always good.

peregrine and i went for a bottle of stout in a bar. it was the day that bernadette devlin had announced that she was pregnant – bernadette, the pint-sized heroine of the battle of the bogside. this was a severe blow to all of the more conservative rural republicans. it was like a death in the family.

in the bar our accents must have got us noticed. i saw one of a group of young men staring searchingly at us. after a while he went out and returned to the bar with an older man. this man very deliberately, and with some air of unspoken authority, came and engaged us in conversation. i thought it best to answer his questions truthfully and without hesitation, while peregrine said nothing. the man soon shrugged and left us – we had been processed by the local intelligence system and judged harmless.

waiting for the tractor to pick us up for the journey home, peregrine and i sat in the sunshine on a low wall. the building behind us turned out to be the army barracks. while we were sitting there, along came a demonstration against the british army presence in crossmaglen. there were half a dozen men of various ages and three or four girls. between them they had several placards on sticks. they spaced themselves out evenly and picketed by walking up the pavement for the length of the barracks, and then back again in the road. a tall bespectacled soldier with an automatic rifle took up position outside the barracks door to supervise this demonstration. we were left sitting in a no man's land, on the wall between the crown forces and the local representatives of the republicans, south armagh sinn féin.

behind the wall were a few straggling rose bushes and on them the last roses of the summer. i plucked a couple of these and handed them to the girl demonstrators as they passed. the soldier was tight-lipped and said nothing. english public school had taught us just how far you can go with the prefects ...

one of the girls taunted the soldier a couple of times:

'come on – we know it's not loaded!'

i wondered if she was right. do you send a possibly inexperienced recruit out with an automatic rifle, to watch a tiny demonstration – *with live ammunition?*

at this time, everyone – soldiers, republicans, and onlookers – was new to civil disturbances. people were still working out the ground rules.

border duty was beginning to take up the time of an increasing number of the guards on our side of the border, but they were not armed, and when called out they often took their time, preferring to give any gunmen in the locality plenty of opportunity to make themselves scarce.

when peregrine went back to england, he was also wearing my greatcoat purchased at cross fair. he asked me if i would like his suit. this was a light tweed, and although he was thin, he was of a similar height to myself and i could just about get into it.

owning this suit was soon to change the course of my life.

mrs collins's dog

i think i began to go slightly mad about this time. i will tell the tale, and you can judge for yourself.

fintan collins had gone back to dublin. life on the dole was very constricting, and a weekly walk to mass to hear father campbell warn about the perils of communism (of which there was very little sign in the free market society along the border) provided limited entertainment. our own entertainment value was declining, as we no longer had the advantage of being the bearers of news from the world outside. to put it bluntly – the customers in mrs mccabe's bar already knew as much as they wanted to know about us.

visitors like peregrine were glad to be invited on summer weekends, but wisely gave laragh a miss in the depths of winter.

after parting with the wolfhound 'murphy', who as well as being intellectually challenged had developed a mysterious disease of the paws, i had at different times kept various dogs, largely for companionship. these included liver spotted dalmations. because of the nature of the place, and my own nature, i always gave my dog its freedom, and never confined it on a lead. a dog that could not follow its master, or would not 'come' or 'stay', when told, was not worth the feeding, and a dog that could not be allowed its freedom, was not worth keeping – either for my sake, or for the dog's own sake.

the monaghan dogs were largely farm sheepdogs. like their owners, some were friendly, a few savage. the other kind of dogs kept were hounds and beagles.

two very different circles of huntsmen lived in the county. the first was represented by the shirley family. monaghan had no pack of foxhounds, but the shirley family – who were the heirs of one of the daughters of the earl of essex of tudor times, and owned the ground rents of all of one side of the main street in carrickmacross – belonged to the neighbouring louth hunt.

laragh had in earlier days been the site of a 'lawn meet' of the louth hunt. in my first winter in the house, when they had been listed in the local paper as meeting at laragh, i got quite nervous in anticipation, and bought in a bottle of whiskey, a bottle of sherry, and polished every glass in the place. the time for the traditional meet came and went, and i eventually walked down the avenue to find that the riders, uncertain of a welcome up at the house, had held the meet in the village instead and were just moving off.

the other hunt in the area were beagles which hunted hares. these were a much less formal affair, although they had their own traditions. each 'member' of the hunt, which spanned both sides of the border, kept a couple of dogs at home. these were long legged beagles, looking more like a big rough fox hound than a purebred show beagle. no notice of the place of the meet was published. it was like an illegal cock fight – you met someone in a car at a certain crossroads, they nodded to you to follow and drove the next part of the way. the pack of hounds brought together in this manner, with each couple responsive mainly to the whistles and shouts of their owner, was somewhat unruly. the peculiar nature of drumlin country meant that when the ill-assorted pack took off, the followers did not run after them, but usually turned and legged it up the hill behind, to get a view of the hunt from the summit. this was also because hares have a tendency to run in a wide circle from the point where they are put up.

if you had met a hunt at a moment when the pack and the hare were hidden from view, you would have wondered at the meaning of a ragged bunch of men and boys, on a crowded drumlin hill top, jumping, waving, cursing, shouting and whistling. there was even a one-legged man on crutches, who 'follied the hunt'.

sometimes the pack would put up a second hare and divide into two. the bookie took me on one particularly exciting sunday hunt, at which the pack split up to follow two separate hares fleeing in opposite directions around a hill – only for both lots to meet head-on in a gateway in a gap between two fields at the other side.

even in that melee the owners were apparently able to identify, and follow the performance of their own muddy couple of hounds.

these monaghan and armagh beagle owners seemed to inhabit a parallel and separate universe to the members of the louth hunt. once, some years after this, two other worlds collided. the louth hunt – all hunt coats, protestant hairnets and plaited manes – were led full pelt for a mile or so into unfamiliar territory by a straight running fox. in a field near the border they came up against a unit of the provisional

IRA — all balaclavas and kalashnikovs — at secret training in a field on a hillside where they would never expect to be disturbed. from their dress, each party could not help but know at first glance exactly who the other party were.

no word was spoken. after a moment's surprise and hesitation, each group turned and went on about its business, as if they had seen nothing, and met nobody.

i was now faced with a lonely christmas at laragh. in other circumstances the bookie and his family would have extended me every hospitality, but living on the charity of your own tenants was a strange and slightly awkward position to be in.

katie, the bookie's eldest daughter, gave me a pound for christmas, and knowing money was tight, gave it to me before the day. she had recently got a job in the office at the creamery.

i had one other asset to cash in. i sold a beech tree for timber and firewood, one that was interfering with the growth of a larger and finer tree beside it. i was too trusting. i came back from the shop to find that the tree feller had 'mistakenly' felled the massive beech and left the smaller one standing. it was a fait accompli that no solicitor or court could reverse, and he knew it.

i had also begun to keep geese. i bought a goose and a gander, and for two years i made them a nest of straw in an outhouse, shut them in, and collected the eggs. the eggs were then placed in a box full of barley on the old kitchen mantlepiece, to keep them at an even temperature until the goose sat, at which time they were all placed under her. each time i tried this the goose failed to sit properly or to bring out goslings.

the third spring my goose disappeared, and i assumed that she, like the recently vanished gander before her, had fallen victim to a fox.

then one day a month or so later she reappeared, coming down the derelict garden followed by eight goslings in single file. this year she had done it her way.

i managed to sell a couple of these offspring, by now full-grown, in time for fattening for christmas. so now i rang fintan in dublin, offering a christmas goose, and hoping for, and receiving, an invitation from his older brother and the latter's new girlfriend, to bring it down with me and to stay for christmas day.

thus early on christmas eve, i arrived in dublin, with money in my pocket, and a twelve-pound goose under my arm, with its neck wrung, plucked naked, but otherwise complete and entire.

i met up with collins the art dealer in the royal hibernian hotel in dawson street. he was with a mrs collins, no relation, upon whom he was busy exercising his mercurial charm. she might have been in her fifties, with a certain amount of heavy jewellery, and a beige-coloured, bored-looking dog on a lead. i immediately gathered that mrs collins was a potential customer, and that i was to moderate my conversation, and play along.

i was rather like a dog on a lead, myself. or perhaps, after the isolation of the country for the last few months, i was like a sailor going ashore after a long spell at sea. the warmth of the hotel, getting no lunch but being plied with unaccustomed gin and tonics, and the tedium of being trapped between collin's unreal charm and mrs collins's aimless chatter, was now my undoing.

real dogs should not be obliged to belong to fat, rich, urban widows.

so i got unsteadily to my feet, and asked if i could take the dog for a short walk. it was obviously an expensive dog, the unusual beige of its coat declared that. like mrs collins's diamonds, for her its whole purpose was to declare that it was expensive – and yet to itself, it was a dog, a creature destined to hunt, scavenge, fight, find bitches, chew bones, piss on trees …

once i had the dog out in the christmas street, he came to life. how could i take him back to his cosseted but tedious confinement in the hotel lobby as mrs collins's ornament? he started to show interest in the unexpected turn his day had taken. round the railings of saint stephen's green we went, marking out the territory in the traditional way as we patrolled each side of the square, pausing to check out interesting smells.

then with the dog's lead in one hand, and the goose under the other arm, i hailed a taxi and set off for collins the art dealer's residence, now in a salubrious part of the distant seaside suburb of dalkey.

i do not remember the journey, or arriving, or how i found the key under the plant pot to get into the house, but the moment that i finally got through the door the telephone rang. collins the art dealer, whose christmas eve i had now well and truly wrecked, was furious to the point of being nearly speechless. where was the dog? what was the idea of taking him away with me? what lunacy had come over me?

within the half hour he had followed me out to dalkey in the daimler, strode into the house, taken up the dog's lead without a word, and slammed out of the house again.

i was in trouble.

i now slipped out of the house and down the hill until i found a taxi. i negotiated a price for the seventy-mile journey to monaghan, fell into the back, and thus spent my entire saved-up christmas funds on retracing the journey that i had made that same morning.

my arrival back at laragh was unexpected. the lights were on in the hall, and the bookie's daughters had my front door unbolted, obviously to receive christmas guests of their own. what could i say? our lives were now intertwined, my social pretensions undermined by the realities of my situation.

inside in the lighted hall was a christmas present, a large and heavy cardboard box covered in english stamps. it was from octavia knox in london.

the contents of the box were more welcome at that moment than almost any other conceivable present could have been. there were tins of beans, tinned soup, cheeses, salami sausage, sardines … provisions, in other words. the kind of parcel that would appeal to people who had recently been victims of a natural disaster.

the way to a man's heart is through his stomach.

i resolved there and then to let the land in the spring, pocket the proceeds instead of paying the overdue rates bill, and – while i still had peregrine's respectable suit – pay a visit to octavia knox in london.

all was not lost. a victory of a kind had been snatched from the jaws of defeat, and i even made it up, later, with collins the art dealer. soon after christmas his new live-in girlfriend rang up to make peace and thank me for the goose. they had enjoyed it but found it strongly flavoured, different from their usual supermarket turkey.

'what did you do, did you stuff it?' i asked.

'oh there was no need,' she said, 'wasn't it stuffed already?'

how happy i could be with either

when spring came i was in debt. the debt was not very large, because i had steadfastly refused to put the deeds of the house into the bank, and my small overdraft was not officially sanctioned. this indebtedness was in the course of being remedied, because i had contracted to sell a five-acre field to a neighbour, peter mccabe, and the deal was close to completion. the sale price was five hundred pounds.

i was sorry to sell off land, even one rushy field, as i was beginning to absorb the values of my adopted country. to sell off land or even hedgerow trees, to raise money, was a sign of weakness if not financial desperation. i had remained a hybrid creature, a cultural mongrel not fully belonging either to my small farm neighbourhood, nor to my 'smart' meath and dublin friends further up the country, and no longer connected to my receding english past.

peter mccabe had a younger sister, janey, who was pretty and red-haired. janey came home for holidays, but worked year-round as a nurse in leytonstone in london. i fell into step with her one day walking home from the shop.

janey knew me from visits i had made to her mother's cottage to negotiate the sale of the field with peter, but a laragh girl, that is to say one who had never been away from home, would not normally walk with a man in public view. for janey to do so, quite casually, was a mark of big-city polish and an almost alien sophistication.

i was now flirting, not with the red-haired janey so much as with an idea. i had passed my twenty-eighth birthday. could i possibly find someone to share my life, who was like me, a creature of two worlds? i was an english fruitcake with a recent icing of irishness – could i find a match with someone who was irish cake mix with an icing of englishness?

it was logically appealing.

but marriage? are we serious here? what has logic to do with it? logic is better kept out of such matters.

as for advice on affairs of the heart, i did not even have a friend close enough to confide in. a local laragh inhabitant might have recognized the symptoms of an isolated bachelor-farmer developing 'notions' about girls. a dublin friend might have guessed that i saw in janey mccabe's auburn hair and pale freckled skin a distant resemblance to the adored, and (by now) stunning, claudia kenny, who was beyond my reach, and who had neither the need nor the inclination to settle for a life of rural poverty and obscurity.

i suggested to janey a meeting for tea in the west end, when i made my trip to london to visit octavia knox. i arranged to let her know, in the spring, as soon as the sale was finally completed, and i had the price of a ticket to go over.

when spring came i laid my plans carefully. when the weather began to turn warmer, the minds of dublin friends would turn to weekends down the country. i invited down dara o'lochlainn, a designer and jazz musician, and his girlfriend, knowing well that his return to dublin would neatly coincide with my need for a lift up to the airport.

the collins brothers were fond of telling slightly exaggerated tales of laragh, about poteen makers, border skulduggery, boar pig riding contests, and the 'good life'. they had built it up, in our dublin friends' estimation, somewhat more than it deserved. laragh was not as wild as its reputation, but it was still a beautiful place to be on a fine weekend.

dara's visit passed pleasantly. the girlfriend was a little taken aback at having to boil a saucepan to get hot water to wash in, and bemused in general at the odd mixture of austerity and grandeur. the house was largely bare of furniture, and the library, the breakfast room, and the pantry, were all far less impressive than their names might suggest.

very early on the morning that we were due to head for dublin, we had got no further than the village when dara's small, elderly car developed a puncture. no problem. he threw the spare out of the boot, jacked up the car and changed the wheel. i stood well back, unwilling to risk oil on my hands, or worse, on my suit. we were about to move off again when it became apparent that the spare was also flat.

we walked back to the post office to ring a garage.

after explaining our problem, we left dara's girlfriend sharing a breakfast pot of tea with the postmistress, and hitched a lift on the milk lorry into carrickmacross, bringing the wheel. there in the town we found that the garage had not yet opened. we enquired in the bar next door. the garage proprietor apparently had a slight problem with monday mornings …

i could see the day ahead leaking away in this fashion until darkness fell.

some voice in my head warned me that my entire life was being gambled away on chance events.

there was only one thing to do. i excused myself from a surprised dara, and walked over to the other side of the dublin road. i hailed the first car that came, with my thumb extended, and it pulled over. was it going to dublin? yes.

we drove off, leaving dara to enjoy, on his own, the local 'pace of life' that he so often enthused about when angling for an invitation down the country.

by four o'clock that afternoon i was sitting down to afternoon tea with janey mccabe in the lobby of brown's hotel in london. she was my guest, but she poured the tea. monaghan men did not pour tea. womenfolk did that.

we were a couple of young people in their twenties, who knew each other. we both knew laragh, and we both knew london, but there was something amiss that i could not put my finger on.

later i decided that it was this: our shared experience of living in the two different worlds, was not the same experience. we were facing in opposite directions, the experience of each of us was a mirror image of the other's. she would always treasure laragh as her home place, but was committed to emerge bit by bit from that harsh background into what was to her the very sophisticated london world. my own journey was the reverse journey, from the impersonal cities towards a simpler, truer life, and an attempt to become rooted in the land of ireland.

we drank our tea, and more tea from the pot, and poured in more hot water and drank more tea. there were plain biscuits. we talked about tentative, inconsequential things, and fell silent. i became distracted by the faint white patch on her knee at the point where the stocking pressed the blood from the flesh. the last time that i had noticed it, had been above muddied wellington boots in a farmhouse kitchen.

she might have been quite alarmed, at the time, to learn how seriously i had thought about her. i never had a chance to take her out again, because that same evening my life took a different turn. this was a day of decisions, and we only ever had that one date. tea in brown's hotel. just an hour and a half. i never kissed her. come to think of it, i never touched her, even accidentally.

is there a pattern here? it was an affair that never was. what was wrong here in brown's hotel?

she did not put a foot wrong, that was what was wrong. i sensed that she too was 'blending' into a new environment. in the fullness of time she would probably have children with english accents – who would go for their holidays to laragh, and find the irish children there wild and good fun, but alien and strange ...

from brown's hotel i went to visit peregrine, in a basement flat in kensington. i rang the bell and a long-haired man let me in. the flat was strangely bare, furnished with decorative tiled walls as if it had once been a turkish bath or something. when i came into the room downstairs there were neither beds nor sofas, but only mattresses on the floor. in the middle of the room on one of these sat peregrine, wearing a kaftan, with a far-away expression on his face.

for meeting him in such a very different place i had half rehearsed a joke:

'do you like my suit?' i said.

(it being of course his.)

peregrine smiled wanly and from a very great distance.

all of my silly english fantasies of one day being married, with the younger son of a duke standing beside me as best man, flew out of the window at that instant. i saw now why tode-kerr had tried to get him out of the country. i knew nothing about drugs, i did not even know the jargon. was he stoned, smashed, high, tripping?

he was just not at home.

poor peregrine.

i was not going to stay the night here.

i nodded to the friend to take me back upstairs and let me out of the locked and bolted door.

so i came to octavia knox's house a day early.

octavia had lost her grandmother since our days at corbally house. she now inherited, and lived in, the grandmother's little house in chelsea.

she answered the door herself and laughed when i announced that i had landed a day sooner than intended.

'you are naughty,' she said, but not in a discouraging tone.

she kept the house exactly as it had been in her grandmother's day, only clearing out one of the bedrooms to rent to a friend, more for company than to make any money from it. the house was tiny and neat, but what was left of its lease would still be worth more than the sprawling house, the village, and all the fields at laragh. a counterpane from a double bed would have covered its garden. it was a typical granny's house, with photographs and paintings, and silver and trinkets in little glass-topped tables. the furniture was gilded and inlaid, and in scale with the tiny residence. the kitchen was still equipped exactly as it had been when installed in the nineteen-thirties.

'have you had any supper? will i start to cook? – or, if you like, there is a little italian restaurant on the corner …'

i had no intention of wasting the little time that we had together with her out slaving in the kitchen. i don't think she really had, either.

'actually, there's a place i have always wanted to go, on the river,' i ventured.

within the hour i was washed and changed. my bed was booked for the night. the flatmate was staying in to wash her hair, and to mind the house, and we were in a taxi on our way to the east end riverside pub – 'the prospect of whitby'.

there above the muddy thames we worked our way through three courses and came to the coffee. we got on famously. comfortable as her london life was, the good times, for her, had been in ireland. she laughed a lot over some old corballis house stories.

i asked her:

'would you live in ireland if you could?'

'it's an ambition.'

'will you marry me?'

she did not bat an eyelid.

'you are naughty. that's a bit sudden.'

175

'well?'

she laughed again. this time she laughed because only now she saw that i meant it. she paused.

'it's very sudden. i will think about it.'

(i thought – *strike while the iron is hot.*)

i said, very seriously –

'i have to go back to ireland. i am not going to ask you again.'

i turned to see if they would bring us more coffee. perhaps she thought i was getting up to go, right now. she laughed again.

'then, i will.'

we sat in silence for a moment, digesting this. more coffee came. i said:

'there might be some opposition.'

she knew exactly what i meant. she said:

'it's not up to them. they'll get used to it. no need to rush them. you'll have to meet my father, first.'

then she laughed again. she made a sort of french shrug as if to say the deal was done, we were having a good supper, and the rest of the world could wait. now i laughed with her too, as all the many implications began to sink in.

the tide was turning. the oily muddy thames eddied below us.

'you are naughty.' she said again.

the shop steward, 1971

getting engaged and getting married in london was going to take a number of trips over to england. octavia wrote to me the following week, a nice long letter, enclosing a cheque for five hundred pounds.

as luck would have it, along with this letter came another in the same post offering an interview for a job. this was a letter sent out by a newly built towel factory. the factory was sited in an isolated field beside a bridge, the bridge being over the river that formed the boundary between county monaghan and county louth. the grants for building factories were apparently higher in the more 'disadvantaged' county, hence the choice of this field.

i was determined not to fall into the trap of becoming a rich woman's dependent, like mrs collins's dog. i went for the interview, and was accepted. i was taken on with twenty or thirty others, all without industrial experience, to train while on the job. i was to work on a four-day shift system as a knotter and greaser, at nineteen pounds per week.

the factory was fourteen miles from laragh. to begin with i commuted seven miles of this on a bicycle, and the remaining seven by car, sharing a lift. if i missed the rendezvous, or the car driver was off sick, all fourteen miles had to be done by bicycle. the bicycle, second hand, cost twelve pounds.

this factory was noisy, very noisy. to talk to someone you either had to lip-read, or beckon them to come outside the door to the car park, or leave it until the next tea break. my job as a greaser was to climb over, under, and around each loom and service its many grease nipples. the knotting part of the job was to join the different coloured threads, when a batch of towels was complete, to the threads appropriate to the design pattern of the next batch of towels.

to begin with we were all very bad at this. the industrial mentality is different from the traditional farm mentality. the men and youths that i worked with had all in one sense or another, been comparatively poor, but they had been their own boss. now they had to learn that a worker in a weaving shed cannot down tools to go to a wake or to hunt down cattle wandering on the road. the lives in which they had juggled many competing demands had to give way to a life in which there was one priority – to keep the looms humming without pause, shift after shift.

the shift system meant long working days, four shifts of twelve hours each, and then half of the weeks were night shifts – but it also left some long three- and four-day breaks.

thus i was able to fly back to london, and meet octavia's father and aunt. her father had been the deputy undersecretary of state at the british ministry of defence. he had also been at the treasury, but was now semi-retired. i went to meet him with some trepidation, but i was expecting to meet some kind of military man, and he was not, he was a mild-mannered civil servant.

octavia's father had married again after his first wife's death, and had a new, young family. it soon became apparent that he was 'neutral' as to his daughter's marriage. her money after all was her own, for it came from her mother's side of her family, a fortune that had been made, strangely, in america. i say 'strangely' because while there are many families who can claim to have sailed to america 'on the mayflower', not many of these live in england, having decided later to come home again.

octavia's mother had died many years before, and for this reason, octavia had sometimes gone to official functions with her widowed father, in her mother's place. she had been, as a child, to number ten downing street, on the day of old queen mary's funeral. this was then an impressive link with the past – perhaps slightly less so now, when few people will even be able to recall exactly who 'old queen mary' was …

i even ventured to debate with octavia's father on the current troubles in northern ireland. he felt that changes in the law would be necessary, to counter sectarian prejudice in both parts of ireland. i reminded him of the act of succession, whereby the monarch, in the united kingdom, could not be a catholic. why not repeal that? it was a thought that *had never crossed his mind*, and it was to his credit that he could see the merit in it.

octavia's aunt eleanor was altogether more formidable. having no children of her own, she had taken it upon herself to see that octavia, her late sister's child, did all of the right things, and this had included 'the season'. the season was a circuit of mostly private dances for debutantes, loved by many, but hated by some, and octavia was one of the latter.

octavia's aunt eleanor's main concern about the wedding was that everything should be done 'properly'. she offered to pay for the entire affair, and by accepting this, we became unavoidably committed to doing quite a lot of things, her way.

first we had to go off to a well-known photographer to have 'the engagement photograph' taken. although the photographer was displaying a long list of former clients, including royalty – his studio was a tiny underground hole of a basement, lit with blinding arc lights.

the lighting was artificial, and so also, when they came back, were the photographs. we did not achieve the ultimate aim of this ritual, which was to have the bride-to-be's face on the front inside right hand page of the magazine 'country life', but for this prominent place there was no doubt very strong competition.

back in ireland i used some of octavia's five hundred pounds to buy calves. i could now see myself able to stock the land, instead of having to let it to the neighbours.

the factory was starting to go a little better. in the end the management brought over a middle-aged woman, doris, from a similar factory in lancashire, england. doris had worked for them there for forty years, and was so proficient, that she stood in front of her loom at ease, arms folded, for hour after hour, while our apprentice weavers sweated and fussed to get theirs going even for a few minutes at a stretch.

one day, with the agreement of the management, an official came down from the irish transport and general workers' union, in dublin, to organize union membership. we were allowed time off with pay to go to this meeting. the separate shifts of knotters, greasers, and weavers knew each other – if only from playing poker together in the canteen in the breaks – but there was also a shed full of girls who did label sewing and packing boxes, with whom we had little contact. in general, few of us were very well known to one another.

these days my morale was high. i had escaped from the sense of being trapped, and was ready to take on new challenges. when the union man started the meeting it quickly became obvious that there had already been some other private meeting. an inside group, however contacted, and for whatever reason, had already planned out the way things were meant to go ...

when dunne, the union official, asked the packing room girls how much they were paid (he probably knew, to the halfpenny, already) and they said it was twelve pounds a week, i said out loud:

'not enough.'

heads turned at this.

dunne now went on to outline the duties of union officials and to announce the names of the two people who he said would make the most suitable shop stewards.

this time i simply said:

'why would they?'

perhaps emboldened by my own rather insolent intervention, a lad at the back said:

'i never voted for them.'

it was true. we had been told who would make the best representatives. we had not been given the courtesy of being asked. we might be new to weaving machinery and jaquard looms up here, but we were not blind to old fashioned politics and underhand skullduggery ...

dunne looked surprised and slightly perplexed as a hum of dissent broke out. he perceptibly began to lose control of the meeting. he said:

'it's union practice. you have to have two representatives.'

this sounded very official and final. the room fell silent. i said:

'but if you didn't give us a chance to back them, in what way do they represent us?'

a girl who had not spoken turned around and said:

'why don't you stand, yourself?'

there was now no going back for either side. twenty hands went up for dunne's most-favoured nominee, and about thirty for me.

they were not actually voting for me – even in the weaving shed they barely knew me – they were voting to show a 'smart-arsed effer from dublin' that he needn't think they could be pushed around.

thus for the first time, and last time, in my life, i won an election. i was chosen with the support of the packing room girls to become a shop steward of the irish transport and general workers' union – headquarters: liberty hall, dublin.

to the directors of the company, as to dunne and the girls of the packing room, i was a completely unknown quantity.

i was not entirely stupid, and i would have been well able to handle the management at our meetings – if they had fought their battles fairly.

– but nothing could have been further from their mind.

happily ever after

how do stories end?

we are about to come to the part in the tale where i get married – you know, the part when the hero marries and lives happily ever after.

it would be a good place to end.

but the observant reader may already have slight reservations. there is no such conclusion as – 'where i get married.' the words are, or should be – 'where *we* get married.' the use of the phrase – 'where i get married' is a little straw in the wind, a subtle harbinger of future troubles. i had already lived too much of my brief life as a solo adventure, a tale with a lone protagonist. by this time for much my adult life i had had no one else to please but myself, and that is not entirely good.

first of all, i had to ask the parish priest permission to marry a girl who is not a catholic.

i called down to his bleak presbytery by arrangement.

we both knew the score. i needed his permission, for one thing, because i wished to be married in a london church that was neither my own parish nor octavia's parish nor even her denomination. he could refuse permission if he saw fit, but knew that i would almost certainly go ahead and marry her anyway, in a church of england or a civil ceremony. then his community would have lost not only me, but also most probably any children resulting from the marriage.

then when the times came around to collect the annual 'dues' — a contribution to the church from each family in the parish (the amount of each donation being read out in public from the altar) — father mcgurk would, at some time in the future, be a couple of contributions short …

in return for his permission, and a letter to the priest in the london parish, octavia was to agree to undergo a course of instruction in the catholic faith, and to allow her children, if any, to be brought up as catholics.

all of this she had already agreed to without hesitation.

my impression is that a girl with marriage in view will usually agree to anything, some girls even agree to attend rugby matches in the rain, if their particular prop forward is threatening to stray …

the parish priest conducted his business in a methodical and businesslike way. like many older people in the parish he addressed me as 'mr' whereas he addressed every other soul in his care by their christian name. this was a dubious distinction and i did not know what to make of it, but i had noticed that murdered protestant paramilitaries were usually also referred to, on the evening news, as 'mr'.

as i was turning to go, he said:

'i have to ask you one question.'

i waited.

'why couldn't you marry a nice catholic girl?'

i smiled apologetically –

'i suppose i did not meet one, father.'

getting married will alter my story in another way: marriage, the traditional end to a fairy story, becomes the first chapter of a different story – a story to which there are usually two versions. you should never tell just one side of a story, unless you intend to publish it as some kind of adversarial document. the full story of any marriage can never be known from the outside, and perhaps should not be told, at all, from the inside. would i like to pick up a book and find such a tale about myself? no, i would not. so i have to apply the same consideration to other people. the reader will just have to take it on trust, that autobiography is fundamentally a branch of fiction. there are always other ways – equally true – in which the same story could be written …

george moore's house

it was clear to us as we agreed to get married, that octavia was not a country person, any more than i was a city person. much as she liked the remoteness (as she saw it), of laragh, she needed a foothold in the city.

london was too far, and we came to the compromise decision that we would trade the bijou chelsea home of her grandmother for a town house in dublin, if a suitable one could be found.

octavia had lived in a street in chelsea, off the king's road, which was so central that she had no need or wish to buy a car. like her grandmother before her she used taxis, and could walk, if she so wished, to nearby restaurants. there was no exact equivalent area in dublin, but soon after our engagement had appeared in *the irish times* and the *london times*, a four-storey over basement georgian house came up for sale in upper ely place. this was near the shelbourne hotel, in a cul-de-sac near a corner of saint stephen's green.

it had once been the house of george moore, the novelist, and sported a little plaque to that effect beside the front door. the right house had indeed come up, but before we had time to get married, and before we were really ready. octavia had booked a last summer holiday for herself in the sun. this was 1971, remember. in a later generation we would have thought nothing of going away together. i rang her in london to lament that the ideal house had come on the market, but sooner than we had planned.

'well, buy it,' she said.

the plump and pleasant auctioneer from dawson street, mr mahony, walked around with me to see the house. to the eye of anyone interested mainly in restoration, it was a delight.

it was a total dump.

it had been the premises of the irish television RTÉ employees' late-night social club. it had been little more than an excuse for after-work drinking, for a group of people whose work often kept them busy until after public house closing times. there was a full-sized billiard table. the carpets were old, filthy, and beer-stained. the house smelt. there were bottles everywhere. but beneath the grime the cornices and marble mantlepieces of the original house were intact, as were all the chair rails, and the panelled double doors between the first-floor drawing room and dining room. The georgian detail was all intact.

mr mahony ignored the filth inside and concentrated on the clean and unaltered facade.

opposite the house on the other side of the road was a deserted and derelict orchard. as upper ely place was a cul-de-sac, there were no buses and no through traffic.

'in a few years,' mr mahony said confidingly, these houses will be sought after – like gold dust.'

but this time i was on my guard. i knew this was just estate agent's talk.

the purchase of upper ely place went smoothly. octavia came neither to the viewing, nor to the auction. in fact i do not even remember the auction. i remember the price – it was twenty-two thousand and five hundred pounds. it was about what we expected. i rang to tell her the good news straight after the auction. she would be back in ireland within a few weeks, well in time to pay the balance and complete the purchase.

i also paid a visit to liberty hall, the new skyscraper on the liffey which was the headquarters of the irish transport and general workers' union. i went up several floors in the lift to mr dunne's office but he was out on business. i asked for a copy of the union guidelines for shop stewards, but they were out of print or something, it was not quite clear what. a senior official looked at me strangely. perhaps it was me, or perhaps no one had ever asked for the rule book before? perhaps they thought my only possible reason for asking for a copy was to conduct some feud against mr dunne himself, or pursue some other devious agenda – or perhaps here in liberty hall, lord peregrine's tweed suit, which had served me so well this year, actually constituted a bit of a handicap.

as the year wore on, the wedding arrangements fell into place. aunt laura was all enthusiasm and support, and would be going. uncle jeremy would be unavoidably absent, elsewhere. i had half suspected that this would be the case. to aunt laura who was louisiana american, i was tall, dark, educated and presentable – not unlike uncle jeremy himself, in his youthful days. to uncle jeremy's own subtle old etonian radar, i probably failed to respond appropriately to certain codes and call signs, and was logged as 'incoming, hostile.' no one is as sensitive to chinks in the social armour as those who might have hidden vulnerabilities themselves.

neither octavia nor her aunt eleanor had a house large enough for a wedding, or a garden large enough for a marquee, so in the end everything was hired or bought. the premises, the caterers, the car, the church, even the present list, were all laid on like stuff obtained by mail order. all we had to do was to turn up on the day, washed and dressed, at these places that we had never been in before (except briefly to check them out). everything else was paid for. it was something of a package deal.

i had a grey morning suit made, and lined up my friend cobby to be best man. we gathered up a contingent of irish-based friends to make a respectable showing on the groom's side of the church, and planned to stay for a party afterwards, on the evening of the wedding.

in the end octavia's friends seemed entirely uncritical of her choice. if anything they were intrigued that she had managed, at twenty-nine, to produce a man without warning, like a rabbit from a hat, and were satisfied that she was going to give them a good party.

cobby and i travelled to england on the liverpool boat. this was a more sedate and ceremonial way to go over than by flying, and you do not have to rush your drinks. we booked ourselves into the ritz hotel, and got small rooms with brass beds high up on a back corridor.

the wedding certificate, when it was eventually filled in, read –

'name – gillies macbain, age – 28, profession – farmer, address – ritz hotel, piccadilly.'

collins the art dealer also came, and antoinette and her latest boyfriend. when you mix the english and the irish, the english become slightly more english, while the irish become determinedly more irish. even if the travelling party would really have preferred to retire to their beds at eleven o'clock, this would have been letting the side down, so those who had travelled over felt obliged to conform to stereotype, stay out on the town, and get riotously drunk.

to any young man marriage is a step in the dark. some who are fortunate enough to come from a stable background, simply set out to recreate the marriage of their parents before them, but others have to make it up as they go along. going into battle is the only comparable challenge. you can practise all you like, but the untried youth has always the nagging doubt – how will he perform as a family man when he actually gets there? the period of the engagement was at some level a period of considerable stress.

the evening before the wedding nearly ended in disaster. i remember little about it, but it seems that at the end of the night out i had decided to walk down the street back home to the hotel in a straight line – straight including up the bonnet of any parked car that came in the way and over the roof and down the boot on the other side …

this resulted in three passers-by, possibly car owners, remonstrating with us. i was in high good humour and only looking for fun, not trouble, and was taken completely by surprise when collins punched all three of them – not hard, but so quickly that not one of the three had time to retaliate before he danced away, fists in the air. cobby saw trouble coming and hustled me away down the street towards the hotel, while collins bobbed around on the footpath, challenging any pursuit. then he, and the three surprised car owners, by tacit mutual consent, slowly backed away from each other.

in the morning there was only one thought in my head – gratitude that the wedding was not scheduled until the late afternoon. i sat on the side of my brass bed in the attics of the ritz, head in hands, while cobby ordered me dry toast and glasses of water from room service. my head was spinning and my eyes suffered a strange kind of hangover dizziness that i call 'horizon flutter'.

in the end we pulled ourselves together. there was a full-length oval mirror in the bedroom. at a distance of three or four yards i did not look bad, the deathly pale complexion actually went rather romantically with the lean grey morning suit, the dark brown hair, and the cream lace cravat.

the weather was good. we retired outdoors to the park where cobby sat under a tree while i walked up and down the grass, with a few crumpled sheets of paper, to rehearse a speech that had been long in the preparation …

at four o'clock we presented ourselves at the church. aunt laura entered immediately ahead of us and the usher in the entrance door said to her –

'bride or groom's side?'

aunt laura, who had come alone from northern ireland, turned and saw us behind her and smiled and said –

'groom's.'

that was big of her. she knew the guest list would be heavily weighted to the bride's side of the aisle. i needed all the support i could get.

octavia arrived on her father's arm. the ceremony itself passed in a daze. i think we did everything correctly as rehearsed. cobby did not lose the ring. my mind was very largely on the volatile mixture of people who had come to see us married. i do not remember hearing a word of the hymns, or the choir singing my own choice – 'saint patrick's breastplate'. octavia was a blur of white lace, and on the way back down the aisle all eyes were on her. this was the one moment that i had not rehearsed in my mind.

with some experience of reading the lesson in school chapel, i tried to look straight ahead down the aisle, while octavia did the more traditional thing and, looking to right and left, smiled as her eyes met those of each guest she recognized.

at the back of the church as we passed out between them, there sat, on one side of the aisle, bridie, wife of 'the bookie' duffy of laragh, county monaghan, in her best frock – and on the other, lady widgery, wife of the lord chief justice of england, in hers.

that was it. done it.

on the steps of the church a bossy photographer tried to control the show, but too late. we quickly broke free, and got into the car. the only thing that i regretted afterwards about getting married was the rolls royce. we only had to travel a few hundred yards. we should have walked down the centre of the road. there is nothing more tacky than a rolls royce at a saturday wedding, for a couple who do not own one and never normally set foot in one. black ones are just as tacky as white ones. even a taxi would have done the job better, but best of all i really would have liked to walk.

champagne and excitement soon restored us all from our fragile state to the high we had so recently descended from. i have a tendency to speak slowly, and to look away from the person that i am speaking to. this social disadvantage is removed when i get up to speak to a crowd. here both the slow delivery and the tendency to avoid looking at anyone in particular both become advantages. i can speak more naturally to two hundred people, than to two. so the speech went well, as did cobby's speech, the cutting of the cake, and the 'going away' – but we only went around the corner to the hotel to get changed, to return again later to the restaurant where the party was to continue.

cobby was not only our best man, but also our companion for the following day's sea-crossing home. i had a theory that disastrous marriages often began with pretentious honeymoons. with this in mind we had arranged the simplest honeymoon possible, by inviting ourselves to stay the night at cobby's house in ireland, before tackling the last thirty miles home. there, in his now beautifully restored house, we crashed out late on the following afternoon amidst the damp green fields, dripping beeches and brambled hedgerows of county meath.

the farmer's wife

octavia was now the wife of a farmer and shop steward. this did not mean a lot to her except the necessity to endure the vagaries of the factory shift system. she did not have to endure this for long ...

the first thing that we did was to order a car. we decided upon a land rover, and to avoid being mistaken for strayed military and becoming accidental victims of some sniper or roadside bomb, we decided upon a powder blue colour. the land rover, with all of its extras minutely specified, was to take six weeks from order to delivery – about the same time that it took to order a book in the dublin bookshops of the time.

meanwhile, five hundred pounds secured a second hand morris estate, and in this i drove to work.

there were several layers of a hierarchy in the factory – between the top management and the workers came a middle layer of shop floor managers and clerical staff. the weaving shed foreman was a lancashire man, lancashire being the original heartland of the textile industry. he frequently came into conflict with the local apprentice weavers, and the many differences between the cultures of industrial lancashire and rural monaghan did not help. i took no particular part in this feuding, but as shop steward it sometimes fell to me to appeal some of the decisions taken by the foreman.

at the monthly meeting between the union and the management the question of safety rails around the top of the looms came up. the management explained how the railings would be an inconvenience to the loom's efficiency of operation, but assured us that they would 'look into' the question of safety and the provision of safety rails.

we were being fobbed off. an unobstructed loom worked faster, though slightly less safely, and more production meant simply, more money. i remembered something that i had read when working in a solicitor's office in england years before. i said to the meeting, quietly, that we accepted the management's reasoning over the safety rails – but could we have it entered clearly in the minutes of the meeting that we had asked for them?

there was a silence. the managing director noticed me, as if for the very first time.

there was no way out for him. i think that he knew what i knew – that in the event of an accident that came to court the request in the minutes would torpedo almost all lines of defence open to the factory management. you might as well write 'guilty' in inch high red ink across the cover of the minute book ... thus it was that more notice came to be taken of my suggestions at meetings, but if this inclined me to any self-congratulation, it would have been premature …

a feud between a ringleader of the weavers and the shop foreman then came to a head. on the surface, at least, it was about timekeeping, but it had become a tedious and personal dispute, or series of disputes, and the meeting to resolve it was likely to be a long and wearisome one. this time i plunged in as soon as the topic was brought up. avoiding the eyes of both the weaver, who was allowed to be present at the discussion of his case, and the foreman – i addressed myself directly to the managing director. i said that i proposed three things: one – that the penalty points against the weaver for deliberately poor timekeeping would be cancelled and that he be allowed to keep his job. two – that in return the weaver would agree to abide by the foreman's shift system without any further challenge. three – that the matter would be closed to all further discussion and all parties would agree not to raise it from this point on. i had shown the managing director the way out, and he took it gratefully.

'done,' he said, and went straight on to the next item on the agenda.

too late, the foreman attempted to launch into his carefully prepared case. the managing director merely raised a restraining hand, and went on with the agenda.

game, set, and match.

this was neat, but too neat. i had only sought to resolve a festering dispute. as the foreman himself saw it, he had failed to show everyone who was top dog in the weaving shed, and i had cheated him of his anticipated victory.

over the following weeks he took his revenge.

first he promised me promotion, to be the minder of a new towel folding machine of awesome technical sophistication. having got my acceptance, he then told me that until the machine was delivered from abroad, which could take some time, the towels would have to be folded by hand. he knew how to neutralize a smart-arse. i was young and lively. hard work would not have finished me off, and i was clearly well-able to counter his manoeuverings at factory meetings and on the shop floor, so his chosen weapon was the infliction of boredom.

for three weeks i laboured at the folding of towels, for twelve hours a day, for three-day and four-day weeks, through the short winter days and through the long winter nights, according to the twenty-four hour shift system of continuous production. at the end of the third week of endlessly folding towels by hand over twelve-hour shifts i gave in my notice and my career in industry was over.

CHAPTER SIX 1972–3

family life

octavia was not a bit put out by my leaving the factory.

those who have worked a shift system will tell you that working at night is no great hardship once you are in the rhythm. the shift system delivers better wages and long three-day 'weekends'. but the changeover is the killer. there is this fortnightly jet lag when you change shift, when you are out of step with normal daily routine, whether waking or sleeping, and nobody likes that.

the months that followed our marriage were full enough, and there was no shortage of things to do. there was a house in london to sell, a house in dublin to restore, and furniture and belongings to pack up and bring over. i realized that the london house was not just a property to octavia, but very much her grandmother's house and a big piece of her childhood. we kept all of her grandmother's possessions, even though the much taller and more spacious house in dublin demanded larger items of furniture.

i spent a lot of time with the builder, with painters, and in auction rooms. once the house in dublin was ours, i installed a camp bed and kept one room to stay overnight in, amidst the paint pots, dust sheets, and stacked-up possessions. i had been concerned that i would not be able to sleep in the centre of the city. there was indeed that distant hum which is the constant background noise in all large cities, but the most noticeable noise on my first night was the wind in the laburnum tree at the back of the house next door.

laragh was only an hour and a half from dublin, a distance that people even consider commuting these days, but in spite of the coming of the motor car, the people's lives at laragh remained for the present locally rooted. it was still a different world. this other world began, for me, when you crossed the bridge over the boyne, below the hill of slane, halfway home.

in the months of our long engagement, i had met octavia's father and aunt, her godmother, and some of her london friends, but also her stockbroker. one day she had said to me 'you had better look at my portfolio,' and thrown a bound file into my lap. this was a list of holdings of shares, and i have to admit, many times more valuable than i had expected.

to become more familiar with this, i had gone, alone, to have lunch in london with her stockbroker. i went expecting to talk about investment, and investment strategies, but this he obviously considered to be his department. he gave me a short tour of his firm's offices, and a long lunch in a cavernous main line station hotel, which he paid for. it seemed that he would give advice, and follow instructions, but not discuss the theory of investment with a layman.

octavia for her part concluded all financial discussions with 'go ahead,' or 'do whatever you want.'

oddly enough, my main concern these days was to set us up for a comfortable family life in ireland, without alienating the friends who had known me in very different times when money was short.

over the hill from laragh a farm came up for sale that consisted of thirty acres of steep south-facing land, with an unoccupied house. this was called 'duffy's' but the original owners were not immediate relations of the bookie's. the likely selling price at auction was four thousand pounds. this seemed to me to be a form of wealth much more tangible than a mere line in a yearly valuation that said –

'1000 shares commercial union insurance @ £4.00 / share.'

i began to harbour ambitions not so much of being a farmer, as, let us admit it, a landowner.

duffy's was to be sold in carrickmacross, by public auction.

this time i knew the form at a monaghan auction. this time i was in no hurry to open the bidding. this time i joined in, bidding unobtrusively until the bidding slowed, and did not panic when the owner and the auctioneer retired for their 'consultations'. all of this was a ritual consummation. all parties knew the form, and this time the show of reluctance on the part of the vendor was matched by my own show of reluctance to bid further – until the auctioneer, unable to bleed the turnip much further, offered to take bids of fifty pounds, and then of twenty-five pounds.

slowly we ground to the climax. auctions are a form of copulation. only the untutored beginner rushes to get it all over with as quickly as possible, and a good irish auctioneer patiently guides his crowd, like a new bride, to heights that she has not experienced before or ever expected to achieve.

'gone.'

mr nugent tapped his book with his stub of a pencil.

the thirty steep acres of duffy's, well-fenced and watered, all in pasture, vacant possession, and free of all encumbrances, were ours.

this time too, i knew not to rush away from the scene of the victory. the auction was held in an upper room of the hotel at the bottom of the main street in carrickmacross, and the hotel basement was also a bar. the under bidders seemed genuine, and were generous in defeat when i returned from the auctioneers' office to complete the ritual in the accepted fashion by buying everyone a drink.

at the same time a creeping doubt entered my soul. i suspected that his was the last farm that i would be allowed to buy. financially, we now had the price of a dozen such holdings, but locally, to go out and 'win' every auction was not acceptable and bound to lead to trouble. this was not going to be an easy way to build a sizeable farm.

'woe unto them that join house to house, that lay field to field, till there be no place, that they may be placed alone in the midst of the earth.'

annus mirabilis

at the beginning of 1972 i was once more unemployed, but busier than ever before. the house in dublin was not finished, but it was taking shape. the restoration had begun with the roof and worked downwards from there. it had got as far as the second-floor bedrooms and we could now spend the night in the house, amongst the plumbers' tools and painters' stepladders.

we were resident in dublin when we heard the news of bloody sunday, the shooting dead of thirteen unarmed marchers in derry. my first reaction was anger at the stupidity of it. i could see at once that there would be a high political price to pay for this outrage. for several years the troubles in the north had been growing, like a distant thunderstorm that was getting ever closer. now it was upon us. there were demonstrations in dublin, and a large white sheet bearing the number '13' in black hung across the facade of trinity college.

i was actually listening to the ten o'clock news in bed, having retired early, when the BBC reporter excitedly announced –

'i can now report that the british embassy has been burned to the ground!'

i sat up with a jolt. this was serious, and surely history in the making. i hastily pulled on my clothes, and leaving octavia in bed, went out into the street.

the british embassy was in the georgian terrace on the far side of merrion square, just around the corner. i rounded the end of the square to see a huge crowd, with the firemen and fire engine standing by in a side street. far from being burned to the ground, the embassy was stolidly resisting being set alight. brilliant petrol bombs arced through the air, but the building seemed to be mostly protected by steel shutters, and only the smallest of flames glittered from within.

to avoid being trapped by the guards, who were present in large numbers, the protestors had laid low the railings at that end of the square. that left them the freedom of the park in the middle to escape into and to regroup, if scattered by a charge. people were still watching from the safety of the windows of the houses on either side of the embassy, but not, i felt, for much longer.

i stood in the middle of the south side of the square, drinking in the almost festive feeling of the occasion. above the heads of this less-involved section of the crowd, i could see a solid line of gardaí, stretching from side to side of the road. here the railings were intact, and the crowd more constricted. i wondered where the BBC reporter could possibly be? in the bushes? in a telephone box in ballsbridge? cowering in his bedroom up in the shelbourne hotel?

then the guards began to move forward. first they came at a walk, in a long line, then they came with truncheons drawn, at a steady jog. the crowd at the front began to retreat. suddenly a neutral and uninvolved stance was no longer possible. there was no time to stop a friendly guard and explain that you only came down the square to see history being made. when the guards broke into a trot, we, the crowd, broke into a run – and running away from the police can be taken as an admission of guilt. suddenly i was indistinguishable from the rest of a crowd bent on political arson. if you were there, you were guilty, and if you were guilty it was now time to get out of the way.

in the middle of merrion square south the guards stopped, a great line of caps and heavy overcoats and truncheons, their panting breath visible in the night air. behind them the street was empty. ahead of them the crowd slowed, and turned. the guards would hold this street if they could, but there were other more desperate characters at loose in the lawns and shrubberies of the central garden, and above the heads of them all, the fire visible in the embassy windows was brightening. the firemen in the side street were still held at bay – their job was to fight fires, not crowds.

with a group of young people, who also seemed to share no great ambition to become involved in physical confrontation with the dublin gardaí, i walked quickly round into merrion street. behind us the blaze was getting a good hold, there would be no saving the elegant embassy building, now. in merrion row doheny and nesbitt's bar was still open. we all fell through the doors into the safety of the pub, unknown to each other, but bonded together by the sharing of common danger and excitement.

behind the bar stood the usual barman in his white apron, arms folded. for the moment he made no offer to serve anyone.

'well,' he said, 'are ye satisfied now, with your night's work?'

every morning in dublin with my coffee in the shelbourne, i read the papers, *the irish times* in particular. for ninety-nine per cent of the time that was where the 'troubles' remained – in the papers, on the television (we did not have one), or obtruding into the odd conversation. only on rare occasions is the average citizen caught up in the action, and for the rest of the time life went on as usual.

at laragh there was the new farm to stock with bullocks, and on the weeks that i was away the bookie had to be the herdsman. although the farm was only over the hill from laragh, the way to it by road, with cattle, was not far short of two miles. i began with a rather thin lot of cattle, friesians mostly, which do not do well under harsh conditions. i had bought the ones in the sale that seemed cheaper, and over the next few months began to appreciate why these particular ones had been cheap. the bookie took no money for his herding, the opportunity for a foothold on the far side of the hill, and an extension of his role in the doings of laragh to another townland and another parish, was reward enough.

some of the cattle – there were only a dozen – were young and had not been castrated.

the bookie's uncle peadar was known as 'the vet'. he castrated the cattle the old way, with a knife, and wooden pegs to clamp the veins until the danger of bleeding was past. i am not very good with blood and operations, and anything to do with testicles can send a sympathetic shiver through the most hardened of male spectators. i opted for a role at the other end of each animal, with the tethers and the nose ring. we had nothing as modern as a cattle crush to hold the animals, neither up there nor down at laragh. as for the amputated testicles, the bookie's sheepdog layed claim to those one by one as each hit the ground in the rocky farmyard.

i liked even less than this business the castrating of young pigs, as the screaming of a pig cuts through you, much more so than the bellowing of cattle.

one day when i was home we were moving cattle back to laragh where there was more shelter. one tall thin bullock decided to jump out of the lane and landed into a flax dam, a steep-sided pit filled with water, about five feet deep.

one of the characteristics of laragh was how many people could appear out of nowhere when something was afoot. i swear that some neighbours arrived upon the scene already equipped with ropes. with so much help, pulling out the beast was not too difficult. getting the ropes under the belly of the bullock, which was underwater, was the hard part of it.

i had no hay or silage for these cattle for the winter, and i was already beginning to suspect that summer grazing thin friesians was not going to leave any profit in the autumn. at the same time it made a lot of work for me, not to mention my obliging neighbours. the land that i now had was too much to farm part-time and alone, and yet too little to justify employing help, even if i had wanted to.

i had hard decisions to take. what i was actually lacking was a farming background. many people do not need to take conscious decisions – for them, what to do next arises naturally from their upbringing. they are surrounded by family and similar neighbours facing similar problems, and coming to similar conclusions.

as the restoration of the house progressed and it became more comfortable, octavia began to spend more time in dublin. i began to see that i could not live a double life as a monaghan small farmer, and among the idle rich in the city, and yet – if we sold the land at laragh –

then as soon as the dublin restoration was completely finished, i would be idle indeed.

octavia was a good cook, and interested in food, but for breakfast, from sheer laziness, rather than make my own coffee, i tended to drift over to the shelbourne hotel and have coffee and toast over there. we had no telephone in dublin. to get one then took up to four years from initial application to final installation. in the meantime the receptionist in the hotel connected my calls.

i was interested in the auction rooms, and apart from our own needs we had a top flat and a basement flat to furnish, which we intended to rent out. we also had surplus possessions to sell. for a time i lived a hands-in-pockets life, between stephen's green and the antique shops along the quays, drinking coffee and thumbing sales catalogues.

an old boyfriend of octavia's, a barrister, was a member of the kildare street club, then in a premises on stephen's green. as a favour to her he arranged for me to be proposed as a member, and obtained the agreement of a seconder. this club was a 'gentleman's club' founded in imitation of the london clubs. i suppose there were also similar institutions in the larger british provincial cities and in the colonies. i was seconded by viscount dillon, father of our bridesmaid, even though i had only met him once.

i ate just one lunch in the kildare street club. there was nothing wrong with the lunch, which was in the 'roast meat and two vegetables' style still current even in the best hotels, but the clubby and exclusive atmosphere — which was what the members paid for — was, to me, utterly claustrophobic. the club members no doubt included many influential people and interesting characters, but my years drinking with sketchley had taught me that down around the corner in the pubs of grafton street — neary's, mcdaid's, davy byrne's, the bailey — were to be found a much wider range of equally interesting characters. routine held few attractions for me, and in the bars you could have your sandwich and pint in a different place every day, wherever your fancy took you.

i realize now that what i liked about the bars was that you could walk away from a character as soon as he became tedious. in the kildare street club you would have to endure him through the full three courses and coffee, and in any case i did not like heavy lunches, and had no professional career for which contacts at the club would have been useful.

for a few months i juggled my time between the drumlin fields of monaghan and the dublin sale rooms. you could still park in some places, for free, around stephen's green, and i might find a space for the muddy blue land rover in ely place, late in the evening, and then leave it there – sometimes even with horsebox attached – for a couple of days. this was not popular with the accountants and solicitors. the parking wardens did not bother me, except once. a warden, refusing to believe that the box was for furniture removal, hassled me for a tip for leopardstown –

'c'mon, you must know something,' he insisted.

after this i even began to park on the double yellow lines. if you let down the ramp at the back and threw a little straw out on to the road, the wardens would never say anything to you.

dara o'lochlainn hailed me once from far down the street.

'i knew it was you,' he said as he caught up, 'no one else wears a pinstripe suit with wellington boots.'

the game was nearly up for me as an aspiring farmer. i put it to octavia that we would never be allowed to carve out a respectable-sized farm of the small farm country around laragh. the only practical way forward was to look for a larger block of better land nearer to dublin.

she let me go back to mr mahony the auctioneer, and before i could tire of spending my days in the auction rooms and second hand furniture shops, i had a new pastime – riding around the counties of south dublin, kildare and wicklow in mr mahony's mercedes, looking at farms.

almost straight away we found an ideal property. merrionstown house in west wicklow had two hundred and seventy-five acres, a small but plain late georgian house, and was thirty miles from the centre of dublin. it had german owners, resident in germany, who therefore employed an irish farm manager – who was willing to stay on. it was a dairy farm, with sixty cows, and the owners were prepared to sell the dairy herd, with all tractors and implements, at a valuation, lock, stock, and barrel.

going home in the car mr mahony said –

'it's a good farm.'

this time i was inclined to believe him. in the morning i went in to the deputy manager of the bank of ireland in the old parliament house in college green. he was doubtful.

'three hundred and fifty pounds per acre? it's a lot of money for land. there's no money in farming, you know. i don't think they are going to give a loan for that.'

'we don't need a loan,' i said.

it had not occurred to me that most other people would not be able to pay as we were going to pay, simply by writing our own cheque. in the end the only thing we bought with a loan was the milking herd, with the intention of paying it off through the monthly milk cheque. perhaps we were advised that this made sense tax-wise, as farmers were now, finally, to be included in the tax net.

looking back i wonder at my own confidence, and at octavia's trusting nature. the new farm was of course in her name, and apart from being liable for the bank loan to buy the cows for one hundred and forty pounds each, there was no contribution towards the purchase from me.

there was no big day of removal, as the furniture that had to come down from laragh was brought down bit by bit, by land rover and horsebox.

i fell into the habit of arriving in the dublin cul-de-sac in late evening. thus the solicitors and accountants who occupied the neighbouring offices arrived in the morning to find me already parked and turned around, ready to face my journey down to wicklow later in the day. i drove out of the city in the mornings and into the city in the evenings, always against the direction of the rush hour traffic.

i was inventing a life. octavia's relations followed our progress from afar. none of them came to visit us.

we now had a georgian house and farm in the country, and a georgian townhouse in the capital city. each property was also set up so that, in theory at least, it could produce an income. that was how people of leisure used to arrange their lives – wasn't it?

the question now was what to do with laragh. octavia regarded it with affection, as the scene of a courtship which had followed, rather than preceded, a proposal of marriage. on the other hand she had no wish to be involved in its practical upkeep. my own good fortune in marrying her had come upon me rather suddenly, and i was not yet prepared to sell it. laragh at least was my own, and it represented to me a solid sense of security that i could never get from a bank deposit or share certificates.

the first move was to sell the thirty acres of 'duffy's' farm over the hill. within a mere twelve months of the last occasion we were back in the dusty auction rooms in carrickmacross. this time the crowd was larger, and the market stronger. the same rise in land values that had hustled us into an early purchase down in wicklow, now meant that the bidding did not pause until it had gone somewhat higher than the four thousand pounds that we had paid for the farm the year before. now it was my turn to pull a long face and withdraw with the auctioneer to the back room. i did so. we returned to announce the traditional formula, that we could not possibly let such a fine farm of land go at such a knock-down price.

the bidding resumed.

at the full five thousand pounds the bidding finally faltered and died. the hammer came down. the farm was sold, and all retired to the bar.

five thousand pounds, less all the fees and other expenses, represented perhaps five hundred pounds profit on the price that i had paid. not a lot. nevertheless my reputation was salvaged from the abyss into which it had fallen when i had sold the thin bullocks for slightly less than i had paid for them. peadar duffy 'the vet' raised the bottle of stout in his crooked hand and summed it up for all present –

'yer the only man that can deal in land!'

when the dublin house was more or less finished, sir dermot and miss talbot came over one lunchtime to have a look at it. i suspected that aunt laura had been boasting about it, and awakened their curiosity. miss talbot did not stay long, but the upstairs double drawing room, typical of the houses in the dublin squares, looked well, and she seemed to approve. octavia's granny's furniture, delicate and inlaid with marquetry, would have been to her taste.

sir dermot lingered longer, and we asked him to stay to lunch, but he generously offered to take us over the road to the shelbourne hotel, instead.

opposite our front door the derelict orchard had gone. it was now a building site and was going to become the royal hibernian art gallery. the day of sites lying derelict and unwanted in the heart of central dublin was rapidly passing. we walked to the hotel. we walked everywhere. if you wanted to get around the city centre an umbrella was more use to you than a car.

the farm at merrionstown was thirty miles from the city centre. at this time the dublin commuter belt which later extended to fifty miles or more, faded away at about twenty-five miles. somewhere as you passed the poulaphouca dam, and went over the bridge where it discharged the infant river liffey, you left the city buses behind and were in the country proper.

the farmhouse at merrionstown had been well-maintained, and while it required things doing to it to adapt it to our needs, these could wait. the farm itself employed the farm manager, and two other men, and for the time being it continued to be run on the same lines as before, with the same friesian herd of cows, hereford bull, 'followers', and one wicklow goat. michael the farm manager coped well, as it is not always easy working for someone who knows far less than you do. he was young, which helped, about five years younger than me.

before the spring was over, octavia became pregnant, and this followed almost immediately upon her decision to put aside contraception. while making no claim to be the most virile of men, i am surely one of the more fertile. in later years i became convinced that to make a girl pregnant i had to do little more than wink at her.

octavia's condition made it more important to finish off the restoration of the dublin house. we wanted to be near the hospitals and doctors when the time came. her gynaecologist was dr karl mullen, a former hooker on the irish rugby team, which gave rise to coarse jokes about the midwife and nurses lining out behind him like the three-quarters at lansdowne road.

as the pregnancy progressed and as octavia became more plump, she tended more and more to stay put, while i motored like a mad thing between monaghan, dublin, and wicklow. a person shares some kind of a centre of gravity with their possessions, and a point comes when the possessions no longer belong to you, so much as your life revolves around them.

the hippies

the friends that i have described, of my bachelor years, were occasionally eccentric, and some, like sketchley, could be called bohemian. octavia's friends tended to date from her days at trinity college, or to be connected to corballis house or to the irish georgian society. i forget who it was who introduced us to the hippies.

like christianity, the hippie cult came to ireland from outside, and the first hippies that i knew were a mixture of nationalities, with only the occasional irish hanger-on.

someone, learning in a casual conversation that we had a vacant farmhouse in monaghan, said that they had friends who would like to 'borrow' a farm. these friends turned out to be the communal proprietors of a vegetarian restaurant down behind the north dublin quays.

this restaurant was a wild success among a certain clientele, but its very success had brought it to the notice of the health authorities. it was in a loft, largely furnished with large cushions and with an aroma of slightly-scented tobacco that still meant little to me, even after my encounters with the film people in glaslough. the commune members tended to keep their children on the premises, and it could be that nappies were changed on the same draining boards upon which vegetables were chopped.

i remembered the starchily permed health inspector who used to demand to see behind the fridges in my own days working in a restaurant. i knew what someone like her would make of it. the hippies were on a loser.

the idea of borrowing a farm was to get some of the women and children out of the way, on a rota, and also to begin to cultivate vegetables of their own with which to supply the restaurant.

the cult of the hippies was attractive. the core belief was that an earthly paradise was possible. the model was a peaceful society that lived humbly, and was made self-sufficient by the growing of vegetables in a way that offered no violence to either man or nature. i was at the same time both attracted to these ideas, and suspicious of the hippies' ability to put them into effect. some of the ideas were self-indulgent. how could we all live with recycled furniture and second hand vans, if no one ever made or bought new stuff?

octavia was less intrigued, but tolerant of anything that did not involve her in personal inconvenience. lending the farm at laragh would actually be less of a permanent commitment than renting it to some tenant, who might then turn out to be reluctant to leave.

i began to discuss with the hippies the terms on which a farm could be 'borrowed'.

bob, the chief of the hippie tribe, had two wives. i never asked, but took it for granted that he was not married to either. we talked a lot about growing vegetables, and the future of the world, but in the end the conditions of the loan boiled down to two basic demands: firstly, there were to be no more than seven people resident at laragh at any one time, however many there were in rotation, and secondly, they were to live quietly and not to alarm the neighbours.

the house was not locked. i would not have to go down and let them in. nor did the house contain any stealable valuables, as the moving of furniture and belongings down to merrionstown was more or less complete. so i agreed to let them set up house themselves. i would go down on the next free weekend and see how they were settling in.

starting a family

early in 1973 our daughter was born.

it happened that miss talbot had asked us out to her new house in dun laoghaire, for dinner. this was a great honour, engineered, i again suspected, by aunt laura. the invitation was accepted with the proviso that as the birth was getting very close, octavia might have to excuse herself from the party at short notice.

as it turned out, the birth, which was easy and straightforward, was early that same morning. the baby was on time and healthy, and would have dark hair like her mother.

i am not one of those fathers who insist upon being present at the birth. if it is going well, they don't need me. if it is going badly, or there is a prospect of a caesarean, i do not want to watch, much less listen from the corridor. in any case, i had recently begun to take my turn at calving cows, and clean and efficient as mount carmel nursing home was – the similarities with the dramas of the calving pen were too close for my peace of mind.

thus it was that once i had admired our new daughter and made a few telephone calls with the news, i presented myself alone at miss talbot's new south dublin residence that evening. why she needed a separate house less than twenty miles from malahide castle was not clear, and i was too in awe of her to ask.

my fellow guests were several young men of the georgian society circle. although miss talbot's late georgian terraced house was modest, compared with the splendours of malahide, some invisible but well-trained domestic was obviously in charge. the highly polished dinner table shone and glittered with gleaming glass and silver. i could not fault it. by candlelight the setting could have been mistaken for a dining room in any of the great houses of ireland.

i went to the supper party on a high, understandably. my new daughter had been born on my thirtieth birthday. i who should have been slightly subdued in the home of my former employer, was almost giddy – full of myself and thrilled by the successful outcome of the day.

the 'georgians' exchanged pleasantries, and gossip about the anglo-irish society to which they belonged, or in which they were aspiring hangers-on. they competed with each other outrageously to amuse their hostess, who took it as her due.

at the coffee stage one of the visitors held up miss talbot's very fine georgian silver sugar bowl.

'this is splendid. the exact twin of teddy winchester's sugar bowl.'

it is a peculiarity of certain aesthetes to know more about people's houses and possessions than the owners themselves know. teddy winchester was an eccentric bachelor landowner in the midlands.

miss talbot shot back –

'then you will have to get him to marry me.'

this convulsed them, but i said solemnly:

'but you would never ever know, would you, whether he had married you for yourself, or for your sugar bowl.'

a slight silence fell.

do i tell jokes with such a straight face that people take me seriously? perhaps i was overstepping some invisible line.

the kind of rejoinder sir dermot would have made? – fine coming from sir dermot, but less than hilarious coming from me.

the laragh commune

when i next drove up the avenue at laragh to visit the hippies i found a van parked in front of the house, and behind it a trailer on which was a sailing boat, and behind that another van. the day was still, bright and warm for so early in the year.

a large dog came out of the house and barked at me. this was a bad start. i did not allow dogs in the house, but had obviously omitted to mention that. dogs are naturally territorial, and i instinctively distrust mild and polite people who own aggressive dogs. when a person says 'hi' and a dog says 'piss off' i tend to believe the dog.

on the floor in the empty dining room sat a long-haired man strumming chords on a guitar. he acknowledged me, but continued his playing, and in the hall i passed two or three more whom i did not recognize. there seemed to be far more than seven people in the house, but bob and his wives were not among them.

i went down the passage into the old kitchen. here there were stacks of unwashed plates, and a cat up on the kitchen table, licking something. i don't like cats in the house either, but the sun was shining and all of the doors were open. like the dog, the cat was apparently free to go where it wanted.

out in the yard i met a young man sitting cross-legged upon the gravel, apparently meditating. then i recognized the sweater that he was wearing. it was mine.

he opened his eyes.

'hi.'

'look,' i said, 'i don't know who you are, and i don't care what you're doing, but i do know that is my sweater you are wearing.'

he looked at me, and without a word he crossed his hands and peeled the sweater over his head and held it out to me, expressionlessly.

'no hassle, man,' he said softly, 'if you are into the property trip.'

he sat there bare chested, eyes closed again, in front of me on the ground. i stood holding the sweater and feeling particularly foolish.

bob and the wives and friends had immediately and without hesitation broken all the conditions of our agreement. there turned out to be nineteen people in residence, of five different nationalities, as well as children and animals. all of my remaining possessions were immediately considered communal, but this was probably inevitable, as bob's own possessions were communal, and newcomers had no way of knowing, even if they cared, what belonged to him and what did not.

bob had very little money, but an endless talent for trading, borrowing, sharing, scavenging, and improvising. his was a philosophy of abundance. the world was full to overflowing with good things, which some misguided people hoarded to the detriment and impoverishment of others, and with precious little gain to themselves. bob and his family were prepared to share out their good things, and mine ...

i gathered up and took back to dublin some of the remaining possessions that i valued.

bob was home the next time i called up. he had acquired, for free, an enormous clydesdale horse. the CIE in dublin still used horses for delivery, though these were being phased out. to turn a horse and flat cart off a wide street, into a narrower street, and without hitting the parked cars on either side, was a considerable skill, but the horse-drawn vehicles were becoming an obstruction to the growing motor traffic. nowadays, of course, with the even greater congestion, they would hardly impede it at all. at the end of their working life the horses were retired, not slaughtered. anyone who could show that they had access to land and a fondness for horses could simply extract one of these clydesdales, for free, from the official retirement sanctuary, sign for it and take it away. so 'max' became the work horse of the laragh commune, except that there was no work for him to do.

i tried to explain to the commune that there was one chance and one chance only each year, to get a piece of land cultivated, and to launch it into production as a garden, but it was no use. there was too great a turnover of people, too much going on, too many disparate characters with too many problems to solve, or to evade, in their dropped-out lives.

the new tenants got up late. in the evenings, which started early, they discussed the self-sufficient life. occasionally i joined them.

it seemed obvious to me that trailing a boat twenty miles to go sailing in dundalk bay was part of a bourgeois lifestyle, and not part of a self-sufficient lifestyle – particularly as the garden remained untouched. no one else seemed able to grasp this. a five-year-old child of the bookie's would have known that either you plant your potatoes in a certain way, by a certain date, or you will go without potatoes. the commune did not know that, but if made aware of it would have considered it an interesting topic for a late-night debate around the fire.

in the end it is often scale which defeats the migrant from the city – which most of the hippies were – and i have more than once seen someone carve out a cultivated patch on a neglected farm. they usually end up in control of about the same amount of land that they were reared on, even if this were only a suburban back lawn.

the hippies also broke the other main condition – not to do anything to alarm the neighbours. for a start a girl was found unconscious by the roadside. she was brought home and quickly revived, but none of them would say what she had passed out from, and local rumour quickly filled in the blank in a number of ways.

the other thing that they did later was to capsize their sailing boat in dundalk bay. this was not particularly dangerous, as the wind was blowing towards the land, but the righted and waterlogged boat drifted slowly northwards to warrenpoint on the county down shore. the few miles that they had travelled by sea became, by road, a journey of many miles around the head of the bay.

far from their promise to be unobtrusive, the hippies now had to pass through the british army checkpoint at the border to get back to their van in the republic. they then had to drive through the border a second time to get back to the shore in county down where their boat was beached. by the third time they passed through the border post on the same evening, the young cockney soldier's gun was shaking in his hands. he had seemingly become prey to deep suspicion of their motives, being unable to fathom what was going on. (was something about to blow up?)

later the military built zigzag walls and massed concrete block houses at the border posts, and hung nets over the slits, so that they could see out, but you could not see them. these elaborate fortresses were to protect the soldiers, not to guard the border, as there were plenty of little back roads nearby with nothing at all on them to mark where the border might lie.

the arrival of a family had unexpectedly made a countrywoman out of octavia. at first, after the birth, she had a monthly nurse to help, and after the nurse had gone, we hired an au pair, a pretty girl from donegal.

octavia began by letting me buy her a large antique pram, and our daughter started her life being pushed around the pond in stephen's green, on the sunnier days. it was the following year, when our second child was born, that the whole business of an au pair, a nursery up two flights of stairs, and walks in the green, began to seem too much trouble. we never took a conscious decision to pull out of the city, but little by little as the children began to walk and explore, it was easier to keep them down on the wicklow farm. there, we had the freedom to leave the front door open and let them run in and out. in dublin the traffic and crowded pavements confined them to the house. but this move happened gradually, and i am jumping ahead of the story ...

the wicklow farm was run as an efficient commercial unit, but within that commercial operation the addition of half bantam hens and runner ducks, a liver and white english pointer, a border collie, and a tortoiseshell cat, gave the appearance of a more traditional family farm.

i bought a shotgun, not for formal shoots but simply in order to get the occasional pigeon or rabbit for the pot, and to keep the crows out of the barley. shooting for me was hunting for the pot. if i went out and met a hare in the back paddock, and shot it, i would bring it back into the house straight away. the job was done. it was for food, not for sport.

after a while i could pluck a pigeon as i walked. it is a job more easily done while the bird is still warm, and it is much better not to bring all the feathers back into the house.

the farm in wicklow was largely self-contained. we had our own silage harvester, and almost all of the machinery we needed, with the exception of a hay baler. at laragh the same amount of land would have made eight or ten family farms, all borrowing, sharing, contracting and hiring, and feuding. these small farms would be economically ten times worse off, but culturally and in their personal relationships, ten times richer – within a comparable acreage.

at harvest time one of the bookie's younger daughters came to stay. she was up early on the harvest day expecting neighbours to arrive, with the usual relays of tea in cans and boxes of sandwiches sent out to feed them. when one solitary man came on a combine, and drove round and around the fields alone, she was disappointed. there would not even be a thrashing to follow, for the combine thrashed the barley as it went along and the grain was hauled to the shed by a single tractor and trailer. the banter of neighbours had been replaced by solitary-looking men in earmuffs, on ever larger tractors, bought with ever larger loans.

civil war?

our lives at this time were lived against a background of civil unrest. i took to attending occasional cattle auctions in the north, where pedigree friesians were cheaper and often came with better milk records and quality. farmers from north and south mingled as they always had done. politics was laid aside in the interests of doing business. on the neat whitewashed dairy farms of south armagh and county down life went on in traditional fashion, with only the occasional low-flying helicopter to interrupt an auctioneer. when one came over, some of the attendance would shrink almost physically, like ducklings in the presence of a hovering hawk.

stopping for a sandwich on the way home, i would sometimes see the television news, of shootings, burnings, petrol bombs and riots, and wonder –

'was i really up there, today?'

the presence of the first black soldiers on the border seemed slightly bizarre to people from rural ireland. to a dairy farmer, tied to his milking parlour twice a day for seven days a week, even people from the next parish are outsiders, if not exactly foreigners.

a black squaddie asked a kerryman stopped at a border checkpoint where he was from:

'annascaul.'

'you wha' man?'

'annascaul, county kerry.'

'you're a long way from home.'

unwisely, the kerryman said –

'you're not exactly sitting under a banana tree, yourself.'

– so the soldier pulled him over and they spent three hours taking his car apart for hidden compartments and concealed explosives, before letting him off to go on his way.

i read the newspaper religiously, every morning. i once reckoned that this took up about thirteen per cent of my waking life. i often wrote letters to *the irish times* letters page, the most prestigious organ for debate on national issues, until the coming of the internet changed everything.

i still feel nostalgia for the great days of *the irish times* letters correspondents. there was a day when they would not have let you away with such an inaccurate use of the word 'prestigious'.

old flame

one morning i was late getting up. i had spent the night in dublin, and as was my habit, i went over to the shelbourne hotel for my morning coffee. it is very easy to get used to being rich. i defy anyone, even the most unlikely winner of the lottery, not to get used to it and begin to take it for granted in about three to six months. this morning, anyway, i came in to the shelbourne as comfortably as if into my own drawing room, and there on the sofa sat claudia kenny.

the sun was shining through the plate glass on to her blood-orange hair, she was backlit on a sofa in the window, unselfconsciously theatrical. after a pause to recover i said:

'how are you?'

but the eyes and the body language had already spoken, before meaningless words could be exchanged.

i had last invited her to meet my aunt and cousin for dinner in snaffles, hoping for a significant occasion – and had met disappointment on that score.

before that i had met her in a steep monaghan potato field. she had appeared to us in a cream linen suit, cool, goddess-like, and inaccessible.

now i could afford to invite her to stay to have lunch in the hotel, to choose whatever she wanted from the restaurant menu … and yet i could not afford to.

it was my turn to be inaccessible.

i now knew ireland, upstairs and below stairs, north and south, east and west, from the wicklow hills to the kildare street club to the small farms on the south armagh border – i had property and land and cattle, good health and a rich wife, a beautiful child, and another on the way, and time on my hands. so did i have everything?

claudia was with her younger brother who made me for some reason uncomfortable because he had grown tall and had the same colouring, and now looked so exactly like her. i sat between them on a low sofa.

after an awkward twenty minutes i excused myself and walked home.

no one gets everything.

over housed

it is a simple fact, that a person can only live in one house at a time. a person with two houses lives in one and worries about the other. we now had three houses, and a lot of my time seemed to be spent in travelling between them and moving possessions.

we had inherited a full-sized billiard table with the dublin house. this i had transferred up to laragh, the only house of the three which now had room for it. the moving had to be done professionally, as billiard tables are made of slate and these heavy slate sections have to be reassembled perfectly even and level for the table to be once again playable.

i began to consider selling laragh. it had only become a refuge for the hippies and an unemployed clydesdale. going up to see the house i realized that the expense of moving up the billiard table had benefited no one except them, and their mangy cat, who slept on it. i made a mental note to talk to bob about the cat, and headed back for dublin.

i knew every inch of the slane road by now, i used to amuse myself by trying to get from laragh to the speed limit sign in finglas, north dublin – sixty miles – without using the brakes. no one believed it could be done. they said that the hill in slane would defeat me – but i used to slow at the brow of the hill above the village, change down to second gear, and roll slowly down the hill. there were no traffic lights on the bridge in those days. occasional lorries missed the turn at the bottom and came to horrible ends crashing through the parapet and into the river boyne below.

the next time i went up to laragh, there was, as so often, no one about. the site of the house was under a steep slope, so that the vegetable garden and the well were in fact above the level of the buildings. at the wall at the bottom of the garden i found two goats yoked together with old bucket handles – one on top of the wall, and the other hanging by the neck. local wisdom asserted that a wandering goat is always travelling in one of two directions – going to do harm, or coming from it. these goats had been enjoying the hippies' vegetable garden. i rescued them by throwing the second goat after the first.

back in the house there was a pool of half-dried cat shit on the billiard table. i had had enough. i took a large piece of sacking, located the cat, and quickly wrapped it around the animal so that it could not claw me. then i rotated the cat's head, one, two, three, and snapped its neck. i marched out of the front door, past the returning hippies in their van, and threw the cat, in the sack, into the laurels.

if this shocks you more than, say, bloody sunday – you may be english, or from the city, and it might be time to reconsider your values.

i had become like the local farmers, able to care for animals, and yet ruthless with them when necessary.

that evening as dusk fell, i made a little speech to the hippies, gathered in the big kitchen around the range. the speech began:

'look, i think this is not going to work out ...'

before i left to return to dublin, a session had begun. a wave of intense relief seemed to launch the company into a party mood. they were once again cast out to drift homeless and hopeless on the tides of the world. they were happy again, and going back to the transient life where they really belonged.

by offering them a farm on which to realize their dreams, i had done a thoughtless thing. as long as they lived in the city, an idyllic life of self-sufficiently growing vegetables was theoretically possible. here upon acres of land, it was painfully clear that it was not.

the desire to change the whole world is sometimes an indication of personal confusion and even weak character. the conviction that the world is in a hopeless mess is often a projection of inner turmoil. if you are ever tempted to embark upon saving the world yourself, check out first the kind of people who have saved it in the past.

you might change your mind.

bob was the dropout son of a new york hotelier. he had certain qualities that had by-passed most of his companions. to keep the peace between two 'wives' and their children, for a start, required diplomacy and copious quantities of homegrown dope.

i never got into the dope, being a nonsmoker by nature. nevertheless there is a thing called a 'contact high'. merely by being among smokers, and with homeopathic-level quantities of scented smoke hanging around in the air, i was able to enter the prevailing mood and the currently fashionable mental state.

bob later lived in county kildare, with some success. we remained acquaintances, and on one memorable visit he was able to offer me rhubarb wine – homemade – a cigar (declined) from home grown tobacco, all beneath two light bulbs which were powered from homemade electricity. the generator was a home carved wooden propeller, mounted up a (stolen or salvaged) electricity pole, which operated upon the back axle differential of a scrapped morris minor, in order to drive the generator and charge an array of linked batteries in the home built conservatory.

outside in his garden he then had discarded plastic cases from computer tapes, opened out like double A 4 cloches, for tender plants. i thought then that i had seen the future – mainframe computers scrapped to help grow home vegetables.

this was brilliant, but you cannot build a civilization upon second hand and recycled discarded stuff. the whole enterprise presumes that there is a wasteful consumer society on the other side of the hill, buying new stuff and throwing out still-useful stuff. the hippies were in fact dependent upon the consumer excesses which they constantly moralized about.

at poulaphouca, near bob's new house, the government erected an experimental wind generator, but it was twenty-five years before the erecting of white wind generator towers became widespread in ireland, with each of them to power thousands of houses – not just one cottage.

bob later moved to a third and more ambitious communal homestead on long island, off the coast of west cork.

he was drowned off a homemade boat, attempting the half mile crossing from the mainland, in unsuitable weather.

lampshades

the ireland of the early 1970s was only just beginning to undergo changes that came in rapid succession as the country adapted to its new position among the nations of the european economic community. it is hard to remember now that there was little or no food in the pubs in rural ireland, and that it was necessary to make the trip to dublin to buy either books or good cheese or real coffee. as for wine, a publican in carrickmacross gave me a few bottles at a discount, because it was 'old.'

one odd thing that was hard to get was lampshades …

i had become engrossed in the breeding up of a pedigree friesian herd. i spent the evenings in wicklow poring over old sales catalogues and milk records. my ambition was to own a bull out of the famous 'terling' herd, the best-known herd in england. when i proposed to make the trip to the annual reading bull show in berkshire, octavia was happy to let me go, and gave me a commission to bring back lampshades from a west end london department store.

it was summer. i took the land rover on the evening ferry to fishguard and drove many miles into wales before stopping at an inn in a village. i got a room for the night and was about to retire when the landlady asked if i would like something to drink before going to bed. expecting cocoa i followed her back down the stairs and went through a door which she indicated to me. here i found myself in a bar in which were several men drinking.

a silence fell on the room. it was well after hours, and for a moment the drinkers must have wondered if they were caught.

after a tentative and somewhat suspicious start, these welsh farmers included me in the general conversation, and i was astonished to realize that i was feeling 'at home'. the conspiratorial atmosphere, the understated contempt for the law, the drink, the topics of rural conversation, the caution with outsiders, the border with imperial england not many miles off down the road … i knew exactly where i was.

in the morning i resumed my journey to the town of reading. i had carefully sifted through the lots in the catalogue before leaving ireland, and it did not take long to view the bulls which interested me. at the auction in the afternoon, i bought two. prices were in a temporary slump. one of the two was 'terling colditz', a bull from the herd which i most admired.

that night i stayed again in a bed and breakfast. i was well-satisfied with my 'raid' on the annual bull sale, and by buying two bulls i had given the other irish friesian breeders something to talk about.

the trip had gone smoothly except for a tendency of the land rover to be difficult to start. it was a diesel land rover of the old kind where the engine required the assistance of heater plugs before you turned it on. the vehicle had to be stopped by a puller which cut off the fuel. it also badly required a wash, but no farmer would be too concerned about that.

i was careful to leave it parked on the brow of a slight hill, and set off again in the morning by letting off the handbrake and slowly rolling down the slope until she coughed into life.

when i came into the heavy traffic at the end of the M4 motorway, i rather wished that i had washed my vehicle to go shopping. i also realized that my limited knowledge of the west end of london did not include a single hill of sufficient slope to restart the thing, once i had stopped the engine.

i drove into the only street that i knew well, the street where octavia's bijou chelsea house had been. i would park and walk.

i had my handkerchief wrapped around the 'puller' to stop me stalling the engine in a moment of forgetfulness. there was nothing to do but chance leaving the engine ticking over. out of consideration for the residents, i carefully turned the vehicle around, so that its put-put-put of blue diesel fumes blew into the roadway, not into the tiny gardens.

it cannot have been more than fifteen minutes before i triumphantly returned with a box of plush lampshades from the soft furnishings section of the 'peter jones' department store. at the corner of the street i met a policeman standing in the middle of the roadway.

'you can't go down there, sir,' he said.

i persisted, but he wasn't having any –

'you can make your way down the next street.'

'but my car is down there.'

'what make is it?'

'a blue land rover.'

'come with me.'

a large hand on my shoulder guided me down the street. in the middle of the street sat the vehicle, still put-put-putting. visible in various gardens were british policemen of several varieties – traditional bobbies, the other kind with flat hats with a chequered band, and plain clothes ones. at the far end of the street a little knot of nannies, charladies, au pairs and small children huddled apprehensively. this was chelsea in mid-morning. as we walked up the deserted street a bunch of men in overalls loaded stuff into a plain van and drove off.

the bomb squad.

i was presented for questioning to another bobby. i was in deep trouble:

1 facing the wrong way in a one-way street
2 leaving the engine of a vehicle running
3 a dirty farm vehicle with an irish registration that indicated a border county
4 suitcase visible in the back (the bomb)
5 handkerchief covering ignition (the wire)
6 parked at the front gate of an important person ...

then i remembered who octavia's neighbours were –

the policeman asked me:

'have you anything to say?'

i gulped. i said – 'i would like to apologize to lady widgery.'

the policeman led me to the front door of her little house, but as we approached it the door opened and lady widgery herself swept out. i started to apologize but she brushed between us without even looking at me.

'i hope they throw the book at you!' she said, and went off up the street.

the policeman exchanged a glance with me. he now knew, and i knew, that i had committed only minor offences. the policeman knew that i could not be extradited from ireland for these, and so did i. all the same, he went through a little charade of taking the address of my nearest garda station in the republic, to which, he suggested, i would have to report.

the excitement was rapidly draining from his day. he had no grounds for detaining me.

'when do you intend to return to ireland?'

holding up the car keys, i said –

'now.'

within less than the hour i was back out on the motorway, and heading for wales.

at fishguard the welsh farmers and lorry drivers from the meat factories were blockading the port, in the furtherance of an industrial dispute, but they let me through. at the customs an officer waved me into a separate lane and asked me questions to do with being on farmland, and even though i had not been, they washed my wheels with disinfectant before waving me through. in the back the big box of lampshades remained unopened. i could have been carrying a month's supply of semtex explosive for all they knew.

the bulls would follow on later. there were quarantine regulations to comply with.

when i got home to the farm, i confessed to octavia what had happened.

'lady widgery?' she said. 'silly old bat was always complaining when my cat pissed on her roses.'

a commercial farm

merrionstown was a commercial dairy farm. i had started farming where the absentee german owners left off, with a farm manager and two experienced farm workers. i did not know enough yet to run it myself, so we kept michael on, the young farm manager, and although he was working for me, i spent much of the time learning things from him.

'terling colditz' and his companion arrived out of quarantine, and i became immersed in the breeding up of the herd.

for mechanical things, on the other hand, i had no great aptitude, although i was able to drive the tractors and, after a while, to plough. nor was i particularly at home amidst the electrical equipment of the milking parlour. although the two farm workers were older than i was, by dint of much practice they were better able for a long physical day's work. only in the breeding of the dairy herd did i find an outlet, as i saw it, for my aesthetic and intellectual abilities. i toured the auction sales of friesians, and whereas at first there seemed to be bargains to be had, i soon found that the cattle i wanted were the ones that made big money. this was an indication that my ability to assess an animal – her conformation, her milk records and pedigree – was steadily improving.

in the winter i walked through the herd in the yard several times a day. we were an autumn-calving winter-milk supplier. there i picked out cows that might be 'bulling', and even though we had two pedigree bulls, we still used artificial insemination to introduce the blood of fashionable sires.

we had a conservative stocking policy. we spread slurry on the land almost year-round, and a good part of the money that we made was sunk back into the herd and the farm.

organic gardening

perhaps through the influence of the hippies, but also because i had time on my hands, i fenced off a quarter acre at the back of the house for a vegetable garden. i was going in precisely the opposite direction to the neighbouring farmers, who had just emerged from the days of homegrown cabbage and spuds to buying everything they needed in the supermarket, plastic-wrapped. the dairy farmers had even stopped drinking their own milk, they sent it all off to the creamery and bought pasteurized milk in a carton from the shop.

at about five thirty every morning the milk lorry came. the driver backed down the yard and connected his hose to our refrigerated milk tank. then he drained the tank through a meter, at the same time taking a small sample for testing. he did this on his own. there was no need, fortunately, to get up to help him.

at one time there was an investigation on to find who was watering the milk. it was clear in the creamery's laboratory that water was being added somewhere, but every time they thought that they had pinned down the culprit, that man's milk passed the following test with no problem.

it took them a long time to work it out.

a particular farmer was adding water to his milk, which was paid for by the gallon, of course. milk is already eighty-three per cent water. this farm was the one, near the end of the collecting run, where the lorry driver stopped each morning for a cup of tea – but this hospitality served a purpose. while the farmer's wife offered the tanker driver a second cup, or even toast or an egg, the farmer himself went out the back to the lorry, which had a carefully arranged metal tray of samples. there each day he extracted his own numbered sample and exchanged it with another one, chosen at random.

back in the creamery laboratory the finger of suspicion was pointing in all directions.

breeding

after a while breeding became an obsession with me. it went far beyond the need to improve the average milk yield of the herd. people will tell you that breeding attractive cattle is a waste of time. not so.

the successful pedigree breeder is a collector, and a selector. every time he sells cattle, he chooses. unless it is a final clearance sale, he has to make choices, not just between good milkers and bad milkers, but between moderately good milkers. of two moderately good animals he will keep the pretty cow, and sell the plain one, every time. gradually, a good-looking herd becomes an indication that it is a highly selected herd.

a herd of plain-looking cattle indicates a collection of other people's cast offs.

the same is true of people.

don't misunderstand me.

this is a pattern in the evolution of attraction:

generation after generation the better off marry the better looking. 'better looking' may vary at different times according to fashion, but there are certain common factors in desirability that persist through different ages. after some centuries of this selection, in a stable society, better looking people are more likely to carry the genes – whatever those happen to be – that are typical of the more successful. they have an increased likelihood of breeding not only better looking daughters, but more successful sons.

so beauty becomes, in time, more than skin-deep.

for a time my obsession with breeding was satisfied among the friesian cows, but also i bred english pointer dogs, half bantam hens, indian runner ducks, and did my best to breed ginger tom cats and tortoiseshell females.

unlike the easy-going cattle, the cats had subversive ideas of their own about whom they wished to breed with, which rarely coincided with my own plan. the cats remained diverse in their colouring.

it was late in the summer when octavia was pregnant again. i began to suspect that with two children to look after she would definitely opt for the country over the centre of the city.

she would settle at merrionstown. it would make sense to sell laragh.

on the market

in february i went to see mr mahony once again, and we arranged to put the house on the market by private treaty.

in those days it often took two years to sell a large house in the country. none of us expected an immediate offer, and we settled down to wait.

'what will you take for it?' mr mahony had asked.

'we'll take fifteen thousand, but let's wait and see what we are offered, first.'

he nodded. but i knew by him that he didn't think we had a hope of getting it.

a couple of weeks later a man came to the door of the house in dublin. he was about forty, dressed in an ill-fitting sports jacket.

'i heard ye're selling laragh house.'

i was immediately suspicious of this man. something told me not to let him into the hall. i stepped out and pulled the door shut behind me. he had an unpleasant but indistinct accent, neither from belfast nor from the border. he made his question sound more like an accusation than a question.

'what are ye asking?'

'it's fifteen thousand,' i said. i thought that would bring the conversation to an end pretty quickly. i knew not to 'come down' in my price for a total stranger in the street, to do so would only set the level that some other conspiring bidder, yet to come out of the woodwork, would begin at. if i refused to reduce my price he would go away.

'i'll give it ye,' he said.

i was completely taken aback. i still did not want him in the house, but what grounds had i for not pursuing this further? what excuse could i make?

so i invited him instead to walk down the street to the shelbourne bar.

we went inside and had a whiskey apiece. i ordered, but he stepped in and paid. then i started to catalogue the drawbacks of laragh, the damp, the roof gutters, the window frames that needed replacing …

'i am very familiar with laragh house,' he said. 'my grandfather worked there. he was the gardener.'

i knew by the way he said it that some deep and long-seated resentment was involved. now i was completely nonplussed. i kicked for touch. i said –

'you will have to talk to mr mahony. he has the sale of it.'

'i didn't come to you through any estate agent,' he argued. 'i heard about it up at laragh.'

but very few people at laragh even knew the house was for sale. he obviously wanted to short circuit the deal, to cut out the estate agent and the fees. i was reluctant to do this. to me, this constituted a form of cheating.

'what has mister mahony done for me?' he asked.

he emphasized the 'mister' to make it almost a sneer.

who was this man? this was my first meeting with frank mcbirney. he was a persuasive man. he had an intensity that pushed past people. he constantly skipped on to the next thing while you were still undecided how you should react to the last thing.

'you would have to put down the twenty-five per cent with mr mahony,' i said.

'ten per cent,' he said. 'this is private treaty.'

'ten per cent with mr mahony,' i corrected myself.

'i'll put it down with your solicitor. ye have a solicitor.'

this was a statement, not a question. there was nothing more to say.

mcbirney finished his whiskey in one go, and went out. he had not even asked the name of the solicitor.

i went home to octavia.

she saw my unease.

'what's wrong?' she said.

'i think i have just sold laragh for fifteen thousand pounds.'

'brilliant,' she said.

– but i was not happy.

a few days later i went to see mr drought, my solicitor, whose office was only across the road in upper merrion street. i wanted him to draw up a contract for the sale of the house. i decided to leave the cottages with tenants out of the sale. although the tenants had consistently failed to come up with the rent, i felt a paternalistic interest in their welfare, and was not prepared to see them put out on the road. i felt that if there was any way, straight or crooked, to put them out – then this particular purchaser would find it. no one acts the landlord more readily than a man who feels that he has suffered under landlordism. no one learns oppression faster than the oppressed.

my solicitor told me that mcbirney had been in contact already, and was anxious to make a quick purchase – mcbirney's wife was selling and vacating a pub on the border, north of dundalk.

as soon as the contract was drawn up, mcbirney was informed by telephone. he didn't like the exclusion of the cottages, which only made me think that my hunch was right. he came down to dublin the same afternoon, to argue the point, and we sat in his car outside the house. it was a brand new three-litre rover.

i argued that the tenants had a hold over the properties. he said that he would not put them out, but he still wanted the cottages included, anyway. i was not going to give in this time, but in the end he persuaded me to include one cottage that was the former gate lodge, at the upper side of the road.

this meant that the map that went with the deeds had to be redrawn.

i had been as tough as i dared, but all the time i was afraid that he would 'kick up' and i would find myself renegotiating the purchase price of the house.

when the contract was ready with the redrawn map, mcbirney and his good-looking but hard-faced wife came down to me in dublin, to meet mr drought in his office. mcbirney put down fifteen hundred pounds in cash, and his wife signed the contract.

again i was a bit wrong footed. i complained to mr drought afterwards, that i had agreed to sell the house to mcbirney, not to her. the solicitor shrugged off the question –

'we are getting fifteen thousand,' he reasoned. 'what did you originally ask for the property?'

'fifteen thousand.'

before another week had gone by, mcbirney rang me again. i agreed to meet him in the hotel bar, as before.

this time he told me what i knew already – that his wife had sold a pub on the main road outside dundalk, and he needed to vacate quickly. he had nowhere to store the bar furniture and various equipment that the new owner was not taking over.

i knew what was coming. he wanted to move stuff in to laragh before the solicitors had completed the conveyance.

i said that i would have to ask my own solicitor about this. again, i was stalling, but again, he just assumed that the deal was done and hustled on with arranging the detail before i had time to object.

on this occasion he allowed me to buy him a whiskey in return, and he began to talk about himself. it was a rambling monologue. a kind of a political speech. he had been reared in belfast because his father had found no work at laragh. he had some hang-up about the mills and the mill owners, and the fact that they had been protestants while all of the mill workers, except the agent and a few trusted foremen, had been catholics.

'religion is a terrible thing. look what people do in the name of religion. people get blown up and shot,' he said.

i did not understand how this was relevant to his father's not getting a job in the mill, and anyway, by his father's time, the day of the flax mills was already long over.

'i was in the blitz,' mcbirney said, 'i was in belfast through the blitz. you won't frighten me easy.'

he said this as though i personally had been with the luftwaffe over belfast. he also spoke of laragh as though i personally had been the employer of the flax mill workers of the 1920s. his opinions had a raw intensity which unsettled me, and instinctively i tried to appease him.

we walked to his car, parked beside the hotel. i expected the rover, but he was driving an almost new jaguar.

'sit in,' he said.

i sat in to the passenger seat. i thought he wanted to demand some further concession, but he only wanted to finish the monologue which he had begun.

'ye would be surprised,' he said at the end, 'surprised, if ye knew how republican i am.'

in the morning i returned to mr drought. i really wanted to know if i was taking a foolish risk letting someone into the property before the balance of the money was paid.

the solicitor said that i could be covered by a standard caretaker's agreement. on this basis we agreed to go ahead with the sale as quickly as possible.

the deal goes sour

we were now preparing for the arrival of a second baby, but at the next opportunity i went up to laragh to take away the remainder of my possessions. it was my habit to go up and stay overnight. the house was cold and unlived in, but i wanted to maintain some kind of a presence at laragh.

when i arrived at the house i found no one about, but inside my few remaining bits of furniture had all been shifted and stacked in one bedroom. this annoyed me, as did the heap of benches, purple and black pub carpets and pub fittings in the hall. outside, the daffodils were coming into bloom. the weather was mild. the heathery hillside opposite was peaceful. the house was isolated on all sides by the lie of the land and by its trees. the slight sense of menace was only in my imagination.

all the same i brought a shotgun with me to the house. it only had a single barrel. it was one of those in which the barrel and the stock come apart, and it could be carried around in pieces in a normal suitcase or bag. i said laragh was a quiet house, and indeed it usually was, but no house is quiet on nights when there is wind in the trees and among the laurel bushes.

in the morning i went down and asked the bookie to come up and lend me a hand to load some bits of furniture into the horsebox. he walked up the avenue sucking on his pipe and saying little. he had met mcbirney on the road one day, and the wife, in the big car. he didn't know much about them.

'racehorses ...' he said.

he said this tentatively. i knew exactly what he meant: 'some people say they have racehorses but you wouldn't know what to believe.'

i guessed then that the bookie was playing it cautiously. loyal friend as he had been to me, he now was figuring how to handle this new neighbour. i could fall out with mcbirney and go off if i wanted to. the bookie had to stay and make the best of it, living beside the new owner. i knew better than to ask what mcbirney might have meant by being 'republican'. that would be only to show the bookie my hand and learn nothing in return.

'you wouldn't know what kind they would be,' – he said, as if reading my thoughts.

back in dublin i was not long in presenting myself in mr drought's office.

'they have gone into the house and moved around the furniture before the caretaker's agreement is signed,' i protested.

mr drought looked at me over his spectacles across the wide leather-topped desk.

'no,' he explained patiently, 'they cannot do that.'

'they've done it,' i said.

i confided my fears to octavia, but played them down so as not to alarm her, someone had once told me to keep a pregnant woman calm and unstressed at all times. we idly speculated what 'the gentry' should do if nouveau riche republicans moved in to 'the big house'.

'burn it down!' we said in unison, and laughed.

'poetic justice!' added octavia. i think she was remembering the major's stories of big houses that were burned in the 1920s.

it seemed important to get back to laragh as soon as possible. octavia had come up to dublin to see her gynaecologist, and was going out to see friends that evening. sinéad, our live-in au pair, was showing signs of restlessness and might not stay with us much longer. better to make use of her while we still had her? looking back, i wonder now if i treated sinead in the benevolent but slightly too patronizing way that i had been used to from my own past employers. anyway, i had no intention of sitting in alone with sinéad, so i got myself invited to stay the night at cobby's house in county meath, which was halfway up to monaghan.

there was also a binmen's strike in dublin and the rubbish was not being collected. i loaded up the horsebox with a fresh gas cylinder to cook with at laragh, and a collection of old carpets and underfelt that we needed to get out of the way in order to complete the final stages of our restoration. finally, i loaded up my patient pointer dog. i seemed to spend my days moving stuff from one house to another.

when i arrived up in meath, cobby himself had been invited out to supper by lady mountcharles. he was slightly smug about being sufficiently 'well in' to be able to ask her if he could bring me along as well. he managed to arrange this.

it was not a party. she had been away and cobby was just being invited to provide an update over supper of county meath gossip, something that was never in short supply. i was always interested in going to new houses, large or small, and i was only sorry that we would be arriving there after dark.

this lady mountcharles was called eileen. i say that because, like the dalai lamas, lady mountcharleses reappear in each generation – and in some generations there can be more than one.

this one and her husband had gone their separate ways, and now lived a few miles apart. this country still had no legal way to divorce, and their situation seemed to be one of those irish 'stand-offs' that could occur between separated couples whose house and land were in ireland, even if they had their other assets elsewhere.

although she was almost a generation older than either of us, lady mountcharles was an elegant and attractive woman. it was a quiet supper for three. i quickly understood that her offer had been to feed us, not to entertain us. it was our role, or cobby's rather, to entertain her. as a single man without a family, cobby had an active social life and could retail the latest local news, spiced with a dry wit.

we did talk about the situation in the north, however, and in the 'bandit country' on both sides of the border. i said a bit sharply that it was time somebody stood up to these people. lady mountcharles looked a little taken aback. the code of the anglo-irish, long bred into them, was to confront nothing and nobody, but to keep the head down and to get on with your life quietly. intensity was very out of fashion. i suppose that it was my personal situation that was beginning to get to me, rather than the political situation. after all, wasn't i a republican myself?

like miss talbot, lady mountcharles had the most inconsequential of suppers laid out with full formality. this was the habit of the aristocracy. the aristocracy? how do you define the aristocracy in an independent republic? i had my own criterion. i would simply include anyone who ate better at home than when they were out!

we did eat well and we must have had a few glasses of wine. i don't remember us leaving, or the journey back to cobby's house. fortunately the way home was by the back roads. people happily drank and drove cars at that time. i don't remember them getting killed on the roads much. there were simply fewer cars, and to be found in the morning asleep in the car athwart some ditch was only something to laugh about at the next party.

the confrontation

in the morning i was up early and off to laragh. monaghan was only thirty miles further down the slane road, but in many ways it was different part of the country.

this time when i drove up the avenue to the house there was somebody there. there was a builder's van parked at the front. i walked around to the side entrance, which i found wide open, passing a heap of rubble as i went.

in the old kitchen i found a scene of devastation. the ceiling had gone. you could see from the kitchen to the ceilings of the bedrooms directly above. a circular hole had been opened out in the floor about fifteen feet in diameter and the rubble of this had been largely cleared away.

that must have been what i passed on the way in. part of the 'breakfast room' had also been demolished.

i was stunned. i was simply speechless. i went through the hall to the front door, but instead of being fastened by the little bolt in the lock, it was nailed shut by a six-inch nail driven deep into the woodwork of the georgian doorcase. i turned to look for something to open it with, but mcbirney had come in quietly behind me. he was holding a hammer. i froze. then i turned and walked back past him as if he wasn't there. my instinct was to carry on doing exactly what i had come up to do, and not to be deterred.

i crossed the hall. he was still right behind me.

'what's the matter with you, man?' was what he said.

i looked into the room called 'the library' to see if any suitable implement was in there for bending the nail. i found a blunt chisel that would do, but before i could get back to the front door he interposed himself between me and the door. in that instant i knew that this was for real. i was in trouble. my house was in bits. even if i managed to regain possession of it, the house was in no shape to show to another buyer.

mcbirney stood between me and the front door. he held the hammer under my nose. the chisel in my hand was down at my side.

i glared at him. he knew by my face that i knew.

he said softly:

'don't try anything … if you want to get home safe tonight.'

i became aware that his wife was standing in the doorway behind us, one hand in her handbag which she held across her.

after a pause, i said, tensely –

'i think i am entitled to look around my own house.'

i went back into the hall and up the stairs and walked from room to room. i was shaking with shock and anger. i would not confront them.

at first mcbirney followed me and then when i persisted in seeing every room and every bit of demolition, he left me. my mind was racing. if i went to the law, the lawyers could take months and might still fail to shift him. if i went to the guards they would only say that it was a civil matter, and refuse to intervene.

i went up the stairs and into each of the bedrooms. i went down the back wing and looked down through the hole in the ceiling to the old kitchen below.

whether he stayed watching me i do not know. when i had inspected every room in the house, i went back to the front door, bent back the nail with the chisel, and opened it to the spring sunlight.

i brought in my gas cylinder, but i left the old carpet felt in the horsebox. then i detached the horsebox from the land rover and drove away, completely forgetting the dog.

at the bottom of the avenue i met the bookie walking on the road. i slid back the window and opened my mouth, but no words came out.

'is something wrong?' he said.

i said: 'i need a drink.'

he went around and got in.

we drove around the hill to mccabe's bar.

old mccabe knew that something was up. people sometimes drank in the middle of the day, but always for a reason. he poured us two bottles of stout, and then two more, and waited patiently for a reason to emerge.

the bookie likewise knew that something or someone had upset me, but was too diplomatic to enquire before i was ready to tell. he might anyway have been keeping an eye on the goings on up at the house on his own account.

all of my instincts were to behave as if nothing had happened. the so-called 'stiff upper lip'. but my upper lip was far from stiff.

i loved laragh. i had had no proper family and no family life until i came to laragh. laragh was more than a house, it was my home, my stronghold, it was my tribal territory. but i had been obliged to buy laragh, humiliatingly, as a foreigner, for as well as finding the purchase price i had had to request and wait for the permission of the irish land commission. thus it took thirteen long weeks, before the house was mine.

i had hated the designation 'non-national'. as soon as i had five years' residence behind me i had made an application for naturalization, and sworn an oath of loyalty in the court in castleblayney, in order to become an irish citizen. the judge did not congratulate me, probably assuming that this was purely a procedure done for convenience. if that is what he thought he could not have been more wrong.

i had even gone further. i was entitled, as many people were, to hold dual irish and british nationality if i wished – but in a time of political unrest i did not like the ambiguity of having dual loyalties. i was determined to go the whole way, and i renounced my british nationality.

this was done by post, and cost thirty shillings.

'thirty pieces of silver,' cobby had commented, dryly.

it seemed to me now that all of my deliberate immersion in ireland had been in vain. i was being pushed back into the unwanted role of absentee landlord. i had read a lot of irish history over the last ten years, and more as a schoolboy before that, identifying all the time with the romantic and oppressed side of the quarrel. doesn't everybody? i had scots-gaelic ancestors, and bore the same name as a hero who had fought and died on the side of the gaelic order in 1746, against the imperial repression of the english. so my not too distant forebears had done more than just wear aran sweaters and sing rebel songs in lounge bars. they had died fighting for independence. did that not count for anything? maybe not.

all of this, logical and illogical, flew through my brain.

the bookie and old mccabe made the best of my silence. they talked about the weather, and the price of pigs, about straying cattle, and the level of water in the lake.

what if i gave in to the pressure, and mcbirney was only a bluffer?

but what if i stood up to the pressure, and mcbirney was indeed some republican godfather? he had many of the signs of being one. whom could i ask? no one. do you imagine that you can just go into the garda station, mention a name, and ask if they have anything on him with regard to subversive activity? and what do you make of a man who has a jaguar car, a rover car, and a hi-ace van, and racehorses, and nobody this side of the border seems to know what he does for a living? and if this man was not a real 'patriot' but more of a crook and a con man, out for himself, did that make him less dangerous, or more dangerous? my head was swimming.

suppose i creep back to the house tonight, barricade myself in, ring the guards, ring the solicitors, and live there, sleeping – or not sleeping – at night, alone with the dog and the shotgun with the bread knife on the bedside table?

why throw away my life standing up to people unknown and unseen, to the neglect of my wife and new family, for money that i did not need and might not get?

but why give away the house that i loved, and retreat from the place and people that i had called home, out of cowardice, and just because of a single threatening remark.

it was too much for me to work out. i went out into the sunlight. i sat on the bench under the pub window, i put my head down in my hands, and i wept with frustration.

after a while old mccabe came out, collected my empty glass, and asked me if i was feeling all right? did i have a sore head?

after a bit i pulled myself together. i went back into the bar.

old mccabe having had no luck in divining what was going on, retreated to his kitchen, and sent out his wife in his place. she might do better.

240

she did. i began to talk. i did not tell the whole story, but i explained that there was demolition work done on the house, and no sign yet of the balance of the money.

the bookie sucked on his pipe and said nothing. mrs mccabe said —

'i wouldn't do business with them people. i'd fire him out of it. i'd batter him out of it.'

i said — 'that's not my way of doing things.'

i suppose we had another bottle or two. time slips by when you are drinking. gradually a resolution took shape in my head. i might be leaving laragh tonight, and i might not, but even if i held on and the sale went through, i would be leaving soon, and there was no way that i was going to creep off with my tail between my legs. if i had to leave, i would leave in style. i would give a party.

i said: 'mrs mccabe. i have something to ask you. would you take a cheque from me?'

she would.

the bookie sucked on his pipe, his dark eyes missing nothing. he knew what was coming.

first i pointed to various bottles of spirits on the shelves, and mrs mccabe passed these over the counter. then she took us out to a locked shed at the back and found us wooden crates of stout, and wooden crates of macardle's ale, and we stacked these into the land rover. then we went back into the bar for minerals for non-drinkers. then the bookie said that more people drank stout than drank ale or minerals. we went back to the shed for more stout, until the back of the land rover was neatly filled. drink is quite heavy in bulk. the tires of the land rover flattened slightly.

'may you die in ireland'

when i had bought laragh, seven years before, mr drought had advised me to make a will. i had protested that i had no close relation to whom to leave my property. mr drought had said that did not matter, to leave it to anyone at all was better than dying intestate and leaving it to the government.

i had taken this advice, and included in the will my funeral instructions, which were that i was to be buried at the 'nearest convenient catholic graveyard.' later i had imagined being buried beside the concrete wall of the parish church graveyard, beside a bend of the road below the milk factory, and disliked the idea, but there was an alternative. at the far end of the lake, beside a little-used boreen, was the original church of the district, an ancient ruin, called chapel mhaoile. here was a peaceful lakeside graveyard, little-used except for the rare case of some very old person who already had relations buried there. like all graveyards, this place had its guardian or sacristan, an elderly local man who knew all the names, the graves and their locations. this was important, as there were many old graves unmarked, and grown over with grass.

i would be buried there.

the request had been made at a time before i was engaged to be married, or had any blood relation in ireland to make arrangements for me, but the parish priest was inclined to make a joke of my request:

'you are surely not intending to die yet!'

when i persisted, pointing out that no one knew 'the hour nor the day', the matter had been arranged. it had been agreed that the bookie could approach the sacristan for me, and between us we could identify a plot.

now on this march day, i wanted to see chapel mhaoile. i felt that i had been threatened – with what, i did not know. rightly or wrongly i felt that the history in the history books, and the troubles that had been swirling all around me for years, had now come and knocked on my door.

what would be my answer?

my answer was that i wasn't giving in. i was going to be a monaghan border man, an ulster man. *no surrender.* the thing i feared most was to be shown up as a coward. i would resist, and go all the way.

all the way to where?

chapel mhaoile was little more than a gable wall and side walls so covered in moss and lichens that they blended into the landscape. here and there were tombstones standing or lying in the grass, but so weathered that few names could be read.

the bookie, who did less thinking than i did, but sometimes at about twice the speed, lit his pipe again and waited.

there used to be gulls nesting on the rocky island in the lake. they only made rudimentary nests, but did a lot of squabbling over territory. there was not much sign of them today. the main road and the creamery lay on the far side of the water a mile away. this was a peaceful place.

there was little to distinguish one part of the old graveyard from another. in the end there was nothing to do except to indicate a broad area of the enclosure.

'out here,' i said, 'out in the middle, not under the wall.'

the bookie nodded.

was i really making arrangements for my own funeral, or was i just making an effort to try and confront my own mortality? to convince myself that my back was to the wall?

the bookie must have known, as a boy, many of the sleepers in that place. he sat in the march sunlight looking over the lake.

i went back to the land rover. in my suitcase, in the front, was my dismantled shotgun. i took it out and fitted the two pieces together. it was not a very distinguished gun, a single barrelled spanish gun with a rubber end to its stock. i found a cartridge in my pocket and inserted it.

the bookie looked on impassively as i fired off a shot into the lake. the noise was enormous and echoed in the stillness. fifty yards out on the water a tiny scatter of spray erupted, and when i broke the gun to load it again a small curl of blue smoke rose from the back of the barrel.

i fired again into the water, and felt better.

for what remained of the daylight hours we toured the locality. we stopped at farmhouses and cottages, up long lanes and narrow boreens to find the houses of people i had met or done business with over the last few years. the feeling of threat and oppression lifted. i remembered a reply of bernadette devlin's when the interviewer asked her if she was not sometimes afraid – (she had lived under the threat of assassination) – she said –

'you live till you die.'

was i really afraid? afraid of what? anyway, if somebody wished you harm, firstly they had to have a plan fully worked out, and secondly they had to know where you were, and right at this moment nobody knew where i was.

i did not really know where i was, myself.

the invitations

we were only within two or three miles of laragh as the crow flies, but there are many hidden lanes, and all roads have to either go around the drumlin or steeply up and over it. few go straight. it is deeply convoluted country. in steep fields and farmyards we hailed all and sundry. some came to meet us. others lay low until they had had time to make a guess at what we wanted. perhaps we were suspected of being on a mission to borrow something. at each stop the bookie said that we were having a 'leaving party' and that everyone was invited.

this was greeted by a certain amount of scepticism, as the bookie was notorious for leg-pulls and jokes, but as soon as anyone took a peek into the back of the land rover and saw the stack of crates in it, they got the message. someone suspiciously asked who else would be going?

'aagh now,' said the bookie, 'the bishop and the captain' (the nicknames of two local farmers), 'the big woman and rosaleen. everybody's going. the guards can come if they like!'

there was no need to tell anyone what time the party would begin at. the party would follow on straight after closing time, it was no good starting a party any sooner.

the day passed pleasantly in various conversations. some of these men i had only met in mccabe's bar. some i had talked to out at cattle marts or auctions, but the bookie knew where each one lived. one or two i had never seen before, added to the list on the bookie's own initiative.

we must have travelled a good few miles from house to house, but all the time more or less within walking distance of home. the people of the valley, like all rural communities, were tight-knit. nowadays everyone has a car. people did have cars then, but had bicycles too, and children walked to school and everywhere else they had to go. most people could get lifts. on a big occasion one car might have to make several journeys, each time bringing four or five more, and later repeat the process to bring them all home again.

at dusk we went back to the bookie's own house, and drank tea. his own expanding family now lived in a smart new bungalow down by the road, leaving his old house up the hill to the goat and the suckling calves. once abandoned, the old house deteriorated rapidly. goats were rapidly going out of fashion, but his was trained to jump up on a table, and this way she could suckle two calves, small ones, but each one taller than herself.

the party

before it was dark, a child was sent through the fields to come back and report if there was any vehicle still up at laragh. if you went far enough up 'the point' – the narrowing belt of trees on the hill above the house – you could see down not only over the avenue but into the yard itself.

the coast was clear.

once it was fully dark we went to laragh, this time in the land rover, with the child between us in the front, and turned the land rover to face down the avenue. the front door, just as i suspected it would be, was again nailed shut, and this time the side door and the back door were both secured. not to worry. at the pantry window was a pane of glass fixed in place not by putty, but only by small tacks, and the pane could be lifted out entire. the resulting hole was just large enough to insert the child. small as he was, he was tall enough to find the bolt on the side door, and open it to let us in. the massive nail hammered into the woodwork at the front door took a little more effort to extract.

i now went about making the best preparation that i could for a party. the first thing to do was to bring in the drink and to set out some of it on a table in the hall. we had extra glasses promised from mccabe's bar on their way, while the beer and stout would have to be drunk out of the bottle.

then it was time to light a fire. the fireplace in the breakfast room had been partly demolished and opened up, and the wall of the big kitchen had gone. instead of a small fireplace in a small room, there was now an enormous open fireplace in an enormous room. fuel was no problem. various timbers from the demolition lay round about and out in the yard. the problem was not to get the fire going, so much as to keep it within manageable proportions, without going as far as sawing up all the timber into short lengths. with the loss of the ceiling above, the electric light had also gone, but soon a good blaze from the fire was enough to light the wrecked room.

the time had gone by very quickly, and i was taken by surprise when the first people arrived at the front door. the arrival of mrs mccabe herself, and her daughter, told me that the bar over the hill must be shut, and soon cars were coming and going and people were arriving at the front door. some of the arrivals were genuinely surprised and sorry to hear that i was leaving, others, better informed, sidled in the door, uncertain still if they were meant to be there – cautious in case the whole thing was some kind of set-up or elaborate joke. some men had wisely come with additional naggins of whiskey or bottles of stout in their pockets, not so much as a contribution to the party as an insurance against the provided hospitality proving insufficient.

the bookie's daughters helped with glasses, tea and minerals. i kept a close eye on the spirits table and served the men as they came in. to many of them, for years, this house had been 'the big house', and yet it was now in chaos, partly demolished inside, and far less well-appointed than most of their own houses, in fact thoroughly out of date in comparison. it was the house of the ulster protestant mill owner who had employed, and fought with, their fathers and grandfathers, grandmothers and great aunts. laragh village was not the remains of an estate, but the salvaged wreckage of an industry.

now the world had moved on, but the place laragh house held in the minds of the neighbours had not. you can tell by reading many a novel about ireland, that people do not live where they imagine themselves to live. we are emigrants from the past, but we continue to carry the old country within us. the world has nearly always moved on a chapter or two from wherever we currently choose to imagine we live. most tourist posters depict an ireland that no longer exists. we conspire in this because that is what people always really want to do – to go back.

this party soon took on a life of its own. at first i was too preoccupied to notice. i was busily anxious that each person coming through the door got a greeting, and a drink. i had a moment of apprehension when two young men unknown to me came in to the hall, they seemed to have a beer bottle each in their hand already, and did not come over to the table but stood by the door, backs to the wall. i slipped out to the bookie in the big kitchen –

'who the hell are those two?'

he took a look around the door.

'no, they're harmless,' he said.

i was happy for people to arrive, but more nervous about anyone leaving. on the other hand, i reassured myself, if word of the reoccupation of the house leaked out, i could not see what anyone could do. there were now too many witnesses. let mcbirney – or worse – turn up if they liked.

the moment then came which every host knows, when there was no more need to push-start the occasion. there was nothing wonderful laid on, just drink, tea, and lemonade (red, and white), but it was as if the ghosts of the old mill owners were hovering close, horrified at the proceedings, but powerless to do anything about it. added to this was the suspicion that we were not meant to be there as far as certain living people were concerned. added to that again was the possibility that the party might be discovered and ended at any moment. there was a 'buzz' at the party.

in the big kitchen an auction had started. a farmer from across the hill was doing his party piece, a passable take-off of the auctioneer in castleblayney, and holding up each of the various builders' tools and pieces of kitchen crockery in turn, to shouts and applause.

some of the wives and daughters thanked me, made their excuses and left. they recognized all the signs, perhaps, of a night that might soon get out of hand.

the spirits were finished. the beer and stout were not finished, but the bottles were all handed out. there was more cheering and shouting from the kitchen. the fire was piled higher with builders' timber. i hoped that some of it was not the new timber. the blaze from the fire lit the whole kitchen.

the guests were getting more drunk than my crates of stout bottles really justified. had someone introduced a supply of the homemade 'katy daly' to boost the proceedings?

then 'the bishop' and 'the captain' excused themselves. this was not their usual form, but they said they were off to check on a cow that was close to calving. the place was a blaze of light and all doors were open. i suddenly feared that the party could end and leave me exposed, alone in the house.

to be ready to depart, i went out and hitched the horsebox to the land rover. the abandoned dog had faithfully waited by the box. then i thought better of it, and unhitched the box again. i might wish to drive off in a hurry. i now began to stack what few portable valuables remained in the house into the back of the land rover.

at the start of the party i had kept control of the door. now there were people who were strangers to me, as well as friends and neighbours, going in and out of the house by various doors to bring wood to the fire.

i met sidney corrigan in the doorway.

'party's nearly over, sidney,' i said, unconvincingly.

sidney had two blue chinese plates in his hands. he fixed me with an unsteady gaze.

'i was helping you load these,' he said.

i did not know whether to believe him. i nodded towards the land rover and he went out into the darkness. had any of the builders' tools gone? i did not know what had been here in the first place. my world was turned upside down. here i was half drunk and like a robber in my own place. not much time. what was left? grab the valuable stuff and to hell with the rest?

this time when i went out i met sidney coming out of the laurels. there were no blue plates in his hands. as soon as he saw me his hands went to his fly which he zipped up ostentatiously. i wondered.

too late to count the plates in the back, now. they were buried under blankets to protect them from breakage. too late.

now the drink really had run out. there was one untouched half bottle of powers whiskey lying unnoticed behind a leg of the billiard table. i took that out to the land rover too, and hid it. the house was emptying, but not fast enough. the enormous fire had died down, whatever supplies of timbers lay around had been exhausted. and still they would not go home. how did mrs mccabe ever empty the bar?

i knew – she called last orders repeatedly, then she flickered the lights. i went out into the stick house where the fuse box sat on the wall and found the big metal lever. i moved this to the up position and felt my way back into the house along the wall.

the house was now plunged into darkness apart from the dying fire, but the last few survivors scarcely noticed. the time for courtesy was gone.

'it's over,' i said. 'we're going. get out. go home.'

it was march, but there was no sense of cold in the very still air. the last guest had gone. i seemed to have travelled a thousand miles since supper last night. the bookie like me was drunk but not to the extent of being incapable. bridie and the girls had long gone home to bed. he lit his pipe, as much i think for the slight light that made, as for the need for a smoke.

'well?' he said.

that meant 'well, what did you think of that for a party, and what now?'

we shared an attachment to laragh and to laragh house, equally deep but totally different in origin.

'i was thinking of burning it,' i said.

'aye,' said the bookie.

this may sound strange, but of all the things that might have upset me, i hated the purple carpets most. purple and black flowered rubber backed carpets – in *my* house.

the bookie now had a choice, to help me or keep out of my way. he kept out of my way. he stood just outside the open door where he would see if anyone came up the avenue, while i stacked the rolls of purple carpet in the angle of the stairs. then i piled on the wooden pub benches and the plastic-backed banquettes. i dragged in the gas cylinder and added that to the pile. i carried in the discarded carpet felt rolls from dublin. finally i went out to the garage and poked around for a small can with a remnant of t.v.o.

i did not even know what t.v.o. was, except that it was some kind of paraffin that went into certain kinds of small grey tractors. i never used it, anyway. it was a leftover from ramsbottom's day.

now i walked slowly up the staircase in the near darkness gradually dribbling t.v.o. into the stair carpet as i went.

at the door the bookie coughed and muttered something. i stiffened. out in the driveway was the sound of footsteps on gravel. it was 'the bishop' and 'the captain' back from calving the cow.

i went out and pulled the door half shut behind me. if they shone their torch inside, the strange stack of chairs and benches would be plain to see.

'the party's over,' i said. 'but i'll find you a bit of whiskey. there's one half bottle in the land rover. you'll have to take it away with you.'

'shine the torch,' said the bookie, swaying slightly, but taking care to stand between them and the door.

their attention was directed to the land rover, from the back of which i now retrieved the last half bottle.

'what did she have?' asked the bookie.

'heifer.'

'hope she's lucky for you.'

i pressed the bottle into the captain's hand.

'now, please go home,' i said.

now the night was still and peaceful. we waited until the voices faded into the distance. to me, silence and darkness mean security – noise and bright lights and people are what make me nervous.

i got a candle from the library and i went from room to room for the last time. i wanted to be sure that no neighbour had stumbled upstairs to sleep it off. the house, thank god, was utterly empty.

now i felt, rather than saw, the bookie behind me, waiting out on the gravel.

i lowered the candle.

the purple flowered carpets were very slow to light, i tried the stair carpet to see if that was any better.

the gas cylinder was in place, with its metal top affixed. the gas was now on, but not lit.

a slow snake of flame slithered up the stairs.

i retreated to the far end of the hall and opened the door wide to let in the night air.

gradually the fire took hold in the pile of carpets and chairs.

i stepped back again, out of the door. we watched in silence.

i said to the bookie: 'i'll give you a lift home.'

we got in to the loaded land rover, the dog in the middle seat between us, but we did not go. we watched.

gradually the orange glow that shone out of the hall door became visible in other windows, as if there were a party in every room. the house would be warm tonight for once. now there were loud crackling sounds.

it was time to go.

at the bottom of his lane i stopped to let off the bookie.

'are you not coming in for a cup of tea?' he asked.

the getaway car

i now imagined that the fire would be discovered. the roads were deserted, but in my fevered mind, pursuit could erupt at any moment – pursuit, or a garda roadblock.

instead of turning for dublin i plunged straight over the main road and towards the back lanes of county cavan. twenty minutes further down the road i was back on another main road for dublin, but from a slightly different direction. now a kind of elation set in. no one knew where i was. i had given county monaghan a party to remember. i had left in style.

mcbirney had tried to give me a role in his personal narrative, his play. i was to stand in for the role of protestant mill owner, the oppressor and exploiter of mcbirney's people, a northern landlord who was fair game. he was to be the hero, the patriot, the cunning native who reclaims the land from the imperialist saxon usurper.

it was a lousy, dated old script.

i lived in a play, too. i also wanted to be cast as the man of the land, gaelic and free – striking at the oppressor and melting away into the night, resourceful and fearless, dashing and elusive.

modesty plays no part in people's fantasies.

the roads were deserted. the country lay open. the official story that the country was protected from the mayhem in the north by constant patrols between dublin and the border by the irish army and gardaí, was not true. the fact was that there was no one about. from the border all the way to the capital, that night, the roads were clear and open. the division of the country was only a division in the mind.

perhaps the 'subversives' actually travelled by day, when there was other traffic to hide among?

outside the hotel in the town of navan, county meath, a man stood out into the road and held out his hand for me to stop. caught?

i slowed to a crawl. behind him a girl stepped out of the shadows. i breathed again. probably someone had missed the lift home from the dance.

i stopped.

'could you give this girl a lift home?' he asked in through the window.

'i can,' i said, 'if she can tell me where to go.'

he helped her up into the passenger seat. there was not a lot of room with all the stuff in the back.

'don't mind the dog,' i said.

it must have been a hunt ball or a big occasion. she was wearing a full-length ballgown. in the orange street light i could not tell the colour. we went on our way, but now i no longer felt the same need to hurry.

men live their lives in compartments. women do not seem to do it quite that way.

somewhere ahead of us in a house in the middle of dublin, i had a wife and a daughter soundly sleeping, the wife due to give birth again in just two weeks' time.

somewhere to the north of us, and behind, the love of my life – another house – was roaring in its death agonies, with no one to hear.

and here in this particular compartment, i was sailing into the pale dawn with a faithful dog and a beautiful girl. i was sure in the early light that she was beautiful, but with both the dog and her luxuriant hair between us, i was seeing little except an occasional glimpse of an elegant neck and firm chin.

there was no need to talk much. the warm and steady hum of the diesel engine spoke for the three of us.

i was disappointed when we came to stone farm gateposts at a crossroads and she said:

'here.'

she stepped down onto the tarmac, holding up the dress, thanking me. it was pale blue, a perfect match for the land rover.

'thanks a million. thanks again.'

she looked baffled when i replied –

'will you do something for me … ? don't tell anyone you travelled with me on this road tonight.'

out of contact

arriving in the outskirts of dublin i turned in towards the phoenix park. i had no intention of going home and waking up octavia at this hour of the morning. anyway she had no telephone, and there was no way to warn her that i was coming.

instead i went and knocked on the door of the new house of collins the art dealer, at the phoenix park back gate.

after a long wait, a bleary-eyed fintan answered the door.

when i told him that i had burned laragh, he brought me in, pulled on some clothes, and made me tea.

bit by bit the story came out. it did not sound such a good story the second time, when collins himself came down to breakfast and i had to tell most of it again. i now conceived the fear that the fire might have gone out, doing little damage but leaving evidence of what had been attempted, and i began to have a fierce hangover from lack of sleep as much as from drink.

by the middle of the morning a plan was made. i parked the land rover in their orchard out of sight from the road. i put my gun away in a cupboard in case i was asked why i was carrying one around. then we got fintan to ring the post office at laragh and innocently enquire if i was at home.

his friend the postmistress's daughter answered.

we could only hear fintan's end of the conversation, but he repeated the words 'to the ground?' for our benefit, giving a meaningful look, and i was flooded with relief. it seemed that no one had seen or heard the fire until half past eight in the morning. in fact it had been reported by a man going to work from a house on the hill two miles away. by that time flames were visible coming up through the roof, which was falling in, a big fire burning fiercely and with very little smoke.

at ten o'clock mcbirney and the wife had pulled in to the filling station in carrickmacross, but this we only learned later. the owner told mcbirney that the fire engine had been called out to laragh.

'i think it's your place.'

mcbirney hadn't even waited for petrol but spun the wheels of the jaguar as he took off up the road.

meanwhile in dublin the collins brothers had a date to go to the races. i decided to go with them. i felt urgently the need to be invisible, to be out of contact, to be missing. the weather was fine, but anyway their idea of racing was largely to do with the socializing in the bar tent.

one of their acquaintances was thelma, a very pretty blonde girl who did announcing on the television. this made me wonder for the first time if all of this was likely to be national news, or just a nine-day local wonder. thelma did not know me but she was by nature direct. after getting a couple of desultory answers to her questions, she said –

'you look pretty rough.'

i suppose i did. hungover, sleepless, unshaven, nervous, preoccupied ...

'my house burned to the ground last night.'

'beat that,' she said as she walked away.

when at last i came home to the house in dublin, octavia knew at once that something to do with the deal at laragh had gone badly wrong.

'i burned it down,' i said simply.

'you are a poet,' she said.

this unruffled response was either from denial, or shock, or from some kind of detachment that comes over heavily pregnant women, a kind of amnesia that insulates them from everything that is not directly connected to the birth.

i did not return to laragh immediately, but by means of a few telephone calls i was able, then and later, to piece together most of the story.

no one saw the fire. no one heard the fire. the sergeant went from house to house in the village and all over the valley. he was heard to observe that never was there a party with so many people at it – and not one of them knew what time they went to it – who they saw at it – how long it went on – or what time they left it.

from my long experience of laragh, i could picture the scene. i had brought about a situation where everyone was a suspect. no one was guilty and yet everyone felt guilty. no one had a motive, and yet everyone had had an opportunity. the bishop and the captain must be feeling particularly nervous, and if sidney corrigan had kept the two blue chinese plates for himself, he would now have to unburden himself of them quickly and quietly. they would be evidence and conclusions could be drawn. i guessed that the last two plates might already be in the river.

on the morning after the party most people for miles around had been hungover, and nobody had heard the fire, even as the roof fell in. at least, nobody was admitting to hearing it. i was prepared to bet that some early risers did see it or hear it, and had gone quickly back to bed to lie low and leave it to somebody else to report it.

of course while the sergeant could glean scant information, there were no shortage of tales elsewhere. 'the party' became a standing joke and grew to mythic proportions. the number of guests and the amount of drink consumed increased with every telling of the tale.

i began to suspect that i had set mcbirney a puzzle. it was not a question of whether he could exact revenge upon me – it was whether he could get away with it. even if some simple accident now befell me he would be suspected immediately. i felt that at that moment that he had had the spotlight turned upon him. who was he? how did he make his money? how could he continue with his 'business' activities while his name was on everyone's lips? how could he now threaten or intimidate people while the simple words 'were you at the party?' brought a grin to everyone's face for miles around?

eventually i went back to laragh. it was the fifth or sixth day. to stay away any longer would invite further suspicion. i had to take a deep breath and face the burned out wreckage.

i went up alone as usual. i did not warn anyone that i was coming. over the boyne at slane, there is a long stone bridge. on the northern bank of the river there is a dangerous corner and a hill up through the village of slane where you need to put the boot hard down to get all the way to the top in third gear.

coming down the hill towards me was the jaguar.

mcbirney's head whipped around as i passed him. his wife was with him. he knew me. there were many land rovers in county meath, but few if any of them were pale powder blue.

i already had the boot down. i could go no faster. when i got to the bend into the village i could see far behind me in the mirror that the jaguar was turning.

i was clear of the village and out on the ardee road when he caught up with me. there was no point in trying to shake him off by turning down side roads, and there was no chance of leaving him behind on the main road. i kept on going.

mcbirney pulled alongside and signalled me to stop. then he pulled the jaguar in front of me and slowed. i was forced to brake but the road was wide and level on this stretch.

i changed into third gear and swung outside of him, and motored on. the jaguar quickly pulled alongside again. he was saying something emphatic but i could not hear, and i was not looking. i did not want to know. again he pulled his car across mine to force me into the verge. this time i was more prepared, and before he had halted i was down into third and pulling outside of him. the third time he caught me again and repeated the manoeuvre more violently. this time there was going to be a collision if he didn't leave me room to get by, and he must have realized it too. my wheels locked on the gravel, but i had room to engage a lower gear and move off, though more slowly this time. if he wanted to question me, i did not want to answer. if he wanted to threaten me, i did not want to hear. if his wife happened to have a gun in her handbag – unlikely – i did not want to be shot, and he must realize that this was no time or place for him to think of doing it.

mcbirney had become the visible person, and i had become the invisible person – hidden in plain sight. looking neither to the left or to the right i remained in third gear, engaged the four-wheel drive, and pressed steadily and determinedly on.

after a while i was no longer being followed.

the interview

in the end the sergeant, having failed to meet me at laragh, came to dublin. octavia gave him tea in one of her granny's best teacups. he must have been very aware of the contrast between this elegant townhouse and the dereliction that was laragh, even as laragh had been before the fire left it a blackened shell.

tactfully, octavia left us alone.

i was very tense, but i was resolved not to tell a lie. the sergeant held the fragile cup in his big hand. he said:

'they were going to come and question you, but i said that i would come myself.'

i took this to mean that he had a fair grasp of the realities of the situation. he asked me many questions. i thought about each and answered carefully and deliberately. he said that the technical bureau had been over the charred remains. had there been any inflammable liquids stored in the house? i said –

'no. except maybe an old plastic container of t.v.o.'

he seemed satisfied.

he wanted to know if i had brought carpet felt to laragh.

i said: 'yes. it was rubbish. there is a binmen's strike on here in the city.'

that seemed to satisfy him, too.

'– and a gas cylinder?'

'to cook my breakfast. i had originally intended to stay after the party.'

'why did you advertise it as a 'leaving' party?'

'i was leaving.'

he listened with interest to my account of not having received the balance of the purchase money, and at this point he made his own terse comment on the situation over the sale –

'no money – no dice.'

the only thing that surprised him was the account of the near-collisions with mcbirney on the slane road. whatever picture had formed in his far from simple mind, this clearly did not quite fit in with it.

he did mention however that mrs mcbirney had immediately accused me of burning the house.

i waited for the big question – had i burned the house?

but the sergeant did not ask it.

★   ★   ★   ★   ★   ★

that is not the end of my story, but it is the end of my story for now. mcbirney was to play a further part in my life, a part that i could not then have possibly foreseen.

mcbirney did not abandon laragh. he put a security guard in the burned-out house, with an alsation dog, but the bookie was undeterred. the bookie went up to see this guard every day, and before he went he used to poke his fingers into the fat of the frying pan on the range – the sausage pan in which bridie had cooked his breakfast. he never reached out to the dog, but after a while the dog learned to go around him and lick his fingers behind his back. after that the bookie could go up to the house across the fields at any hour he wanted. the dog did not mind him. the bookie could then take a look around and report back to me the next time we met.

* * * * * *

it is sunday morning.

against the wall of the graveyard the men stand in the sun and talk. the women are already inside, all seated on their own side of the chapel. the altar boys, all boys, are in their vestments and ready. the men wait until the last possible minute, when the priest has rung the bell, before going in to mass.

the bookie is standing alone under the wall when the bishop and the captain approach him, one from each direction. other men turn to look as these two lean menacingly over him, until their noses almost touch his jacket lapels.

'do you smell scorching?' the captain says to the bishop …

it is sunday morning in ireland. *no one knows anything. everyone knows everything.*

a sting in the tale

mcbirney caused me further trouble when he took the stand in my divorce case, which – like 'riverdance' – split into two shows running separately, one in dublin, one in belfast. this suited the fee gobblers, and was possible in the legal and constitutional context of the time.

i was even required to take a psychological examination – separately in each jurisdiction.

i was appalled. what if it were to be found fully sane by a dublin psychiatric evaluation and absolutely crazy by the equivalent evaluation in belfast? and as the landrover rattled over the metal bridge in aughnacloy where the old bridge over the border had been blown up – what would happen to me? going from sane to crazy and then back again the same evening from crazy to sane, how was i expected to feel?

my solicitor sighed. he said we would face that if and when we came to it.

i hope to write about that also, if god spares me, and my publisher and his manuscript readers think that it can be pulled off without leaving too much innocent blood on the canvas.

mcbirney admitted to me years later that the fire had done him a lot of damage. he died 'on the run' in new york, leaving the many who were looking for him unpaid. he had an amazing high court record:

fought 19 cases. lost 19 cases. paid up: £ zero.

outside the box

the coffin was flown back to ireland and buried in the tiny graveyard of the little painted corrugated church at laragh.

a burial of the big house gardener's grandson – a catholic – planted among the memorial stones of the old protestant mill owners.

when i heard about it months later i commented to the bookie that he must have been a very strange and bitter man to make a political protest even out of his own funeral.

the wee black bookie sucked on his pipe.

'maybe it's not him in the box, at all,' he said.

A NOTE ON THE LETTERING

capital or uppercase letters originate from the letters that the romans used to carve in stone with hammer and chisel.

lowercase letters, on the other hand, originate in various early mediaeval forms of handwriting with pen or brush, and have a more rounded form.

we have become so used to seeing the two alphabets mixed that we are no longer aware of the confusion.

the author believes that the imposition of capital letters upon children (and adults) who are learning to read, thus making forty or more letters to master rather than twenty-six, is unnecessarily conservative, and perverse. there are no capital letters except in unicameral form (meaning – all letters in capitals). capital letters are retained in one instance only, to indicate acronyms, thus: CIE, BBC, IRA, etc.

bicameral mixing of upper and lower case is therefore avoided. there are no other new conventions to learn. for emphasis an italic font is used – a third form, originating from italian renaissance handwriting.

for most readers the slight initial irritation caused by the unfamiliar disappears after two or three pages, and the eye adjusts as it has to adjust to the many advertising and display fonts that it encounters in the course of a normal day.

decorated or illuminated hand drawn initial letters such as those in the famous book of kells can be very beautiful, but the expense of these would of course be beyond the means of any publisher.